"Exemplary reflections from today's frontline warriors that will disconcert liberals but inspire young people who want to live the struggle in the revolutionary tradition of Robert F. Williams, the Watts 65 rebels, and Deacons for Defense and Justice."
—Mike Davis, author of *Planet of Slums* and *Old Gods, New Enigmas*

"This anthology resists police and vigilante murders. It is not an easy read. We will not all agree with its analyses or advocacy. Yet its integrity, clarity, vulnerability, love, and rage are clear. As a librarian who archives liberators and liberation movements, I recognize essential reading as a reflection of ourselves and our fears. With resolution, this text resonates with narratives of mini-Atticas. The 1971 prison rebellion and murderous repression by government and officialdom reveal the crises that spark radical movements and increasing calls for self-defense. This volume offers our cracked mirrors as an opportunity to scrutinize missteps and possibilities and hopefully choose wisely even in our sacrifices."
—Joy James, author of *Resisting State Violence: Radicalism, Gender, and Race in U.S. Culture*

The George Floyd Uprising

Edited by Vortex Group

The George Floyd Uprising
Vortex Group © 2023
This edition © 2023 PM Press

ISBN: 978–1–62963–966–6 (paperback)
ISBN: 978–1–62963–981–9 (ebook)
Library of Congress Control Number: 2022931956

Cover design by John Yates/www.stealworks.com
Interior design by briandesign

10 9 8 7 6 5 4 3 2 1

PM Press
PO Box 23912
Oakland, CA 94623
www.pmpress.org

Printed in the USA

Contents

Dedicated to all those murdered by police and all
those who took great risks in fighting back

Welcome Back to the World

Vortex Group

In the summer of 2020, the United States experienced its most intense wave of social unrest in at least half a century. After months of eerie quiet during which the world was enthralled by the COVID-19 pandemic, the streets were suddenly flooded with people. Following the death of George Floyd at the hands of the Minneapolis police, multiracial crowds took to the streets night after night, fighting the police, looting, and eventually burning down the Third Precinct, as well as entire commercial blocks across the city and in neighboring St. Paul. The revolt soon spread to cities large and small across the country.[1] Police cars were set on fire, luxury shopping districts were looted, and the president had to hide in the bunker of the White House. Even as the National Guard was deployed and curfews were repeatedly announced in dozens of cities, in the streets it seemed as if anything was possible.

By early June, the rioting had birthed alongside it a mass social movement that unfolded over the course of the summer. In addition to daily mass demonstrations and marches, an entire array of creative forms of collective action were spawned. In Seattle, New York City, Atlanta, and elsewhere, occupations of plazas, parking lots, and city streets fashioned themselves into "autonomous zones" and sought to keep police out.[2] The movement regrouped and experimented with how to reproduce itself. Elsewhere, iconoclastic demonstrations tore down monuments to the Confederacy and colonialism, occasionally sending local police to the hospital along the way.[3] In Portland, Trump's decision to send in federal forces revivified and deepened a months-long stretch of militant demonstrations, drawing in thousands of new combatants from all walks of life and provoking a wave of solidarity demos elsewhere.[4] Smaller yet seemingly prepared and experienced crowds attacked the infrastructure of the carceral state and clashed with police. A DHS/ICE office in Atlanta and a courthouse in Oakland were each briefly set on fire, and a juvenile jail under construction in Seattle was burned down. Everywhere, a new generation of would-be revolutionaries were finding each other in the streets, developing a shared tactical sensibility, and getting organized to take the initiative.[5]

Throughout the summer and into the fall, rebellion would continue to erupt in a different city nearly every week: Chicago, Kenosha, Rochester, Lancaster, Louisville, Wauwatosa, Philadelphia. Each new explosion brought with it practical innovations, as "frontliner" tactics first popularized in Hong Kong and Chile in 2019 were rapidly adapted and developed in various US cities. It also brought with it fierce reprisals on the part of the state, ranging from grotesque and indiscriminate violence toward uneventful crowds to summary executions of activists in broad daylight, as occurred with Michael Reinoehl.

As the summer turned to fall, the deadly climax of the Kenosha rebellion provoked a strike among the major league sports teams in the NBA, WNBA, MLB, MLS, and NHL. Solidarity demonstrations inspired by the events in the US began taking place across the globe. Anti-police riots would soon spread to Mexico, Colombia, Nigeria, France, and elsewhere, continuing the global exchange of insurgent tactics that had begun the year prior in places like Haiti, Hong Kong, and Chile. All told, more riots took place in the summer and early fall of 2020 than during the entire "long, hot summer" of 1967, and more people in this country participated in the resulting social movement than at any other time in American history.

•

As the George Floyd uprising unfolded throughout the summer, several sorts of commentaries began to emerge around it. Much of the writing in both mainstream and left-wing publications praised the social movement that had emerged and particular activist groups or organizers they saw as central to it, without offering much in the way of critical commentary. Often this writing attempted to provide context for the uprising by rehearsing histories of policing, segregation, inequality, and earlier anti-racist movements. It also attempted to provide a political framework by debating the implications of the movement's demands, such as defunding or abolishing the police, for public policy. Editorials would celebrate the official protests during the daytime, while passing over the rest in silence. Almost nowhere were the riots taken seriously on their own terms, nor were their potentials and limitations reflected upon.

The book you're holding in your hands offers a very different perspective on that long, hot summer. Rather than policy proposals, the writings collected in this anthology reflect the movement's efforts to engage its limits on its own terms. What you'll find here are strategic reflections from within the heart of the storm, marked by an urgent fidelity to the insurgent spirit of the uprising. They offer a record of theoretical and pragmatic wagers made by active participants as they survey the successes and failures of the movement, while sketching out the new revolutionary horizons opened up along the way. At the same time, this anthology is by no means a comprehensive statement on the uprising, but rather a curated collection of writings from a specific revolutionary tendency. Each of these texts was written as an intervention in a particular moment in the unfolding of the revolt, often situated in a particular place. Nonetheless, a set of key themes weaves throughout the texts.

What binds the authors here together is a perspective that orients toward uprisings and mass movements as potential openings for a revolutionary rupture. Rather than seeking new and better arrangements with ruling powers, they share a commitment to deepening and widening social struggles, consciously working to prolong the interruption of capitalist society by inviting wider sections of society to take part in the hostilities, thereby holding open the space in which something new might emerge. It is this commitment to transformative escalation that leads them to take combative practices such as riots, occupations, and looting seriously as political forms in their own right, rather than understanding them solely through their relation to activist campaigns or policy. Through the eyes of our authors, such belligerent and even violent acts appear not merely as an ugly yet predictable outcome of state oppression but as generative, even creative, events through which territory is reconquered from police control, while social groups suspend their resentment and fear and forge new and tentative alliances.

At the same time as this creativity allowed the movement to reach new heights, it also inevitably hit upon its own limits. The present anthology wrestles with a series of logistical and strategic questions that have reemerged within all twenty-first-century uprisings. Each text concerns itself with the movement's fluctuating social composition, its forms of organization and coordination, the spread and reach of its tactical innovations, and the debates that surround it. Rather than simply a celebration of the uprising, these texts should, thus, be read as a debate happening in real time over the impasses and limits the uprising encountered:

- Movements have to constantly innovate their tactical repertoire to stay dynamic and ahead of the police.[6] How did the introduction of *frontliner* tactics first developed in Hong Kong and Chile impact the US rebellion? How did they spread from city to city, transforming along the way? How did the street fighting in Seattle open the space for the City Hall Autonomous Zone, thereby laying a template for similar experiments in Atlanta, Louisville, New York City, and elsewhere? How did innovations like looting by car spread from Chicago to Louisville to Philadelphia, allowing much smaller crowds to disrupt an entire city? Why did certain tactics spread across contexts, while others didn't? How was technology (weapons, protective gear, lasers, cars, communications, etc.) able to facilitate this? And how did the nature of the tactics adopted by the movement limit the possibilities for its growth overall? For instance, how did the separation of political riots from storefront looting place a ceiling on the spread of the movement as a whole?
- Mass disruptive activity requires a high degree of coordination. However, in today's cycle of struggles this rarely arrives externally through the agency of political parties, activist groups, nonprofits, or conspiracies but tends to be an immanent and emergent feature of the movement itself. How were the crowds that laid siege to the Third Precinct in Minneapolis or that stormed Manhattan's SoHo able to organize themselves in the absence of any external coordinating body? How did the internal heterogeneity and combination or "composition" of different roles within the crowd make this possible? How much of this success was due to factors like rhythm, ritual, and territory, which help to confer consistency and momentum on events?
- The more intense and generalized struggle becomes, the higher degree of coordination it will require. What were the obstacles that prevented these riots from generalizing and drawing in wider segments of society? Why was the uprising unable to

spread to workplaces, schools, or other places where it could have exerted a different kind of leverage? How and where was the uprising able to maintain its disruptive edge, while still pulling more and more people into the street? As the composition began to break down, how were different factions able or unable to find a basis for meaningful coordination? How might revolutionaries intervene in and contribute to these processes?

- Looking beyond the movement's heroic accomplishments, our authors also interrogate the counterinsurgent implications of many popular activist slogans and proposals. To what extent was the defeat of the struggle attributable to state repression? How did co-optation, recuperation, and opportunistic reframing from within the movement succeed in realigning the stakes of the conflict along lines amenable to the existing order? Was the call to "defund the police" a radical demand or an effort to displace the agency of the street movement back into the hands of politicians and policy makers? What are we to make of the paradoxically disarming spectacle of leftist militias?
- Identity has played a complicated role of containing and narrowing struggle at one extreme, while providing the language and unity for expanding the struggle at the other extreme. How does race manifest itself in the moment of the riot? Do white radicals have to listen to moderate Black protesters who are calling for peace and order? Is it helpful to understand the uprising as driven by the Black radical tradition, or has the latter exhausted itself? Can we understand, fight, and build a new world through gestures and tactics alone?

Answering such questions requires a fine-grained attention to the internal fabric of the rebellion, which can only be attained by a deep commitment and a willingness to take risks. Rather than regurgitating the platitudes of the past or claiming to have all the answers, our authors challenge readers to think critically about what exactly happened during the uprising, warts and all.

•

In spite of a shared commitment, there are tensions that run throughout the texts. Our authors diverge around a number of key political, social, and strategic questions, such as race and identity, abolitionism and reform, and the role of weapons and ethics.

The Black struggle has served a singular role in American radical politics, often acting as the igniting element that sets wider layers of society into motion.[7] While the George Floyd uprising was unique in the diversity of its participants, the composition of the uprising often broke down over the course of the fall as separations around race reemerged. Our authors differ both in how they make sense of this terrain and how they propose to move and act within it. On the one hand, in such a context, any decision to prioritize the agency of participants due to their race or ethnic identity risks reasserting social separation rather than dissolving it. While some authors lean into categories of race and ethnicity to explain the precarity of these tenuous alliances, others worry more about the risk of reifying frameworks of identity and instead attempt to develop a new conceptual language centered on actions and practices. Some authors find fertile ground in drawing off of frameworks from the Black radical tradition, while others are skeptical about whether any inherited framework is adequate for the moment we find ourselves in.

A second productive disagreement concerns how revolutionaries ought to orient themselves with the social movement that ensued in the wake of the riots. While some authors insist on a qualitative difference at the level of practices between the social movement and what they term the *real movement*, a difference that could even place them in direct antagonism, others emphasized what they viewed as a relationship of reciprocity and complementarity between the rioters and peaceful protesters.

This tension is also found in the diverging interpretations of the demand to defund the police. As a result of the uprising, calls to abolish or defund the police—once the niche domain of activists and radicals— were now being debated in the mainstream. In trying to engage with debates over the meaning of the movement, the authors differ in what tack they take. While Shemon sees the demand to defund the police as part of an effort to recuperate the uprising, Jarrod Shanahan and Zhandarka Kurti argue that we should see the radical content between reformist demands. Relatedly, while some of the authors attempt to intervene in debates around the meaning of abolitionism, others argue that revolutionaries should attempt to articulate a totally separate pole than any of those currently on offer. For example, whereas Shemon distinguishes between "revolutionary" and "reformist" currents within the existing abolitionist discourses and practices, Adrian Wohlleben instead distinguishes the "demolitionist" wave of attacks on police infrastructure from the "social movement apparatus" broadly construed, seeing in the language of "abolition" an effort to translate the real movement back into a dialogue with existing power structures.

Another disagreement revolves around the question of guns. As the summer progressed, it became impossible to not address the use of arms, especially after the climactic violence of Kenosha. The authors here try to tread a careful line, avoiding the twin temptations of pacifism and the fetishization of armed struggle. Rather than speaking from the certainty of moralism or abstract revolutionary theory, their interventions address the concrete impact that weapons have on the strategic maneuverability of situations. A number of texts express the concern that taking up arms lent itself to the creation of specialized groups that tended to separate themselves from the rest of the movement. This, in turn, lent itself to an endgame in which the escalation of violence would generate situations in which fewer and fewer people could participate, reducing the uprising to periodic episodes of armed conflict between quasi-militarized groups and evacuating any liberatory potential it once had. The strategic limits of such an outcome became painfully visible in the autonomous zones in Seattle, Atlanta, and Louisville. On the other hand, evoking the legacy of John Brown, Idris Robinson insists that in the specific context of America's racial nightmare the use of arms *is* still necessary to open up a crisis in which revolutionary change is possible. On his reading, the race treason to which Michael Reinoehl's actions attest should not be subordinated to a purely strategic calculus, since the violence that subsumes Black people in this country obeys a qualitatively different rationale.

•

The year 2020 will be remembered alongside 1968, 1917, and 1848. For a brief but glorious moment, people took part in a mass assault on the established order unlike any the USA has witnessed in our lifetime. The texts collected here stand as a testament to what people were able to accomplish, not only at the level of tactics, strategies, and theory but also at the level of ethical sensitivity and social complexity—a pedagogy of the oppressed.

For much of 2020, that strange plague year, anything seemed possible—anything except a return to normal. But, today, more than a year after the riots, anything other than the crushing inertia of the present state of things seems unthinkable. Some readers might justifiably ask: Was anything achieved through it all? Was it worth all of the risk? If it was, this wasn't because the insurgents "won" and succeeded in defeating their enemies, but because the experience of the uprising, with all its dangers, all its limits, all its prisoners and martyrs, offers a forecast of the challenges the future holds in store.

It is only by opening oneself to the joys, to the experience of power, to the confidence and lucidity of the uprising that a serious conversation about its obstacles can be had. In assembling this volume, our aim is to preserve a record of the aspirations and frustrations forged in those fires, which offer living proof of an *other* political rationality. We hope that future generations will take the time to learn from the George Floyd uprising, to soak up the intelligence it was able to produce, while discarding the debates and dilemmas that no longer feel pertinent.

For the last decade, we've seen a global sequence of struggles unfold. As each successive wave crashes, it leaves in its wake a new generation of revolutionaries whose task is to incorporate the lessons of the movements that preceded them, so as to leap over them. This book, then, is a modest offering to this new generation, as well as a tribute to all those who found among the broken glass and smoldering rubble something that felt true, something they won't easily let go of, all those for whom the idea of returning to normal last year felt not only derisory but suffocating.

In the face of despair, Rosa Luxemburg reminded her comrades that "revolution is the only form of 'war'—and this is another peculiar law of history—in which the ultimate victory can be prepared only by a series of 'defeats.'"[8] The point is not to make a virtue out of losing but to toughen our resolve and prepare for the battles still to come.

Nothing presently available is sufficient.

September 2021

FIRST THERE WAS FIRE

The Siege of the Third Precinct in Minneapolis: An Account and Analysis

Anonymous

The following analysis is motivated by a discussion that took place in front of the Third Precinct as fires billowed from its windows on day three of the George Floyd Rebellion in Minneapolis. We joined a group of people whose fire-lit faces beamed with joy and awe from across the street. People of various ethnicities sat side by side talking about the tactical value of lasers, the "share everything" ethos, interracial unity in fighting the police, and the trap of "innocence." There were no disagreements; we all saw the same things that helped us win. Thousands of people shared the experience of these battles. We hope that they will carry the memory of how to fight. But the time of combat and the celebration of victory is incommensurable with the habits, spaces, and attachments of everyday life and its reproduction. It is frightening how distant the event already feels. Our purpose here is to preserve the strategy that proved victorious against the Minneapolis Third Precinct.

Our analysis focuses on the tactics and composition of the crowd that besieged the Third Precinct on day two of the uprising. The siege lasted roughly from 4:00 p.m. well into the early hours of the morning of May 28. We believe that the tactical retreat of the police from the Third Precinct on day three was won in large part by the siege of day two, which exhausted the precinct's personnel and supplies. We were not present for the fighting that preceded the retreat on day three; we arrived just as the police were leaving. We had been across the city in an area where youth were fighting the cops in tit-for-tat battles while trying to loot a strip mall—hence our focus on day two here.

Context

The last popular revolt against the Minneapolis Police Department took place in response to the police murder of Jamar Clark on November 15, 2015. It spurred two weeks of unrest that lasted until December 2. Elements of the crowd repeatedly engaged the police in ballistic confrontations; however, the response to the shooting coalesced around an occupation of the nearby Fourth Precinct. There, organizations like the NAACP and the newly formed Black Lives Matter asserted their control over the crowds. They were often at odds with young unaffiliated rebels who preferred to fight the police directly. Much of our analysis below focuses on how young Black and brown rebels from poor and working-class neighborhoods seized the opportunity to reverse this relationship. We argue that this was a necessary condition for the uprising.

George Floyd was murdered by the police at 38th Street and Chicago Avenue between 8:20 and 8:32 p.m. on Monday, May 25. Demonstrations against the killing began the next day at the site of his murder, where a vigil took place. Some attendees began a march to the Third Precinct at Lake Street and 26th Avenue, where rebels attacked police vehicles in the parking lot.

These two locations became consistent gathering points. Many community groups, organizations, liberals, progressives, and leftists assembled at the vigil site, while those who wanted to fight generally gathered near the precinct. This put over two miles between two very different crowds, a spatial division that was reflected in other areas of the city as well. Looters clashed with police in scattered commercial zones outside of the sphere of influence of the organizations, while many of the leftist marches excluded fighting elements with the familiar tactic of peace policing in the name of identity-based risk aversion.

The "Subject" of the George Floyd Uprising

The subject of our analysis is not a race, a class, an organization, or even a movement, but a *crowd*. We focus on a crowd for three reasons. First, with the exception of the street medics, the power and success of those who fought the Third Precinct did not depend on their experience in "organizing" or in organizations. Rather, it resulted from unaffiliated individuals and groups courageously stepping into roles that complemented each other and seizing opportunities as they arose.

While the initial gathering was occasioned by a rally hosted by a Black-led organization, all of the actions that *materially* defeated the Third Precinct were undertaken *after* the rally had ended, carried out by people who were not affiliated with it. There was practically no one there from the usual gamut of self-appointed community and religious leaders, which meant that the crowd was able to transform the situation freely. Organizations rely on stability and predictability to execute strategies that require great quantities of time to formulate. Consequently, organization leaders can be threatened by sudden changes in social conditions, which can make their organizations irrelevant. Organizations—even self-proclaimed "revolutionary" organizations—have an interest in suppressing spontaneous revolt in order to recruit from those who are discontented and enraged. Whether it is an elected official, a religious leader, a "community organizer," or a representative from the "revolutionary" left, their message to unruly crowds is always the same: *wait.*

The agency that took down the Third Precinct was a *crowd* and not an organization, because its goals, means, and internal makeup were not regulated by centralized authority. This proved beneficial, as the crowd consequently had recourse to more practical options and was freer to create unforeseen internal relationships in order to adapt to the conflict at hand. We expand on this below in the section titled "The Pattern of Battle and 'Composition.'"

The agency in the streets on May 27 was located in a crowd, because its constituents had few stakes in the existing order that is managed by the police. Crucially, a gang truce had been called after the first day of unrest, neutralizing territorial barriers to participation. The crowd mostly originated from working-class and poor Black and brown neighborhoods. This was especially true of those who threw things at the police and vandalized and looted stores. Those who do not identify as "owners" of the world that oppresses them are more likely to fight and steal from it when the opportunity arises. The crowd had no interest in justifying itself to onlookers and was scarcely interested in "signifying" anything to anyone outside of itself. There were no signs or speeches, only chants that served the tactical purposes of "hyping up" ("Fuck 12!") and interrupting police violence with strategically deployed "innocence" ("Hands up, don't shoot!").

Roles
We saw people play a number of roles.

Medical Support

This included street medics and medics performing triage and urgent care at a converted community center two blocks away from the precinct. Under different circumstances, this could be performed at any nearby sympathetic commercial, religious, or not-for-profit establishment. Alternatively, a crowd or a medic group could occupy such a space for the duration of a protest. Those who were organized as street medics did not interfere with the tactical choices of the crowd. Instead, they consistently treated anyone who needed their help.

Scanner Monitors and Telegram App Channel Operators

This is common practice in many US cities by now. Police scanner monitors with an ear for strategically important information played a critical role in setting up information flows from the police to the crowd. It is almost certain that much of the crowd was not practicing the greatest security when accessing the Telegram channel. We advise rebels to set up the Telegram app on burner phones to stay informed while preventing police stingrays (false cell phone towers) from gleaning their personal information.

Peaceful Protesters

The nonviolent tactics of peaceful protesters served two familiar aims and one unusual one:

- They created a spectacle of legitimacy, which was intensified as police violence escalated.
- They created a front line that blocked police attempts to advance when they deployed outside of the precinct.
- Finally, in an unexpected turn of affairs, the peaceful protesters shielded those who employed projectiles.

Whenever the police threatened to use tear gas or rubber bullets, nonviolent protesters lined up at the front with their hands up in the air, chanting, "Hands up, don't shoot!" Sometimes they kneeled, but typically only during relative lulls in the action. When the cops deployed outside the precinct, they frequently found themselves facing a line of "nonviolent" protesters. This had the effect of temporarily stabilizing the space of conflict and gave other crowd members a stationary target. While some peaceful protesters angrily commanded people to stop throwing things, they were few and grew quiet as the day wore on. This was most likely because the police were targeting people who threw things with rubber bullets early on in the conflict, which enraged the crowd. It's worth noting that the reverse has often been the case—we are used to seeing more confrontational tactics used to shield those practicing nonviolence (e.g., at Standing Rock and Charlottesville). The reversal of this relationship in Minneapolis afforded greater autonomy to those employing confrontational tactics.

Ballistics Squads

Ballistics squads threw water bottles, rocks, Molotov cocktails, and fireworks at police. Those using ballistics didn't always work in groups, which protected them from being targeted by nonviolent protesters who wanted to dictate the tactics of the crowd. The ballistics squads served three aims:

- They drew police violence away from the peaceful elements of the crowd during moments of escalation.
- They patiently depleted the police's crowd control munitions.
- They threatened the physical safety of the police, making it costlier for them to advance.

On the first day of the uprising, there were attacks on multiple parked police SUVs at the Third Precinct. This sensibility resumed quickly on day two, beginning with the throwing of water bottles at police officers positioned on the roof of the Third Precinct and alongside the building. After the police responded with tear gas and rubber bullets, the ballistics squads also began to employ rocks. Elements within the crowd dismantled bus bench embankments made of stone and smashed them up to supply additional projectiles. Nightfall saw the use of fireworks by a few people, which quickly generalized in days three and four. "Boogaloo Bois" (Second Amendment accelerationists) had already briefly used fireworks on day one, but from what we saw they mostly sat it out on the sidelines thereafter. Finally, it is worth noting that the Minneapolis police used "green tips," rubber bullets with exploding green ink tips to mark lawbreakers for later arrest. Once it became clear that the police department had limited capacity to make good on its threat and, moreover, that the crowd could *win*, those who had been marked had every incentive to fight like hell to defy the police.

Laser Pointers

In the grammar of the Hong Kong movement, those who operate laser pointers are referred to as "light mages." As was the case in Hong Kong, Chile, and elsewhere in 2019, some people came prepared with laser pointers to attack the optical capacity of the police. Laser pointers involve a special risk/reward ratio, as it is very easy to track people using laser pointers, even when they are operating within a dense and active crowd at night. Those who use laser pointers are particularly vulnerable if they attempt to target individual police officers or (especially) police helicopters while operating in small crowds; this is still the case even if the entire neighborhood is undergoing mass looting. (The daytime use of high-powered lasers with scopes remains untested, to our knowledge.) The upside of laser pointers is immense: they momentarily compromise the eyesight of the police on the ground and they can disable police surveillance drones by interfering with their infrared sensors and obstacle-detection cameras. In the latter case, a persistently lasered drone may descend to the earth, where the crowd can destroy it. This occurred repeatedly on days two and three. If a crowd is particularly dense and visually difficult to discern, lasers can be used to chase away police helicopters. This was successfully demonstrated on day three following the retreat of the police from the Third Precinct, as well as on day four in the vicinity of the Fifth Precinct battle.

Barricaders

Barricaders built barricades out of nearby materials, including an impressive barricade that blocked the police on 26th Avenue just north of Lake Street. In the latter case, the barricade was assembled out of a train of shopping carts and a cart-return station pulled from a nearby parking lot, along with dumpsters, police barricades, plywood, and fencing materials from a condominium construction site. At the Third Precinct, the barricade provided useful cover for laser pointer attacks and rock throwers, while also serving as a natural gathering point for the crowd to regroup. However, at the Fifth Precinct, dozens of individuals filled the street with a multirow barricade when the police advanced on foot toward the crowd and succeeded in pushing people a block back. While the barricade limited the police advance and allowed the crowd to regroup outside the range of the rubber bullets, it soon became clear that the barricades also limited the crowd's ability to retake territory, as any attempt would be dangerously exposed. The barricade had to be partially dismantled to facilitate a second press toward the police lines. It can be difficult to coordinate defense and attack within a single gesture.

Sound Systems

Car sound systems and engines provided a sonic environment that enlivened the crowd. The anthem of days two and three was Lil Boosie's "Fuck the Police." Yet one innovation we had never seen before was the use of car engines to add to the soundscape and "rev up" the crowd. On day two, this began when a guy parked his pickup truck behind the crowd, facing away from it. When tensions ran high with the police and it appeared that the conflict would escalate, the driver would redline his engine and make its modified exhaust system roar thunderously over the crowd. Other similarly modified cars joined in, along with a few motorcyclists.

Looters

Looting served three critical aims.

First, it liberated supplies to heal and nourish the crowd. On the first day, rebels attempted to seize the liquor store directly across from the Third Precinct. Their success was brief, as the cops managed to resecure it. Early in the standoff on day two, a handful of people signaled their determination by climbing on top of the store to mock the police from the roof. The crowd cheered at this humiliation, which implicitly set the objective for the rest of the day: to demonstrate the powerlessness of the police, demoralize them, and exhaust their capacities.

An hour or so later, looting began at the liquor store and at an Aldi a block away. While a majority of those present participated in the looting, it was clear that some took it upon themselves to be strategic about it. Looters at the Aldi liberated immense quantities of bottled water, sports drinks, milk, protein bars, and other snacks and distributed these items on street corners throughout the vicinity. In addition to the liquor store and the Aldi, the Third Precinct was conveniently situated adjacent to a Target, a Cub Foods, a shoe store, a dollar store, an AutoZone, a Wendy's, and various other businesses. Once the looting began, it immediately became a part of the logistics of the crowd's siege on the precinct.

Second, looting boosted the crowd's morale by creating solidarity and joy through a shared act of collective transgression. The act of gift giving and the spirit of generosity were made accessible to all, providing a positive counterpoint to the head-to-head conflicts with the police.

Third, and most importantly, looting contributed to keeping the situation ungovernable. As looting spread throughout the city, police forces everywhere were spread thin. Their attempts to secure key targets only gave looters free rein over other areas in the city. Like a fist squeezing water, the police found themselves frustrated by an opponent that expanded exponentially.

Fires

The decision to burn looted businesses could be seen as tactically intelligent. It contributed to depleting police resources, since the firefighters who were forced to continually extinguish structure fires all over town required heavy police escorts. This severely impacted their ability to intervene in situations of ongoing looting, the vast majority of which they never responded to (the malls and the Super Target store on University Avenue being exceptions). This has played out differently in other cities, where police opted not to escort firefighters. Perhaps this explains why demonstrators fired in the air around firefighting vehicles during the Watts rebellion.

In the case of the Third Precinct, the burning of the AutoZone had two immediate consequences. It forced the police to move out into the street and establish a perimeter around the building for firefighters. While this diminished the clash at the site of the precinct, it also pushed the crowd down Lake Street, which subsequently induced widespread looting and contributed to the diffusion of the riot across the whole neighborhood.

The Pattern of the Battle and "Composition"

We call the battles of the second and third days at the precinct a *siege*, because the police were defeated by attrition. The pattern of the battle was characterized by steady intensification punctuated by qualitative leaps due to the violence of the police and the spread of the conflict into looting and attacks on corporate-owned buildings. The combination of the roles listed above helped to create a situation that was unpoliceable, yet which the police were stubbornly determined to contain. The repression required for every containment effort intensified the revolt and pushed it further out into the surrounding area. By day three, all of the corporate infrastructure surrounding the Third Precinct had been destroyed, and the police had nothing but a "kingdom of ashes" to show for their efforts. Only their precinct remained, a lonely target with depleted supplies. The rebels who showed up on day three found an enemy teetering on the brink. All it needed was a final push.

Day two of the uprising began with a rally: attendees were on the streets, while the police were stationed on top of their building with an arsenal of crowd control weaponry. The pattern of struggle began during the rally, when the crowd tried to climb over the fences that protected the precinct in order to vandalize it. The police fired rubber bullets in response, as rally speakers called for calm. After some time passed and more speeches were made, people tried again. When the volley of rubber bullets came, the crowd responded with rocks and water bottles. This set off a dynamic of escalation that accelerated quickly once the rally ended. Some called for nonviolence and sought to interfere with those who were throwing things, but most people didn't bother arguing with them. Those who did were largely ignored or else the reply was always the same: "That nonviolence shit don't work!" In fact, neither side of this argument was exactly correct: as the course of the battle was to demonstrate, both sides needed the other to accomplish the historic feat of reducing the Third Precinct to ashes.

It's important to note that the dynamic we saw on day two did not involve using nonviolence and waiting for repression to escalate the situation. Instead, a number of individuals stuck their necks out very far to invite police violence and escalation. Once the crowd and the police were locked into an escalating pattern of conflict, the objective of the police was to expand their territorial control, radiating outward from the precinct. When the police decided to advance, they began by throwing concussion grenades at the crowd as a whole and firing rubber bullets at those throwing projectiles, setting up barricades, and firing tear gas.

The intelligence of the crowd proved itself as participants quickly learned *five lessons* in the course of this struggle.

First, it is important to remain calm in the face of concussion grenades, as they are not physically harmful if you are more than five feet away from them. This lesson extends to a more general insight about crisis governance: don't panic, as the police will always use panic against us. One must react quickly while staying as calm as possible.

Second, the practice of flushing tear-gassed eyes spread rapidly from street medics to the rest of the crowd. Employing stores of looted bottled water, many people in the crowd were able to learn and quickly execute eye-flushing. People throwing rocks one minute could be seen treating the eyes of others the next. This basic medical knowledge helped to build the crowd's confidence, allowing them to resist the temptation to panic and stampede, so that they could return to the space of engagement.

Third, perhaps the crowd's most important tactical discovery was that when forced to retreat from tear gas, it is important to refill the abandoned space as quickly as possible. Each time the crowd at the Third Precinct returned, it came back angrier and more determined to either stop the police advance or make the police pay as dearly as possible for every step they took.

Fourth, borrowing from the language of Hong Kong, we saw the crowd practice the maxim "*Be water.*" Not only did the crowd quickly flow back into spaces from which they had to retreat, but when forced outward the crowd didn't behave the way that the cops did by fixating on territorial control. When they could, the crowd flowed back into the spaces from which they had been forced to retreat due to tear gas, but when necessary the crowd flowed away from police advances like a torrential destructive force. Each police advance resulted in more businesses being smashed, looted, and burned. This meant that the police were losers regardless of whether they played defense or offense.

Finally, the fall of the Third Precinct demonstrates the power of ungovernability as a strategic aim and means of crowd activity. *The more that a crowd can do, the harder it will be to police.* Crowds can maximize their agency by increasing the number of roles that people can play and by maximizing the complementary relationships between them.

Nonviolence practitioners can use their legitimacy to temporarily conceal or shield ballistics squads. Ballistics squads can draw police fire away from those practicing nonviolence. Looters can help feed and heal the crowd, while simultaneously disorienting the police. In turn, those going head to head with the police can generate opportunities for looting. Light mages can provide ballistics crews with temporary opacity by blinding the police and disabling surveillance drones and cameras. Nonviolence practitioners can buy time for barricaders, whose works can later alleviate the need for nonviolence to secure the front line.

Here, we see that an internally diverse and complex crowd is more powerful than a crowd that is homogenous. We use the term *composition* to name this phenomenon of maximizing complementary practical diversity. It is distinct from *organization*, because the roles are elective; individuals can shift between them as needed or desired, and there are no leaders to assign or coordinate them. Crowds that form and fight through composition are more effective against the police, not only because they tend to be more difficult to control, but also because the intelligence that animates them responds to and evolves alongside the existing situation on the ground, rather than according to preexisting conceptions of what a battle "ought" to look like. Not only are "compositional" crowds more likely to engage the police in battles of attrition, but they are also more likely to have the fluidity that is necessary to win.

As a final remark, we may contrast composition with the idea of "diversity of tactics" used by the alter-globalization movement. "Diversity of tactics" was the idea that different groups at an action should use different tactical means in different times or spaces to work toward a shared goal. In other words, "You do you, and I'll do me," but without any regard for how what I'm doing complements what you're doing, and vice versa. Diversity of tactics is activist code for "tolerance." The crowd that formed on May 27 against the Third Precinct did not "practice diversity of tactics" but came together by connecting different tactics and roles in a shared space-time as the situation required.

The Ambiguity of Violence and Nonviolence on the Front Lines

We are used to seeing more confrontational tactics used to shield those practicing nonviolence, as in Standing Rock and Charlottesville or in the figure of the "frontliner" in Hong Kong. However, the reversal of this relationship divided the functions of the "militant frontliner" (à la Hong Kong) across two separate roles: shielding the crowd and counteroffensive. This never rose to the level of an explicit strategy in the streets; there were no calls to "shield the throwers." In the US context, where nonviolence and its attendant innocence narratives are deeply entrenched in struggles against state racism, it is unclear if this strategy could function explicitly without ballistics crews first taking risks to invite bloodshed upon themselves. In other words, it appears likely that joining ballistics tactics and nonviolence in Minneapolis was made possible by a tacitly shared perception of the importance of self-sacrifice in confronting the state that forced all sides to push through their fear.

Yet this shared perception of risk only goes so far. While peaceful protesters probably viewed each other's gestures as moral symbols against police violence, ballistics squads undoubtedly viewed those gestures differently, namely as shields or as materially strategic opportunities. Here again, we may highlight the power of the way that composition plays out in real situations by pointing out how it allows the possibility that totally different understandings of the same tactic can coexist side by side. *We combine without becoming the same, we move together without understanding one another, and yet it works.*

There are potential limits to dividing frontliner functions across these roles. First, it doesn't challenge the valorization of suffering in the politics of nonviolence. Second, it leaves the value of ballistic confrontation ambiguous by preventing it from coalescing in a stable role at the front of the crowd. It is undeniable that the Third Precinct would not have been taken without ballistic tactics. However, because the front line was identified with nonviolence, the spatial and symbolic importance of ballistics was implicitly secondary. This leaves us to wonder whether this has made it easier for counterinsurgency to take root in the movement through "community policing" and its corollary, the self-policing of demonstrations and movements within the bounds of nonviolence.

Fact-Checking: A Critical Necessity for the Movement

We believe that the biggest danger facing the current movement was already present at the Battle of the Third Precinct—namely, the danger of rumors and paranoia. We maintain that the practice of "fact-checking" is crucial for the current movement to minimize confusion about the terrain and internal distrust about its own composition.

We heard a litany of rumors throughout day two. We were told repeatedly that riot police reinforcements were on their way to kettle us. We were warned by fleeing crowd members that the National Guard was "twenty minutes away." A white lady pulled up alongside us in her van and screamed, *"The gas lines in the burning AutoZone are gonna blowwww!"* All of these rumors proved to be false. As expressions of panicked anxiety, they always produced the same effect: to make the crowd second-guess its power. It was almost as if certain members of the crowd experienced a form of vertigo in the face of the power that they nonetheless helped to forge.

It is necessary to interrupt the rumors by asking questions of those repeating them. There are simple questions that we can ask to halt the spread of fear and rumors that have the effect of weakening the crowd: "How do you know this?" "Who told you this?" "What is the source of your information?" "Is this a confirmed fact?" "The evidence seems inconclusive. What assumptions are you using to make a judgment?"

Along with rumors, there is also the problem of attributing dispro-portionate importance to certain features of the conflict. Going into day two, one of the dominant storylines was the threat of "Boogaloo Bois," who had shown up the previous day. This surprised us, because we didn't encounter them on day one. We saw half a dozen of them on day two, but they had relegated themselves to the sidelines of an event that outstripped them. Despite their proclaimed sympathy with George Floyd, a couple of them later stood guard in front of a business to defend it from looters. This demonstrated the limit of both their solidarity and their strategic sensibility.

Finally, we awoke on day three to so-called reports that either police provocateurs or outside agitators were responsible for the previous day's destruction. Target, Cub Foods, AutoZone, Wendy's, and a half-constructed condominium high-rise had all gone up in flames by the end of the night.[1] We cannot discount the possibility that any number of hostile forces sought to smear the crowd by escalating the destruction of property. If that is true, however, it cannot be denied that their plan backfired spectacularly.

In general, the crowd looked upon these sublime fires with awe and approval. Even on the second night, when the condominium development became fully engulfed, the crowd sat across from it on 26th Avenue and rested as if gathered around a bonfire. Each structure fire contributed to the material abolition of the existing state of things, and the reduction to ash became the crowd's seal of victory. Instead of believing the rumors about provocateurs or agitators, we find it more plausible that people who have been oppressed for centuries, who are poor, and who are staring down the barrel of a second Great Depression would rather set the world on fire than suffer the sight of its order. We interpret the structure fires to mean that the structures of the police, white supremacy, and class are based in material forces and buildings.

For this reason, we should assess the threat posed by possible provo-cateurs, infiltrators, and agitators on the basis of whether their actions directly enhance or diminish the power of the crowd. We have learned that dozens of structure fires are not enough to diminish "public support" for the movement—though no one could have imagined this beforehand. However, those who filmed crowd members breaking the law while fram-ing them as provocateurs posed a material threat to the crowd. For in addition to bolstering confusion and fear, they empowered the state with access to information.

Postscript: Visions of the Commune

Ever since Guy Debord's 1965 text "The Decline and Fall of the Spectacle-Commodity Economy," there has been a rich tradition of memorializing the emergence of communal social life in riots. Riots abolish capitalist social relations, which allows for new relations between people and the things that make up their world. Here is our evidence.

When the liquor store was opened, dozens came out with cases of beer, which were set on the ground with swagger for everyone to share. The crowd's first beer of choice was Corona.

We saw a man walk calmly out of the store with both arms full of whiskey. He gave one to each person he passed as he walked off to rejoin the fight. Some of the emptied liquor bottles on the street were later thrown at the police.

With buildings aflame all around us, a man walked by and said to no one in particular, "That tobacco shop used to have a great deal on loosies.... Oh, well, fuck 'em."

We saw a woman walking a grocery cart full of Pampers and steaks back to her house. A group that was taking a snack and water break on the corner clapped in applause as she rolled by.

After a group opened the AutoZone, people sat inside smoking cigarettes as they watched the battle between cops and rebels from behind the front window. One could see them pointing back and forth between the police and elements in the crowd as they spoke and nodding in response to each other. Were they seeing the same things we were seeing?

We shopped for shoes in the ransacked storeroom of a looted Foot Locker. The floor was covered wall to wall with half-destroyed shoeboxes, tissue paper, and shoes. People called out for sizes and types as they rummaged. We spent fifteen minutes just to find a matching pair, until we heard the din of battle and dipped.

On day three, the floors of the grocery stores that had been partially burned out were covered in inches of sprinkler water and a foul mix of food that had been thrown from the shelves. Still, people in rain boots could be found inside combing over the remaining goods like they were shopping for deals. Gleaners helped each other step over dangerous objects and, again, shared their loot outside.

As the police made their retreat, a young Somali woman dressed in traditional garb celebrated by digging up a landscaping brick and unceremoniously heaving it through a bus stop shelter window. Her friends—also traditionally dressed—raised their fists and danced.

A masked, shirtless man skipped past the burning precinct and pumped his fists, shouting, "COVID is over!" while twenty feet away some teenage girls took a group selfie. Instead of saying, "Cheese!" they said, "Death to the pigs!" Lasers flashed across the smoke-filled sky at a police helicopter overhead.

We passed a liquor store that was being looted as we walked away from the best party on Earth. A mother and her two young teenagers rolled up in their car and asked if there was any good booze left. "Hell, yeah! Get some!" The daughter grinned and said, "Come on! I'll help you, Mommy!" They donned their COVID masks and marched off.

A day later, before the assault on the Fifth Precinct, there was mass looting in the Midtown neighborhood. A young kid who couldn't be more than seven or eight years old walked up to us with a whiskey bottle sporting a rag coming out the top. "Y'all got a light?" We laughed and asked, "What do you wanna hit?" He pointed to a friendly grocery store, and we asked if he could find "an enemy target." He immediately turned to the US Bank across the street.

June 2020

Theses on the George Floyd Rebellion

Shemon and Arturo

"The working class in every country lives its own life, makes its own experiences, seeking always to create forms and realize values which originate directly from its organic opposition to official society."
—C.L.R. James, Grace Lee Boggs, and Cornelius Castoriadis

1. The George Floyd Rebellion was a Black-led multiracial uprising. This rebellion cannot be sociologically categorized as exclusively a Black rebellion. Rebels from all racialized groups fought the police, looted, and burned property. This included Indigenous people, Latinx people, Asian people, and white people.

2. This uprising was not caused by outside agitators. Initial arrest data shows that most people were from the immediate areas where the riots took place. If there were people driving in from the suburbs, this only reveals the sprawling geography of the American metropolis.

3. While many activists and organizers participated, the reality is that this rebellion was not organized by the revolutionary left or by the so-called progressive NGOs. The rebellion was informal and organic, originating directly from working-class Black people's frustration with class society, particularly the police.

4. Not only was the police state caught off guard by the scope and intensity of the rebellion, but civil society also hesitated and wavered in the face of this popular uprising, which quickly spread to every corner of the country and left the police afraid and in disarray.

5. The police displayed many weaknesses during the initial rebellion. Up against a few hundred protesters, departments were easily

overwhelmed and forced to concentrate their forces in particular hot spots. Once police arrived in one area of conflict, people would retreat and move on to another location to do more damage. Conventional warfare, with its emphasis on superior force and weaponry, failed to counter a series of flexible, decentralized, rapid maneuvers focused on looting and property destruction.

6. The most militant and widespread phase of the rebellion was from May 26 to June 1. After June 1, the rebellion was not only repressed through police and military force but was also politically repressed. Aside from the police, National Guard, and vigilante crackdown, the uprising was politically repressed by reformist elements of the left, which reacted to the riots by blaming them on outside agitators. In some places, "good protesters" went so far as to detain "bad protesters" and hand them over to the police.

7. Black NGOs, including the Black Lives Matter Foundation, hardly had any relationship to the militant phase of the rebellion. In fact, such organizations tended to play a reactionary role, often preventing riots from escalating and spreading. Black NGOs were the spearhead of the forces dividing the movement into "good" and "bad" protesters. The social base of Black NGOs is not the Black proletariat but the Black middle class and, most importantly, a segment of the radicalizing white middle class.

8. The uprising has been put down for the time being. Many NGOs and middle-class people will make a buck off the brave efforts of those who fought and died during that first week, but these rebellions will return. This isn't over.

9. This uprising was about racist police violence and racial inequality, but it was also about class, capitalism, COVID-19, Trump, and much more. It was a reflection of the ongoing struggles that have been happening since the last global recession (2008–2013). Now the world economy is once again in recession.

10. This rebellion opens up a new phase in the history of Turtle Island. A new generation of people have experienced a powerful movement and, in the face of ongoing crises, are unlikely to sit back and accept them. The rebellion has produced a new subjectivity—the George Floyd rebel—initiating a set of processes with many possible outcomes, which will be determined by various trajectories of class conflict.

11. This uprising is the tip of the spear in the struggle against the miserable conditions of the pandemic. The pandemic is only going to worsen the living conditions of people around the world, and as a result we can expect more rebellions across the planet.

12. The ongoing daytime protests are a contradictory product of the rebellion, drawing in large crowds, more middle-class and whiter. This composition certainly helps to create a nonviolent and "good protester"–type atmosphere, but that is inseparable from the Black leaders who advocate this type of politics. At the same time, the expansion of the daytime protests allows for greater participation, which is important.

13. The nighttime riots had a limit in the sense that they did not draw larger sections of society into their activity. Riots, looting, and attacking the police are a young people's and poor people's activity. Many working people had sympathy with it but stayed at home. This shows that riots by themselves are not enough.

14. Many other struggles merged with the street riots, including transit workers refusing to collaborate with the police in transporting detained protesters, prisoners going on hunger strike in solidarity with the rebellion, the creation of autonomous zones, and the occupations of empty buildings. Still, it is unclear how this rebellion connects to the simmering workplace struggles that are unfolding in the context of the pandemic. It seems there are historical and future connections to be made. To what extent were those involved in the workplace struggles in the winter and spring involved in the summer riots? To what extent will the rioters continue the struggle at work?

15. Unions often view police and prison guards as workers in need of protection, instead of seeing them as the armed thugs of the bourgeoisie that they are. Despite the long history of police being strikebreakers, much work remains to be done on the labor front when it comes to police and prison abolition. Without the transit workers, logistical workers, sanitation workers, medical workers, and others, the abolitionist struggle is doomed.

16. Considering the low unionization rates, many workplace struggles will be chaotic, explosive, and unmediated by unions or any other kind of official organization. Unions will come in and attempt to control them and co-opt them. Can the struggles in the workplace

bypass the labor bureaucracy and feed back into the struggles in the streets? If they can, we will enter a new phase of struggle.

17. To reconsolidate its power and prevent revolution, the bourgeoisie scrambles to grant reforms and concessions: some police get fired and charged; the budgets of some police departments get cut; some schools and universities cancel their contracts with police; some racist statues are removed; Trump signs an executive order providing more resources for police accountability; the Minneapolis City Council votes to disband its police department. This is a common pattern in capitalist history—the ruling class responds to revolutionary crises by restructuring itself in a way that allows it to stay in power.

18. What must be done through the self-activity of the proletariat, other elements of society are attempting to do through petitions, voting, legislation, and policy change. Reforms are a commendable goal in a racial capitalist system that clearly prioritizes policing over life. However, we must keep in mind that bourgeois society wants to keep this rebellion as narrow as possible, making it only about George Floyd, about slashing police budgets and redistributing the budget to other areas of society. But this rebellion is about something much more. It is about the deep injustice felt by a people that no amount of reform can extinguish.

19. Abolition entails the material destruction of the range of policing infrastructures. Abolition occurred from May 26 to June 1. As a result of widespread rioting, more has happened in a week to discredit and limit police power than has occurred in many decades of activism. Here we see the revolutionary potential of abolition in its fullest sense, opening up a brief moment of solidarity between the different fractions of the proletariat, causing a national crisis and cracking open the door to a new world.

20. Not everything that took place during the uprising was empowering and liberating. The same problems that existed before continued during the rebellion—racism, transphobia, homophobia, competition for meager resources. All of that doesn't suddenly disappear in a rebellion. The crucial work of building a new world remains to be done.

21. We have yet to answer the full meaning of this rebellion. Is the content of Black Lives Matter only about those who are racialized as Black, or does the Black struggle take on a larger content?

22. Comparisons of this rebellion to 1968 are wrong. This rebellion is different on many levels. It is Black mayors and Black police commissioners who govern in many cities. It was a multiracial proletariat that rebelled.

23. Can the Black proletariat lead the other racialized fractions of the proletariat in the upcoming years? This is a question that goes back a century with W.E.B. Du Bois, Harry Haywood, C.L.R. James, Claudia Jones, and Fred Hampton all trying to devise various coalitions in this country or overseas in an attempt to defeat racial capitalism and empire. They all knew that the Black proletariat could spark a broad rebellion but could not defeat its enemies on its own.

24. The desire for multiracial solidarity is always fraught, as the histories of racism have shown. The development of solidarity will be tense, difficult, and will depend on objective circumstances and strategic choices. Of greatest concern is that solidarity might come at the expense of Black liberation. To prevent this, efforts must be made to respect and support the autonomy of the Black revolutionary struggle.

June 2020

A Gift for Humanity:
The George Floyd Rebellion

Inhabit

The storming of the Third Precinct lifted the veil of fear. As it went up in flames, so did the self-assured certainty of the old world. More than half of the country believes burning the precinct was justified.[1] All the institutions have lost legitimacy: the government, the cops, the media, the economy. The law has shown itself for what it is: sad, scared men draped in a Blue Lives Matter flag crying when the lights go out. Liberalism and its peace treaties are in tatters. This is really the end of an era, the breakdown of an intolerable order. Now we must learn to inhabit the ruins we have given ourselves.

The racial nightmare in this country is an atrocity without comparison. Every nation-state is founded on massacre, but the *unique* violence of chattel slavery, the juridical categories of race, and the direct line from slave catchers to present-day police is specific to the US. The liberal order may apologize profusely for its racist history, but these are crocodile tears. They believe racism is part of human nature. They tell us we need cops to protect us from an evil within, that left to ourselves we would be crueler than their whips or prisons. But the truth is *they* wrote this order into law precisely because we didn't accept their paranoid view of life.[2] Confronted with revolts in the early colonies, the planter class punished servants and slaves by codifying race and enshrining whiteness.

Since the invention of the legal concept of a "white" person, race has marked some as capable of becoming human, while separating out others as always less than human. It's a refinement of the old colonial order in which Christians were the privileged subject. It's a weapon used by elites to divide us, granting privileges to some at the expense of their dignity. There is one history where we see Europeans fighting each other viciously for access to whiteness. There is another history, parallel and diffuse, of those who wished to hold on to their dignity by searching for ways to deactivate, destroy, or escape this racist civilization. Every movement traverses these two histories and must decide upon which of the two they will stake their future. Barring a few exceptions, social movements in the US have sided with the racial order. Each time a revolutionary upsurge shook the foundation, a more optimized racist solution emerged to put people back in their place.

•

From the first slave revolts to the George Floyd Rebellion, this other history beckons us to burn it all and not look back. With each of our defeats, even the dead are sent back to the fields. The racial order mutilates history—first with its minstrel shows, now with its branded content. Politicians feign somber expressions and kneel for photo ops. Amazon ads say: "We see you." Gushers collaborates with Fruit by the Foot to celebrate Black Lives. Soon they're going to tell us that the Black Panther Party was a civil rights organization that wanted to uplift Black entrepreneurs. It's not because the elites *don't get it*. It's because their system relies on Black suffering and racist lies—and its latest version includes self-flagellation for clicks. They will always find a way to profit from it.

Brands and billionaires repent, but the racial nightmare is woven into the social fabric. We see it in our jobs, housing, the media, courts, schools, hospitals. We see it in how Black and Latino people are denied access to medical care and are forced to work amid a pandemic to keep the economy afloat. After the upheaval of the 1960s, urbanists frantic to save capitalism restructured the social landscape along racial lines. The police—a murderous gang emancipated from the law—decide who lives and who dies on this terrain. Everyone knows cops kill. They kill regardless of their own ethnicities, and they kill Black people dispropor- tionately. The cops kill Black Americans, because Black life has been and continues to be considered *disposable*. Slavery, Jim Crow, ghettoization, private prisons—the US is a slaughterhouse.

All manner of reforms have come and gone, even a Black president. But Obama presided over Trayvon's lynching, Tamir's slaying, and Mike Brown's murder. What's left? Generations have prayed, paid, marched, sat-in, voted, cried, and given their lives. Should kids born after 9/11 hurry up and wait? We are sick and tired of this hell. It's not surprising that the cry of Ferguson was "Burn this bitch down." No wonder that's got more appeal than Biden telling people that if they don't vote for him they're not Black. The chorus of "Fuck the police" has resounded for almost thirty years. The days after the Third Precinct burned were a crescendo built upon the 1992 LA riots. Like Ferguson, Minneapolis spread because people didn't back down and demonstrated a courage we all yearn for. A generation is waking up to the realization that body cameras, woke cops, sensitivity training, and "community policing" are all bullshit. If we want to end the racial nightmare, it's going to take all of us digging up the roots of this rotten society.

•

Everyone hates the police. Our rage is justified; it begins with racist murder but encompasses the indignities we each suffer at their hands. In trying to repress the movement, their stupidity and brutality have turned millions against them. Thousands defied the curfews, braving arrest and violence. Traffic halted, bridges blocked, windows smashed, stores looted, statues toppled, cop cars set ablaze—such is the fury they set loose with the murder of George Floyd. Even the National Guard had to be demobilized, because they were faced with a conflict they could not win. The government preferred to save face and prevent defections by bowing out of a situation over which they did not have control. Watching the police flee the Third Precinct, we learned they are not invincible. For once, we defeated them in the streets. How do we make their retreat permanent?

This rebellion cannot be separated from our tumultuous epoch. The American uprising echoes the experimental advances made in Hong Kong and Chile last year and continues to develop tactical innovations in real time. We've seen tear gas doused and umbrellas used as shields and to protect anonymity. Cops' personal information gets leaked, department sites get hacked, and people listen to police scanners to convey the cops' actions to their friends in the streets. "What to wear to a protest" infographics go viral, and engineers build sound-deflecting anti-LRAD shields. Barricades ring autonomous zones to protect against cops, as well as the far right's vehicular attacks. We have new technical means of communication and coordination to keep us moving together, one step ahead of our enemies.

Every movement has its hang-ups. Not a week had gone by before the various activist/organizer cliques began scolding anyone daring enough to fight back. We've all seen them: people who are obsessed with telling others what to do or guilting them into playing an assigned role. Showing up in the middle of a rebellion just to give the order to disperse before the cops do proves you're out of touch with reality. We shouldn't trust every dumbass with a megaphone, and we need to understand the nuances of "leadership."

A march can be "led." Everyone can stay in line and do only what the leaders approve. But it wasn't marches that broke the hold of the police-enforced racial order; it was an uprising. In an uprising, leadership emerges from moment to moment: Who displays courage? Who pushes past their own fear, inviting the rest of us to confront our own? Who refuses to stand by and watch the intolerable? Who sees the relation of forces and opportunities in a clear way? Anyone who has entered such a situation knows the impossibility of following any pre-appointed leadership. You follow the intelligence that emerges from the crowd. You contribute your part, then step back and allow others to do the same. In those situations, the person with the megaphone is usually left in the dust.

This is a complicated and confusing moment. There is no shame in not knowing what to do. We are a generation without victories, without a tradition to teach us what it means to fight and win. Our collective intelligence will only come from being there and experiencing it, without preconceived notions of what it is or what it should be. All the rules, roles, and identities are going to get broken as we figure out how to undo the American nightmare. An uprising is not a Zoom call.

•

There is no outside to the movement. Parasites come from within. A dying liberalism, white or Black, crops up as a real hurdle to the radical leap we need. Some shamelessly do the work of the police, while others hide their agendas behind mission statements.[3] If they get their way, the end of the police will not be the end of policing. We already see abolition being diluted into palatable reforms in elaborate rebranding campaigns. Cops are learning to speak like nonprofits. Mayors call out white privilege to delegitimize the revolt—identity politics weaponized as counterinsurgency. Politicians pretend to listen, while ensuring that protests are subject to heavy surveillance. Under pressure from their workers, tech companies promise not to sell facial recognition technology to the police, but what else is that shit even good for?

"Broken windows" gives way to the "snitch in the screen." If progressives attempt to drain the movement of its vitality, it's because their political goal is to achieve in the industry of crime and punishment what Amazon has in retail—optimized, on-demand, always-on policing. Their reforms entail a perverse version of *transformative justice* that hinges on deeper racial ordering, with silicon chips rather than nightsticks and prisons. The site of incarceration might change, as in the case of electronic monitoring, but the fact of control won't. The irrational prejudice of the beat cop is outperformed by predictive algorithms whose insidious outcomes are perfectly logical and built to spec. The bias in the machine conflates race with crime. The historical legal construction of race in the US is now outmoded by intelligent machines acting on data sets. Instead of the gavel or the badge, a computer decides who gets to be human and who is always less than.

Cutting back on the number of cops on the street, only to put more in the cloud, is just the latest user update to the familiar cycle of revolt and repression. As police departments are defunded, Silicon Valley will be eager to seed the next wave of technological solutions to the problem of crime and unrest. In the historical collision of the pandemic and the anti-police movement, "contact tracing" might become the latest attempt to control an ungovernable populace. All your qualities calculated and policed. Your health, your neighborhood, your habits, your movements, your friendships, your immigration status, your genetic makeup, your skin color, your job, your finances, your search history, your protest attendance—each one coded as variables in their perfectly calibrated nightmare. Hell by design.

·

In crisis lies possibility. Our time has been upended. COVID-19 and the George Floyd Rebellion form a wedge bending the continuum of time at the present. These simultaneous events are a wellspring, where the sad legacy of the racial nightmare and the tradition of incomplete revolutions rise to the surface. The uprising proves that normalcy is far more lethal than the pandemic. The lockdown interruption of the economy has exposed everyone to just how cruel the system is. Those forced to stop working realize just how unnecessary work is. Those forced to keep working realize just how expendable they are. Pent-up energy from months of isolation erupts in the streets—contesting the reign of the police and the economy they defend. Is that store closed down for the quarantine or the riots? Hard to say.

There is unrest in every state. A generation is learning what it means to live and fight. The racist urbanism that structured our cities is being torn apart. Landscapes are being reconfigured with the art of distance and the spirit of rebellion. Outside the burning Third Precinct, laughter and speeches. Outside the burning Wendy's, sideshows with dirt bikes and cars doing donuts. In cities everywhere, fireworks and gunshots in the distance. The mood of this uprising oscillates from rage to exuberance, from celebration to seriousness—somewhere between block party and civil war.

The rebellion is wildly diverse in terms of who is taking part and why they're out there. We are now a month into the unrest, punctuated by sudden intensities, as the police kill again or people in the next city show themselves to be as fearless as Minneapolis. As statues come down amid cheers, it feels like we're witnessing the fall of a regime, but we aren't the only ones watching it happen. There are many forces at play and countless ways this can go. As the rebellion converts urban hell into popular inferno, we have to dream about what can fill the ruin. If we don't, our enemies will.

•

Minneapolis set a tone of ferocity. The Capitol Hill Autonomous Zone in Seattle set another. A choice between clearing the way or laying the path is a false dichotomy. We need to exert force that gives us room to grow and to cultivate material power that gives us the capacity to exert force. Rebellion deepens by increasing the distance between our world and theirs, but it also spreads by incorporating what exceeds their order—all those whose labor is redundant or whose creativity is meaningless under capitalism. Each autonomous zone constitutes a radically open commune, contingent on who moves through it. Right now, we need to expand the ways people can participate in the uprising by extending its revolutionary horizon. If the zones of autonomy are to resonate, they must be able to convert our passions, skill sets, and creativity into practical solutions.

Asking *practical* questions signals that the uprising is serious. A revolution needs to eat, rest, and care for its injured. We need places where we can catch our breath together, whether it's an autonomous zone or a safe house away from the front lines. This is how it is now: street medics must learn how to treat gunshot wounds. As coronavirus cases rise again, we will need not only vigilance about everyone's safety but also the knowledge to care for the sick. If nurses in New York applauding protesters is any indication, defection in the medical industry is not off the table. Such measures aren't only practically necessary for the rebellion to endure, but testify to the ethical truths of the movement. We can give one another the care that the state and its racist order have denied.

The heart of revolution is communal. Revolutionary gestures proliferate, set in motion in Minneapolis and Seattle and reverberating outward. These gestures bring with them advanced propositions but also a certain amount of baggage. Half measures and activist jargon can portray the movement as role-playing. It's important the autonomous zones go all the way—keep the cops out and break down the activist cliques. As housing security and unemployment insurance expire for millions of Americans, expect to see more zones of autonomy and more kinetic spikes of intensity. The short-lived seizure of a hotel in Minneapolis is just the beginning. A looted Target opened the possibility for the redistribution of goods, making common what was prohibitively enclosed. Private property must be abolished in practice through use. We need to increasingly convert hostile environments into territory, enemies into friends. Strip malls and urban architecture are terrains we have to radically reimagine. What questions have to be answered to turn the footprint of a ruined big-box store into habitable space? How do we make these into something dignified, beautiful even? What bioremediating plants can be cultivated to heal the soil in vacant lots? What laws must be ignored and whose authority must be disregarded in order to grow food at scale in city parks?

Urban areas tend to be the sites of the fiercest battles, but movements have to exceed them to survive. Small towns and rural areas have their own revolutionary part to play. The backwardness of the countryside is something of an urban myth. Acting with tact and speaking truth, you'll find people there who are just as angry about the cops and elites as in any hood in the city. Racism should be openly confronted where and how it appears in these places, but don't expect people to follow the script of anti-racism that has been forged in the Ivy Leagues. Holding everyone in your small-town rally to the "high standards" of Twitter dialogue could destroy opportunities for building a common force. The toxic legacy of racism is literal too and will be even harder to dislodge than the last Confederate monument. Whole swaths of the countryside have been devastated by industrial production—a system for which Black lives have always been expendable. With the right alliances, the historical dispossession of Black farmers can also be reversed and new maroon communes can strengthen our collective fist.[4]

Global logistics have made most cities fatally dependent on outside inputs. So it's no surprise that small farms are in demand during a pandemic when you have to depend more on local food systems than the global market. As crises overlap and accelerate, converting farms and other local production into hubs along an autonomous corridor might be the way to stitch together a durable revolutionary force across the shattered capitalist landscape. The hinterlands, depopulated but traversed by supply chains and critical infrastructure, remain a social contradiction of the regime and one of its strategic vulnerabilities. So too might they become our strength, from the opportunities for systemic disruption to the possibilities of freedom and refuge they offer, waypoints on an exodus from the uneven violence of a changing climate.

•

The police marked a moment in human history when a civilization created a fundamental distinction in its social fabric and democratically gave the right reserved for the sovereign to a privileged warrior class. The spartan aesthetic and gritty Punisher imagery popular in police culture revealed how the cops really saw themselves as different and closer to the heavenly elites than the rest of us. The police were paid tribute in upper-bracket wages, earning higher salaries than even those who die in war.

To undermine this legacy, we must reenvision duty. Revolutionary struggle creates the conditions for selfless acts. We often elevate comrades who've been forged in the fight, but it's important to remember *they've also lost themselves there.* We need fighters, but their mixture of adrenaline, ethical fervor, and trauma cannot function as the constituent element of the worlds we are building. Heroism should be honored, but heroes cannot be the source of judgment. This is how every revolution has created a new police force and popular heroes have become the new tyrants. We need to constantly ground ourselves in love for daily life, to tend to the wounded souls of those who've found their heroism and bring them back down to earth. Our duty is to repair the world. Reparation—the historical undoing of white supremacy, the states that have enshrined it, and the economy it has served—will require heroic acts from every corner of existence. The burden to serve cannot be the sole task of our fighters. Each of us has unique potential to perform an exemplary act. We have an obligation to cultivate strength and the capacity for heroism in everyone.

How will we handle interpersonal conflict and harmful behavior? Who will judge? There is no uniform order that can be mapped onto the earth. There is a unique way of inhabiting each place. Repairing a damaged world will be messy and contingent on our shared values. Maybe in some autonomous zone there will emerge an irregular council of grandmas whose wisdom is respected. Maybe elsewhere long conversations facilitated between those in conflict will mark the way. It's not up to us to create a blueprint and judge others by it. What's demanded of us is that we accept a deeper sense of responsibility to nurture our relationships with vulnerability and care. We may need to grow up—to demonstrate revolutionary discipline by discussing the complexities of relationships with each other, learning patience and forgiveness, knowing where to draw harsh lines, and owning the agency of our bodies. Finally, we may still fuck up, and we may still need a period of exile to reflect.

•

The legal origins of race and the police share a common denominator: both are political techniques to govern who can become human and which lives are allowed to live. Some of the fundamental laws that established race in the US legally forbade love between servants and slaves and restricted Africans, even freemen, from possessing arms. Their merciless law has meant the cops are the first response and, at the same time, have the final and often lethal say. Practically, abolishing the police will mean the violence they hold can no longer be the first resort in any situation nor the exclusive burden of any particular section of society. Like love, the capacity for force is something we all must understand that we have at our core. We must honor each other by cultivating it and deciding *how not* to use it.

We must love each other with more intensity than law can govern. The history of Black struggle in the US has blessed this uprising with a repulsion to captivity and the instinct to cultivate joy in *fugitivity*.[5] Law functions by forcibly attaching us to qualities that are only useful and profitable for the order of racial capitalism, draining worlds of their complexity and segregating bodies according to multiplying redlines. We have to break out of this imprisoning logic by establishing authentically diverse worlds. Collective autonomy can only be born by materially breaking down the borders of racial order. The history of resistance to all forms of slavery has shaped Blackness in the US. The George Floyd Rebellion has shared this gift with humanity, proving we have always exceeded the ways that we are governed.

Human drama will not vanish when the thin blue line finally disappears. The stakes will only get higher. As their time comes, we can expect the police will be even more frightened than they are now, lashing out as a new world renders them an artifact of the racial nightmare. There will be more defectors among their ranks, disgusted by their own atrocities. They will have to learn to live with the burden of their actions. Like anyone else who harms their communities with predatory acts, they will have only the mercy of that community and their own will to change. Our task is to untangle judgment from transcendental law. For each other, we must welcome the end of *policing*—emancipating ourselves from the urge to cancel human beings. We must permit ourselves atonement and grace. Assuring someone learns from their mistakes hinges on their bonds with people willing to forgive them. We must likewise learn how to be responsible for our capacity to take or give life, for someday we may be asked to be wise enough to pass judgment. As a revolutionary process settles all debt, may the racial nightmare finally come to a close. May the year of Jubilee finally arrive.

June 2020

Prelude to a Hot American Summer

Jarrod Shanahan and Zhandarka Kurti

"The most dangerous creation of any society is the [person] who has nothing to lose."[1]
—James Baldwin

In the unfolding of social antagonism, which drives human history, there are spectacular moments when a hitherto invisible threshold is crossed and great masses who have long appeared to suffer in silence thrust themselves onto center stage to claim their place as breakers of chains and makers of history. The 2010 self-immolation of Tunisian street vendor Tarek el-Tayeb Mohamed Bouazizi was one such event. The 2016 plan to construct the Dakota Access oil pipeline across sacred Indigenous land and water was another. Now, the police murder of George Floyd, played and replayed millions of times around the world, has set alight a great wave of struggle the likes of which the United States has not seen in half a century. Racist violence and oppression are not a new feature of American society; they are intrinsic to American capitalism, which is to say, intrinsic to the country itself. George Floyd is only among the latest in a pantheon of victims whose lives ended at the deadly nexus of racist exploitation and violence that holds the country together. So why George Floyd, and why now?

In a better world than ours, any death as callous and senseless as Floyd's murder would spark scenes of righteous indignation like those we have seen in the past month. But in the contemporary United States, defined as it is by a banal daily spectacle of pointless, slow violence and wasted life—especially the lives of working-class Black people—the events set in motion by the murder of a regular working-class man on a nondescript American street require a closer look. In particular it is worth exploring how a rebellion against police violence and systemic racism took root during a global pandemic, pushed into the mainstream the hitherto marginal movement to divert police funding to much-needed social services, and opened new horizons for liberation—and recuperation—unimaginable just weeks before.

In the months leading up to George Floyd's murder, the coronavirus brought much of the global economy to a halt, placing at least thirty-six million Americans on some type of unemployment, while laying bare the shocking inadequacy of American public infrastructure to protect vulnerable people, especially Black people, from the physical and economic ravages of COVID-19. "The old African American aphorism 'When white America catches a cold, black America gets pneumonia,'" writes Keeanga-Yamahtta Taylor, "has a new, morbid twist: when white America catches the novel coronavirus black Americans die."[2] But the disaster extended far beyond Black America. As COVID-19 ravaged the world economy, many Americans who previously considered themselves secure, or even middle-class, were confronted with the specter of interminable joblessness, a dire lack of hospital beds and health services for all but the superrich, and the startling fragility of a world market on which we are all forced to depend for subsistence. Meanwhile, politicians and business elites openly debated the magnitude of human sacrifice necessary for the cause of getting the economy moving again. But this kind of macabre calculation is nothing new. For decades, the US ruling class has shirked the brunt of sluggish profit rates, capital flight, and recurring economic crisis by stripping away the standard of living of working people, replacing the proverbial carrot of wealth redistribution with the stick of policing and incarceration.[3] Recent national strike waves in education and nursing, as well as behind prison walls, including a recent strike at Rikers Island against New York City's disastrous handling of COVID behind bars, have demonstrated that many sectors are ready to fight back against a society whose central figure of social reproduction is the policeman's club.[4]

Alongside the fear of impending death lurks the prospect of a life of poverty, as Americans watch their livelihoods crumble, bills amass unpaid, mortgages and rents come due and past due, and the most substantive relief comes in the form of a one-time $1,200 check. Is it any wonder that the horrific sight of a man slowly choked to death while pleading for his life has found such widespread resonance? Thus, while building upon the Black Lives Matter (BLM) movement and the long tradition of Black radicalism that came before it, the unfolding rebellion against racist policing in the United States is inextricable from the COVID crisis, its lethal consequences, and the picture it has emblazoned on many Americans' minds of a capitalist society in decline. Perhaps we have at long last reached the breaking point. "When history is written as it ought to be written," wrote C.L.R. James, "it is the moderation and long patience of the masses at which [people] will wonder, not their ferocity."[5]

Get in the Zone

> "Shout-out to my friends at home on the couch! I did it! I'm here! I'm the man!"[6]
> —protester outside the burning Third Precinct

In this moment of great upheaval, one thing that is certain is that American cities are no longer ghost towns. "COVID is over!" declared a shirtless yet masked protester, pumping his fist amid the flames of Minneapolis.[7] Tens of thousands of people march on previously deserted boulevards and highways, weaving along and crisscrossing the overpoliced streets of New York, Chicago, DC, and Philadelphia, but also along the Main Streets of smaller cities and towns across America. Groups of demonstrators, at once jubilant and enraged, move through streets made impassible to auto traffic, scattering into meandering snake marches, reconverging by accident amid cheers of joy. These street scenes have furnished an organic anarchic environment for a wide range of tactics, whether they be anti-cop graffiti, expropriation of goods, pitched battles with the police, or simply feeling the power of shutting down the streets without permission. We've seen COVID mutual aid networks immediately repurposed to provide food, water, and masks to sustain protesters throughout the course of long marches, while these practices are also taken up by individual people announcing their free wares with signs on their backpacks or cars. In Chicago, cars parked along march routes, distributing hand sanitizer through the driver's side window. Simultaneously, "car blocs" provided a safer way for people vulnerable to COVID to participate—and snarled traffic in the process, often with passengers protruding through sunroofs, waving signs and dancing.

Anyone with a social media account and a few followers can call a demonstration, and while the would-be middle managers of utopia might bemoan the amateurism of it all, countless young people are learning by doing. In many places, these youths are proving braver and more tactically ingenious than old guard organizers who follow the familiar peaceful protest script.

In the US, unpermitted marches and infrastructure blockades call to mind the BLM movement at its post-Ferguson peak.[8] But unlike the previous wave of BLM protests, we have seen far more violent confrontations with police and widespread militant tactics. We have seen police cars set on fire, businesses targeted, and goods expropriated in cities big and small. In Minneapolis, fire consumed the city for days. The now-infamous Third Precinct, home to Derek Chauvin and his accomplices, was set afire along with an AutoZone, a Target, a liquor store, other local businesses, and a condominium building under construction.[9] Nearby, protesters worked out inside a ransacked Planet Fitness. Locals were spotted mowing their lawns in gas masks. For a time, police were nowhere to be found. Afraid and outnumbered, they awaited relief from the National Guard. In Greece, demonstrators hurled firebombs at the US embassy in Athens in solidarity with those protesting the death of George Floyd. Clashes with police have also marked anti-police actions in Mexico and in England.[10] In the latter, a statue of a prominent slave trader was torn down and consigned to Bristol's harbor, formerly a key node in the Atlantic slave trade.[11]

In New York City alone, at least forty-seven police vehicles have been damaged and at least thirteen of them torched by protesters.[12] Broken glass lined the streets of Fordham Road in the Bronx, Brooklyn's Atlantic Avenue, and Manhattan's SoHo.[13] In Chicago, roughly one hundred police cars have been taken out of service, and friends report spotting others out on patrol with broken windows and covered in anti-cop graffiti.[14] In Atlanta, protesters climbed the sign in front of CNN headquarters, spray-painted anti-police messages, and waved the Mexican flag.[15] In Philadelphia, a statue of the notorious Frank L. Rizzo, an enduring symbol of police abuse and racism, was attacked and defaced.[16] In Nashville, protesters set fire to the courthouse.[17] Police departments and courthouse buildings were targeted by protesters in other cities, including Dallas, Denver, Phoenix, and Portland.[18] In Denver, protesters smashed the windows of the Colorado Judicial Center.[19] In Portland, protesters smashed windows and set fires inside the Multnomah County Justice Center while correctional staff manned the first floor.[20]

Confronting the cops, protesters have tossed bottles, bricks, and Molotov cocktails, have returned volleys of tear gas cans, have shot fireworks, and—following the examples of Hong Kong and Santiago—have used lasers to impair cops' vision, even forcing a helicopter to retreat in Minneapolis.[21] In Seattle, protesters have beaten back police and opened a cop-free "autonomous zone."[22] Even the "hands up, don't shoot" tactic pioneered in the streets of Ferguson, often misunderstood as a symbol of pacifism, can in fact be a confrontational tactic when facing down a police line, as it was in the siege of the Third Precinct.[23] At least thirteen protesters have been killed thus far and hundreds more injured by police tear gas and rubber bullets.[24] While chemical agents are prohibited by the Geneva Convention, American police deploy them domestically. In Louisville, Kentucky, the National Guard shot and killed David McAtee, an owner of a barbeque restaurant known for giving cops free meals.[25] In San Jose, police rubber bullets maimed a local activist who worked to educate cops about their "implicit biases."[26]

Municipal governments firing and pressing criminal charges against police murderers—a central demand of the original Black Lives Matter movement—has not slowed the rebellion's momentum. After the Minneapolis police took the rare step of firing four of its own and the district attorney took the even rarer step of filing murder charges against them, the rebellion continued unabated. Three days after George Floyd's killers were charged, the streets of Washington, DC, erupted in flames. The headquarters of the AFL-CIO, a defender of the police unions in its ranks, was smashed and defaced.[27] Afraid of the potential and looming danger to the White House, as protesters clashed with police and set the guardhouse on fire, officials turned off the exterior lighting and President Trump hurried off to hide in a bunker.[28] That same day, the National Guard was called in to Washington, DC, Georgia, Kentucky, Wisconsin, Colorado, Ohio, Tennessee, and Utah.[29]

Interviews with Minneapolis protesters reveal growing frustrations over the inability of so-called police reform to stop police murders. One young Black protester pointed to the fires consuming the Third Precinct as he stated: "We are living through hundreds of years of discrimination and a bunch of stigma that we face every day. We tried peaceful protesting, we tried every different direction, and this was our last resort."[30] According to one poll, over half of Americans believe that the burning of the Third Precinct by protesters was justified—a higher approval rating than Donald Trump or Joe Biden.[31] But the rebellion's unfolding is not unopposed, nor are its enemies simply the cops.

Don't Believe the Hype

> "These people who judge us should take a city bus or a cab through the South Bronx, the Central Ward of Newark, North Philadelphia, the Northwest section of the District of Columbia or any Third World reservation, and see if they can note a robbery in progress."[32]
> —Kuwasi Balagoon

Aided by their mouthpieces in the press, state officials have done everything in their power to divide the rebellion into "peaceful protesters" and "rioters"—the latter portrayed as looters and opportunistic riffraff out to destroy the fabric of communities. In this lexicon, many tactics in which no human body is harmed are classed as "violent," including the destruction of inanimate objects, the expropriation of commodities for use, and self-defense against police who have, in fact, been initiating violent encounters all over the country. Befitting a society that privileges the value of private property over human life, so-called looting has proven to be a particularly divisive issue. Interestingly, however, debates around expropriations, as with those around arson, have focused almost solely on the targeting of small businesses, with a noticeable lack of sympathy for chain stores like Target and Wal-Mart. Similarly, during the 1965 riots in Watts, Black small business owners painted "Blood Brother" on their storefronts. While the term is no longer in vogue today, signs declaring businesses "Black-owned" have sprung up across cities like Chicago and New York.

"I grew up around these buildings," a protester in Minneapolis proclaimed as the blocks around the Third Precinct went up in flames. "Fuck these buildings. I used to get tacos here. Fuck them tacos. Fuck this shit, man. Fuck it all!"[33] Despite widespread evidence of rebellion by local residents, the timeless racist myth of the outside agitator has been resurrected once more.[34] Claims of outside agitators in Minneapolis, St. Paul, Sacramento, DC, Houston, and Miami—to name a few—were contradicted by arrest data, which showed that the militant street tactics were largely conducted by locals.[35] Additionally, proponents of this theory have yet to explain how outside agitators can be present in nearly every city simultaneously. Patronizing rumors have swirled that a single white outside agitator "started the riot" in Minneapolis, as if one person could force thousands to adopt militant tactics if they weren't already good and ready.[36]

A still more effective fabrication pushed by liberal politicians and the mainstream press builds off the minimal presence of white supremacists on the fringes of these massive street actions to argue that legions of undercover white supremacists are driving all confrontational tactics. This racist narrative, which denies agency to non-white people and forecloses their ability to take radical action, functions alongside a bevy of misinformation spread by cable talking heads and sensationalist scholars like University of Chicago historian Kathleen Belew, who float reckless conspiracy theories that ascribe Black agency to white people, such as the debunked stories about "bait bricks" left by police to lure hapless rubes into breaking the law.[37] The conservative counterpart to these canards is the similarly unproven invocation of "antifa" lurking behind every transgression of respectability and law, echoed by Trump himself.[38] Those spreading disinformation are aided by a lack of information discipline in activist circles, where outlandish rumors are spread at fever pitch, often free of factual substantiation, creating needless panic.

The counterinsurgency strategies we have seen are largely nothing new. In the time since Watts and the birth of Black Power, entire urban political machines have been erected to prevent Black insurrection, with police forces "diversified" and Black and brown radicals either bought off, marginalized, incarcerated, or murdered.[39] Novel in the post-1968 moment is the growth of the third-party sector, or nonprofits, as the managers of working-class misery.[40] The proximity of these community-based nonprofits to large foundation money and Democratic Party coffers helps them fund programs that offer meager support to working-class people, and mostly positions them to broker relationships between working-class residents and employers, landlords, and carceral state officials.[41] Key to this alliance is keeping the peace with the cops, even though this is mostly a one-sided deal. It is no coincidence, then, that the most confrontational direct action in Minneapolis was taken outside the power of the local politicians, faith leaders, and nonprofits, or that we have seen considerably less confrontational direct action where these forces have gained control of the movement.

Things Fall Apart

"Everybody's trying to shame us. The legislators. The press. Everybody's trying to shame us into being embarrassed about our profession. Well, you know what? This [badge] isn't stained by someone in Minneapolis. It's still got a shine on it, and so do theirs, so do theirs. Stop treating us like animals and thugs, and start treating us with some respect! That's what we're here today to say. We've been left out of the conversation. We've been vilified. It's disgusting. It's disgusting."[42]
—Mike O'Meara, president of the New York State Police Benevolent Association

In 1968, Richard Nixon could count on large numbers of white Americans, the "silent majority," to heed his calls of "law and order." Today, the geography of recent protests shows many rural, majority-white areas as the scene of spirited and at times confrontational BLM protests.[43] This is significant, as over the past four decades the growth of a massive security and carceral state in tandem with the destruction of the post-war welfare state has relied on the assent of a critical mass of the working- and middle-class white people who form the popular base of this "law-and-order" coalition with the US ruling class and leading politicians of both parties.[44] The predominant role police play in many domains of social life—education, drug addiction, mental health, homelessness, sex work, etc.—derives in large part from the success of this coalition, which alongside the hollowing out of the welfare state has fueled the rise of what we today call "mass incarceration."[45] In 2017, Black Youth Project 100, Law for Black Lives, and the Center for Popular Democracy compiled an overview of police budgets across American cities to demonstrate how massive investment in law enforcement has gone hand in hand with diminished investment in social safety nets and basic infrastructure in working-class communities of color.[46]

The present recalls another decisive moment: the urban crisis of the 1970s, when this coalition solidified. Just as the rug of post-war prosperity was pulled from beneath the feet of working-class people, a critical mass of white Americans threw in their lot with the forces of police and prisons against the threat of Black and brown radicalism.[47] Simultaneously, police and prison guards, as custodians of the law-and-order coalition, were able to maneuver and secure a comfortable position for themselves in exchange for overseeing the imposition of austerity with brute force. Since then, generations of Americans have seen their pensions privatized and taken away, the public sector being the first on the chopping block of liberal mayors' budgets, community programs offering free services shut down, public housing obliterated in all but a handful of major cities, and homelessness now a permanent feature of working-class life.[48]

Today, even in the most liberal cities, COVID-19 is already providing the ruling classes with the opportunity to further cut job security, housing, services, and youth programs. Police budgets, on the other hand, are already seeing an increase—no doubt anticipating the fiery potential that a growing working-class immiseration could translate into. It should hardly surprise us that amid the ravages of COVID, animosity toward the police as the central figure of social reproduction for the American working class, especially its most violent forms, is on the rise. In New York City, this hostility has assumed a catchy slogan.

"NYPD Suck My Dick"

"Tension is high, man these niggas is irate
You can see it in they eyes, they wanna violate
Screaming out 'Oink! Oink! Bang! Bang!
Gang! Gang! Gang! Gang! Murder! Murder!'
Murder they mind state"
—Vic Mensa, "16 Shots"

Central to the present rebellion is open and bitter hostility toward the police. "Mom, I have to go," a young Minneapolis protester was overheard saying on the phone. "Fuck the police. Mom, okay, fuck the police. I'll call you later. Fuck the police."[49] The classic anti-police slogans "Fuck 12" (numerical slang for police) and "ACAB" (all cops are bastards), derived respectively from hip hop and punk subcultures, have escaped these niche lexicons and become ubiquitous on protest signs, shop windows, city walls, and even cop cars, coast to coast. The most popular chant in New York City—"NYPD suck my dick!"—is driven by Black youth but embraced by all but the most puritanical. On Chicago's South Side chant leaders evoke local rapper Vic Mensa's anti-cop anthem "16 Shots" by counting to eleven, at which the crowd rejoins "Fuck 12!"

The rebellion's banner victory thus far was overtaking and destroying the Minneapolis Police Department's Third Precinct. Credit for whatever reforms follow in the weeks and months ahead is due in no small part to the revelers who put this building to the torch. We imagine it will be difficult, moving forward, for reformers and radicals alike to sit through endless municipal budgetary meetings and community town halls after Minneapolis has demonstrated how effectively a critical mass of pissed-off people can cut through the red tape. It remains the most significant fact of the entire rebellion that the people of Minneapolis found it suitable to skip these niceties and simply destroy the building where Derek Chauvin suited up the day he killed George Floyd. The Third Precinct was also where Chauvin and his accomplices later filed a falsified story about Floyd perishing of natural causes, which was passed along by their superiors to the press and would likely have passed as truth had the murder not been caught on tape by a courageous Black teenager named Darnella Frazier.[50] One can only guess how many such falsehoods have been cooked up within the precinct walls that the good people of Minneapolis decided were no longer fit to stand.

The siege of the Third Precinct contrasts profoundly with the events of 2015, when the MPD murder of Jamar Clark spurred a nearly month-long occupation outside of the officers' precinct.[51] This action was effective and befitted the political moment when it occurred, but we are in a new era. This time around, within three days of George Floyd's murder, the offending precinct was up in smoke. The popular slogan of the 2016 Parisian uprising, *Tout le monde déteste la police* ("Everyone hates the police"), far better encapsulates the tenor of the present moment than the cliché about "bad apples," a cliché that begs the question: Why don't the good apples blow the whistle or quit?

Today's burgeoning anti-police zeitgeist has been aided tremendously by the cops themselves. In the present rebellion, the task of mediating antagonisms between police and the policed has largely proven impossible. Not even the most liberal cities have been able to control their cops. Thanks largely to social media, Americans have seen police use all tools at their disposal, including stun hand grenades, tear gas, rubber bullets, and even police vehicles, to attack protesters. Dangerous projectiles like tear gas canisters and rubber bullets are fired directly at protesters' heads, in contravention of their intended "nonlethal" use. Police brutality has also not spared so-called peaceful protesters, even when they are white, nor has meting out brutality been limited to white cops. Their brutal street tactics have reliably injected fresh impetus to the movement with each new viral video, and the conspicuous solidarity that they show one another as the tide of public opinion turns against them has made the bad-apples narrative impossible to swallow. For instance, when two Buffalo cops were disciplined for brutalizing seventy-five-year-old Catholic Worker organizer Martin Gugino, the entire riot squad resigned from their voluntary post in protest, making their allegiances clear to all.[52]

Police unions are also fueling the growing polarization by material necessity, since they stand above all else both for the freedom of individual cops to wield violence any way they see fit and for the boundless expansion of the police in terms of both their numbers and the scope of their power.[53] By their very nature, police unions oppose efforts to chasten and downsize police departments, just as they are prone to slander the victims of police violence to help exonerate the murderers they represent. Thus, the head of the Police Officers Federation of Minneapolis predictably dubbed George Floyd a "criminal" and his supporters "terrorists," winning few supporters save for those presently hiding behind badges.[54] Further, as politicians scramble to pass symbolic concessions to a movement that has them terrified, police and their powerful unions have largely proven unwilling if not incapable of budging an inch, besides the occasional corny "taking a knee" with protesters, sometimes as a prelude to brutalizing them.[55]

The Color Line and Other Barricades

"Today I saw a storm at sea
Its bilious white and black
It spent its forces as if it knew
The power of its back."[56]
—Claudia Jones, "Storm at Sea"

Along with opposing the police, this movement also takes direct aim at the racial violence of capitalist society that the daily violence of police perpetuates and upholds.[57] Floyd's death also came on the heels of the police murder of Breonna Taylor, a Black woman gunned down in her own home by cops executing a "no-knock" warrant, and the shooting death of Ahmaud Arbery, a Black man killed by a former cop and his son in broad daylight as he jogged down the street. These cases were only two of the latest and most high-profile in a seemingly endless cascade of white supremacist terror reminiscent of the old Jim Crow. What Floyd allegedly did to warrant a summary execution is completely beside the point, but the fact that it was the trifle of passing a counterfeit $20 bill amid a global pandemic that has rendered over thirty million Americans unemployed provokes all the more anger. This aspect of Floyd's case also calls to mind the stories of Eric Garner, Michael Brown, and Sandra Bland, who perished at the hands of the state after trifling encounters, catalyzing the first incarnation of BLM. The limits of liberal police reform and the continuous police killings have left young people with no choice but to be "fed the fuck up!"[58]

As the cultural winds shift quickly away from the decades-long worship of police, big companies are getting in on the act, with anti-racism taking the place of the COVID-canceled Pride Month as the flagship of corporate virtue-signaling. But young protesters know better than to wait for Bank of America to release a statement of support for the movement. Around the nation, bank windows have been broken and banks set on fire. In one protest photo shared on Twitter, a young Black girl is posing in front of a boarded-up Minneapolis bank adorned in graffiti that reads: "This is for all the overdraft fee$." The most powerful fight against racism and white supremacy remains in the streets, where people are taking risks in concert and struggling together to overcome the historical legacy of racism through direct action aimed at building a better world. This is also the primary site where racial divisions can be broken down through the process of shared risk-taking, magnified now even more by a global pandemic. As one piece of graffiti on a Philadelphia trash can proclaimed: "To all the white ppl out here with us: you a real nigga!" This is by no means a unanimous sentiment, however, as plenty of people have stepped in to instruct white people in ornate detail on the proper way to behave in this moment and thereby preserve their distinct social existence as white.[59]

If social media are any indication, people are doing important work breaking these walls down in workplaces and homes through debates over just exactly what it will take for the American police to stop killing Black people. People are disagreeing and drawing the line with family members over dinner and all over social media. One young person tweeted: "I lost my aunt today.... She's not dead, just racist!" Conversations about racism, police violence, and white supremacy are dividing family members, causing important frictions and divides not seen perhaps since the late 1960s. White members of the Black Lives Matter Tennessee Facebook page have publicly shamed family members, friends, acquaintances, and local businesses that still proudly display Confederate flags and memorabilia. Importantly, these conversations are also happening in Latino and Asian communities. In New York City, a video showing Dominican men defending stores against alleged Black looters went viral and sparked important discussions and solidarity protests among Latinos and African Americans.[60] In Chicago's South Side, Mexican organizers sponsored a solidarity rally to bring together African American youth and Mexican youth, and local activists organized a truce between street families, after considerable violence and tension engendered by the chaos of the rebellion.[61] While tactics have remained largely street demonstrations, confrontations, and expropriations and have yet to penetrate "the glass floor" into the abode of production, the rebellion is doing necessary work to challenge the color line in American society and lay a foundation for future offensives against capital.[62] It is also important to watch the ways that multiracial struggle and collective risk-taking are destabilizing boundaries in the streets.

These questions around racist police violence and white supremacy have exposed not only American police to public scrutiny but all other institutions that reproduce white supremacy—including obvious vectors like prisons and multinational corporations and less obvious ones like public schools, which are often defended as inherently good for working-class people of color but simultaneously abet the "school-to-prison pipeline" and other forms of racial differentiation from an early age.

We imagine that the swirling boardroom conversations and the anti-racist training workshops that will unfold over the next year, even if successful, will only incorporate a small handful of Black Americans into the upper echelons of corporate America and the nonprofit sector. They will also do very little to stem the tide of a growing number of discontented youth who are perpetually kept out of the material comforts afforded the petty bourgeoisie, and from whom the coming COVID depression will likely strip whatever illusions remain that social mobility is still possible in the United States. Today's young people are already the generation most hostile to capitalism and amenable to "socialism." Many are now finding in the streets the means to this end that they failed to win with Bernie's ballot box "revolution," as *Jacobin* flails and flounders to say anything relevant to the youthful leaders of this rebellion. Today's horizon extends far beyond voting or a more diverse 1%. Most telling in this respect is the present demand to defund the police.

"Starve the Pigs"

"A lot of people in the bourgeoisie tell me they don't like Rap Brown when he says, 'I'm gon' burn the country down,' but every time Rap Brown says, 'I'm gon' burn the country down,' they get a poverty program."[63]
—Stokely Carmichael, Free Huey rally

While Democrats and nonprofits call for "reform," the recent history of Minneapolis, where the rebellion began, provides us with front-row seats to the tragicomedy that this entails. Beginning in 2012, Janeé Harteau, the city's first female and openly gay police chief, vowed to overhaul the force and embraced change along lines advocated by the Obama administration.[64] In 2015, in the aftermath of the Ferguson rebellion, Minneapolis was selected by the Department of Justice as one of six cities to undergo reform efforts as part of Obama's national My Brother's Keeper initiative. In three years, $4.75 million dollars were spent to collect data and come up with a list of evidence-based practices to repair community-police relations.[65] The result was Harteau's "A New Police Model," aimed at shifting the MPD to so-called community policing. The initiative was widely resisted by the cops. Two years later, a damning report by the Department of Justice accused the MPD of failing to discipline officers charged with misconduct.[66] The MPD found loopholes to avoid police suspensions and other forms of discipline and instead sent its officers to "coaching sessions," which amounted to reading the police manual out loud.[67]

In 2016, the MPD rewrote its policy regarding the use of force and instituted new rules that required police officers to intervene when fellow officers were being abusive.[68] Other changes were introduced, including training on procedural justice, implicit bias, and crisis intervention.[69] Yet these changes were never embraced by the rank and file. A year later in the wake of the MPD murder of forty-year-old Australian American Justine Damond, Chief Harteau quit her post.[70] In 2018, the MPD was lauded for leading the nation in terms of embracing procedural change despite yet more public outrage over a police killing, this time of a thirty-one-year-old Black man named Thurmon Blevins.[71] Since 2000, the MPD has killed 195 people, most of them working-class and disproportionately Black.[72] Today, the usual calls for police reform and accountability, which constituted the mainstream demands of the 2014–2015 cycle of struggle, seem dated and hopelessly inadequate.

Like Stokely Carmichael in the 1960s, many of today's young protesters have learned from the fire of Minneapolis that riots, for better or worse, are often the main pathway to forcing the state to grant real material concessions to working-class people. Before the present rebellion, the last time that New York City was placed under curfew was on the eve of the Harlem Riot of 1935, which forced Mayor Fiorello La Guardia to consider the city's housing problem and build the Harlem River Houses, a housing project built to accommodate working-class African Americans and Puerto Ricans. Against this historical backdrop, today's protests have moved straight for the jugular: police budgets, which are representative of the hollowed-out welfare state, the material power of police unions, and the base of the law-and-order coalition itself. After surveying a litany of failed liberal policing reforms that do little to reduce police power and growing working-class misery, sociologist Alex Vitale concludes: "The only leverage that remains is to starve the beast."[73]

In a move to appease protesters and piss off another DC resident, Donald Trump, DC mayor Muriel E. Bowser had "Black Lives Matter" painted in bold yellow lettering near the White House. A day later, protesters decided to add their own messaging: "Defund the Police." The calls to defund the police have grown louder and have become a dominant political voice, drowning out liberal demands like Campaign Zero's #8CantWait program, which proposes a list of procedural reforms promising "to bring immediate change to police departments,"[74] another way to build a more efficient police power. Abolitionists have called such liberal demands "dangerous and irresponsible."[75] A basic abolitionist criterion for non-reformist reforms is the litmus test of whether they strengthen the power, social scope, and funding base of the police—which most liberal reforms like #8CantWait surely do.[76]

Following the groundwork laid by organizations like Critical Resistance, Black feminist theorists, and the tireless work of police and prison abolitionists who have shown time and time again the limits of police reform, the campaign #8toAbolition has released a set of demands to defund the police. Defunding the police is only one part of a broad agenda that includes their removal from schools and other social welfare institutions, the channeling of resources toward free and accessible public transportation, health infrastructure that supports free care and treatment services for low-income residents, cancellation of rent without burden of repayment during the pandemic, banning evictions, removing police from shelters and other social welfare institutions, repurposing empty buildings to provide shelter to the homeless, and more bread-and-butter redistributive policies. In short, the #8toAbolition campaign sees defunding of the police as part of a bigger struggle to redistribute resources and redefine society based on need, not the profits amassed from exchange.

One of the most significant developments of the present rebellion has been its embrace of this hitherto marginal demand. The fact that a large number of protesters can today imagine a world without police, instead of yet another quixotic movement toward "police reform," is an important political development that deserves our unyielding support. No other anti-police protest in past or recent history has offered up the demand to defang police in favor of building what can be seen as a move toward social democracy for Black America. Every anti-police riot in American history from 1919 to the present has ended with an acknowledgment of the material conditions shaping police violence against Black Americans but has arrived at two main solutions: police reform and the promise of job opportunities for Black youth. Today, such crumbs are too little, too late. Further, Trump's response to the protest movement has been to beat the war drums demanding a reinforcement of law and order reminiscent of Nixon in the late 1960s. His attorney general William Barr had no qualms about sending the military to respond to protesters outside the White House.[77] The breaking of ranks of the US ruling class on how to respond to the rebellion represents a rare opportunity to push a radical agenda into the mainstream. By taking aim at police budgets, the vanguard of the anti-police movement is launching what could potentially become the opening salvo against the capitalist social order that makes police necessary.[78]

Politically, the defund demand is an example of how the more radical tendencies of BLM have seized the moment and dealt a successful blow to calls for still more police reform along these same old lines. After the first wave of BLM protests dissipated and was channeled into liberal talking heads and Democratic Party cheerleaders, smaller BLM groupings began to direct their energy into local organizing. This coincided with a wave of Democratic Socialists of America (DSA) chapters springing up in major cities and electing young progressive candidates to defeat Democratic Party machines in city council, senate, and local district attorney offices. In Minneapolis, three BLM organizations have been pushing local city council members to reduce police budgets and invest that money in a social safety net. MPD150, Black Visions, and Reclaim the Block have argued for more funding allocated to working-class communities of color, as opposed to police, jails, and prisons. During Super Bowl weekend, Black Visions Collective members blocked and shut down Metro Light Rail, which was only accessible to ticket holders and out of reach for low-income Black residents.[79] In New York City, the No New Jails NYC campaign against a plan to expand the city's jail system created important networks and publicized a broad vision for prison abolition in the city, rooted in defunding police and prisons and investing in public services for working-class communities of color hit hardest by the scourge of mass incarceration.[80]

Minneapolis and New York City are not the only cities where debates about defunding the police are taking place. On the heels of the Minneapolis city council decision, Democratic Socialist alderman in Chicago Rosanna Rodriguez-Sanchez penned an op-ed demanding that similar measures be taken up in Chicago.[81] In Los Angeles, the local Black Lives Matter chapter has been pushing for the defunding of the police department and has taken this opportunity to win more public support for its work. In response to Campaign Zero's #8CantWait, LA Action Network drafted a document calling it out as an example of "superficial reform" and demanding the defunding of the police. Like many city councils around the nation, LA has been overseeing budget cuts to various social service programs and departments, while increasing the scope and size of the police force. Amid the protests, the mayor agreed to increase the budget cut to the LAPD to $150 million, which would be redistributed to the city's various nonprofit agencies. Organizations like LA Action Network argue that this is a drop in the bucket for the kind of investment that is needed in working-class communities of color.

Part of the struggle waged by abolitionists will be to prevent defunding and other non-reformist reforms from being hijacked by liberal nonprofits seeking to absorb the gains of the movement and secure lines of funding for their own urban poverty programs. This is not the defunding vision that is advocated by abolitionists like Ruth Wilson Gilmore and the organization Critical Resistance. Yet the tension between a social democratic horizon and communist vision remains one that the protest movement will have to grapple with. Even within the present rhetoric of revolution, defunding can easily become about taking from one sector of the capitalist state to benefit another, which falls within the horizon of capitalist social democracy. In the pursuit of non-reformist reforms, abolitionists must continually check in with themselves: Have we simply become left Keynesians?

Toward a Long, Hot Summer

> "There are decades where nothing happens; and there are weeks where decades happen."
> —commonly attributed to Vladimir Ilyich Lenin

Not since the late 1960s, when the Black Panthers enjoyed widespread popularity among young people and chants of "Off the pigs!" echoed in demonstrations across the US, have the American police been forced to adopt such a defensive posture. Fifty years of right-wing politics and Hollywood copaganda have worked tirelessly to paper over the contradictions between the cops and the people they police, which are presently laid bare. The cancellation of the dehumanizing TV show *COPS* is the perfect bellwether of the mythos of "not all cops" going up in smoke before our eyes.[82] This is a moment for radical change, not piecemeal reform. "Action speaks louder than words, bro," a masked Black youth told reporters, as they stood outside looted burning stores in Minneapolis. "Fuck all that talking."[83] The expropriation of commodities, especially when it has involved large chain stores with little connection to the neighborhoods they exploit, has garnered more sympathy among ordinary Americans than during the 2014–2015 wave of protests. The sentiment that human life is worth more than a bank or a Target store is indisputable, especially amid a global pandemic. But this tactic seems already to have run its course, revealing a series of potential limits awaiting those who aim to push the struggle further.

For starters, expropriation and property destruction on the local scale has clear limitations: once you empty a box store, it will not be refilled until order is restored. When you burn down a (non-carceral) piece of infrastructure, you foreclose its reappropriation for prosocial uses. The tactics that have arisen in this moment, while far more militant than those of previous cycles of struggle, have yet to take hold of the supply chains that will keep goods flowing to help reproduce a sustained insurrection. On the other hand, social reproduction arising within long marches, such as the organized distribution of food and water, along with street medics

THE GEORGE FLOYD UPRISING

and the short-lived Minneapolis hotel—taken over by protesters and used to house the houseless—are examples of experimentation in reproducing the movement for an extended horizon, which must be built upon moving forward.[84] Similarly, manifestations of this movement in workplaces have thus far been relegated to questions of diversity of staffing and the ideological racism of individual bosses, which are important components of everyday anti-racist class struggle but lag far behind the building of autonomous counterpower presently unfolding in the streets.

These limitations are only exacerbated by the prospect of co-optation by the nonprofit industrial complex (NPIC), especially organizations operating under the aegis of the Ford Foundation, a counterinsurgent force battle-tested against the 1960s Black Power movement.[85] The abolitionist sidelining of Campaign Zero's #8CantWait, discussed above, represents an important early victory in the war of position against the forces of NPIC recuperation, but history warns us that the money and seats at the table that become available to grassroots organizers in times of great upheaval are a perennial risk to the movement. Thus, the most pressing limitations of the present rebellion present themselves in the tactical divide between temporary street militancy and sustained social reproduction of the rebellion, on the one hand, and between reform and revolution within the growing abolitionist ranks, on the other. The degree to which these barriers are overcome will depend on militant struggles within workplaces, alongside struggles within and *against* labor unions and nonprofit organizations, which will play out against the backdrop of heightened austerity.

On this last point, it is worth keeping in mind that reducing police budgets to zero across the country and appropriating all of this money for improving the lives of working people would still be a drop in the bucket toward redressing stark class divides and differentials of power that define class society, especially where class intersects with the color line, and this says nothing of the demands of Indigenous people for sovereignty and the return of stolen land or the pressing necessities demanded by the underdevelopment and political turmoil of vast areas of the globe wrought by American imperialism. In short, we should not kid ourselves that a simple redistribution of funds from one sector of the state to another is adequate to realize the project of human emancipation, or even to meet the moral imperatives of the most basic internationalist anti-racist praxis. The wisdom of decades of abolitionist activism instructs us that demands such as defunding the police are means to a broader end of class struggle against the very existence of class society, and not ends in themselves.

Recent critiques of defunding the police, however, have argued that reducing policing will only gain mass working-class support if it is part of a broader social democratic fight to expand the social safety net.[86] Yet this fails to account for how four decades of austerity measures have not only relied on prisons and police but also on the welfare functions of the state to punish and discipline the poor and the unemployed. While we join those who advocate shifting resources from police and prisons toward more redistributive state functions, we must not romanticize the welfare state under capitalism and must never forget that white supremacist punitive power has shaped the functioning of all governing institutions, including social work, homeless services, education, and far beyond. For a working-class person, the threat of incarceration and the disciplinary imperative to complete a mandated program at the local welfare office to meet workfare requirements serve the same punitive function. Moreover, for the past four decades, police and prisons—while expensive at face value—have proven a whole lot cheaper for the ruling class than guaranteeing the basic demands of free health care, housing, education, and other minimum demands for a comfortable and dignified life, which capitalism in its present moribund state is almost certainly incapable of providing.[87] Thus, while reducing the penal arm of the state in favor of rebuilding robust welfare is laudable, this horizon must by necessity be broadened toward a more generalized attack on class society itself, one that aims not just at economistic redistribution but at the conquest of power, the means of production, and the land itself by the working class.

With these perils in mind, we recognize, with great hope, that the mainstreaming of the abolitionist vision speaks to a growing disenchantment with liberal police reform and to a popular acceptance of the fact that working-class people have very little to show for their blood, sweat, and tears except for well-equipped local police departments. In New York City, as a million people face evictions amid COVID, police officers show up at peaceful protests brandishing their new "turtle uniforms" (riot gear) and expensive shiny toys. In this moment, abolitionists wisely embrace non-reformist reforms like defunding the police as a challenge to conspicuous police consumption and power amid large-scale working-class immiseration. The campaign #8toAbolition advances a platform dedicated to creating free public transportation, mental health and other health care services for low-income New Yorkers, a ban on evictions amid COVID, and many other social goods. But, again, we would be remiss to not remind young revolutionaries of the lessons from the historical defeat of the last mass movement of the present magnitude, that of 1968. To paraphrase Kristian Williams: counterinsurgency doesn't only come dressed up in riot gear, it also comes as your friendly neighborhood community-based nonprofit organization.[88] In the coming months and years, many revolutionary-minded individuals within the NPIC will likely have to choose between their structural position as mediators of the class struggle and their political commitment to advance this struggle.

As the US ruling class grapples to contain and redirect the militant energy driving the present rebellion, we should do everything in our power to make this task impossible.[89] Facing a horizon of stagnant capitalist growth, a global health pandemic with no vaccine in sight, looming austerity cuts, and the daily persistence of racially disparate police violence, what kind of *normal* can we expect to return to besides the outcome of a class struggle decided in favor of one or the other of the contenders? In its process, we envision protest movements underway and ahead providing ample opportunities for working-class people to continuously do the experimental work of claiming their emancipation. Current and future protest movements will, in Marx's words, "have to pass through long struggles, through a series of historic processes, transforming circumstances and [people.]"[90] To this effect, our role is to participate in these societal transformations, to fan the revolutionary fires, and to help a new generation sharpen the contradictions between reform and revolution.

July 2020

How It Might Should Be Done

Idris Robinson

I want to begin with a shout-out to what happened here last night and to the working class of the city of Seattle, to the rebels of the city of Seattle. I really liked what I saw, that's why I'm here, you know, to feel that vibe. I would also like to send my solidarity to comrades in Greece. It was they who allowed me to experience insurrection for the first time in 2008. The lessons I've learned and the experiences I had there have been so valuable this time around, even though we are in a much different social context. Moreover, a comrade was recently killed at the hands of the police there. To the fallen comrade Vasillis Maggos I want to say: rest in power.

My title demands a little bit of explanation. It is a reference to Nikolay Gavrilovich Chernyshevsky and the novel he wrote from inside a Czarist prison.[1] Lenin borrowed the title for his 1902 pamphlet *What Is to Be Done?* which provides answers to what he calls "the burning questions of our movement." Among other questions: What does it mean to constitute a vanguard party? How do we spread consciousness from this vanguard party to the working class? How do we move beyond strikes to a full-on revolutionary political struggle?[2] Later, in 2001, a text entitled "How It Is to Be Done" appeared in the journal of the French collective Tiqqun.[3] Rather than stating what our goals or objectives should be, Tiqqun sought to shift our focus to the means and the techniques of struggle. Instead of thinking about ends, they thought about the means that we should employ.

My aim here is far less ambitious. As for the grammatical construction, "might should," from the southern dialect—I tried to Blackify the title a little bit. But it's also serious, because these are in fact tentative theses and proposals: I'm perfectly okay with being completely wrong about every single thing I put forward today, just so long as it creates a deeper discussion on strategy. What I really want to do is open up this discussion, and I want to leave it for people to engage with it as they want to and to push it further. At the same time, I want the dialogue to be honest. There's a kind of prevailing posture of cynicism, nihilism, and democratic moralism that holds back insurrection. I think now is the time; we are experiencing an uprising on a scale that many of us have never lived through. Even if we compare it to present events in Greece, this thing has gone much further. There are far more martyrs in this struggle than there were in the Greek uprising. The time has arrived for strategic thought and reflection.

It's, of course, weird to find myself saying this in America, the most counterrevolutionary place on the globe. But we must reorient ourselves, and take these questions seriously. The stakes have been raised to the next level; they're extremely high now. It's time for us to think seriously about them.

1. A militant nationwide uprising did in fact occur. The progressive wing of the counterinsurgency seeks the denial and disarticulation of this event.

The obvious is not always so obvious.

We all saw it. We all saw what happened after the murder of George Floyd. What occurred was an extremely violent and destructive rebellion. It was a phenomenon the likes of which we have not seen in America in forty or fifty years. Very few of us have experienced anything of this magnitude: a precinct was immediately torched in Minneapolis, after which entire cities went up in flames—New York, Atlanta, Oakland, Seattle. Comparisons were quickly made with the riots after Martin Luther King Jr.'s assassination. However, I think that we've gone further in this case, that 2020 went harder than 1968, and we're not done yet.

Despite all of this, the reformers have the audacity to claim that all of this never actually happened. They are trying to make the burning cop cars disappear, to extinguish from memory the police stations on fire, as if it didn't happen. Again and again, I hear the same script: someone comes on the news, a political activist gives a talk, and we hear them say something like "the protests were peaceful and nonviolent; they stayed within the bounds of law and order." No: cops being shot at in St. Louis is not within the bounds of law and order. They're doing their best to make the event disappear. One has to wonder what planet they are on that a torched police station appears within the bounds of civility.

This delusion is something that we need to think about. Ultimately, it's more than a delusion. It unites veritably all the progressive liberals who chatter on about what's been going on over the past summer. From the Biden democrats through virtually all of the mainstream media not affiliated with Fox News to the Black Lives Matter™ people, the agenda pushed by all these groups is the claim that the insurrection did not take place. I even read a recent study by some sort of consulting firm that sought to prove through quantitative means that there was a very civil nature to the protests.[4]

The fact is, whatever data or graphs they draw up, nothing will erase the fact that police cars were on fire in dozens of American cities. So why do liberals feel the need to jump through such incredible hoops in order to erase this insurrection or this uprising? Why is it that the most violent wings of law and order—e.g., Attorney General William Barr—are today the only audible voices willing to acknowledge that the uprising occurred? We need to think this through.

What is at issue is more than just a momentary lapse of sanity; it is a strategy of denial, a counterinsurgent strategy of reform par excellence.

Unconsciously, liberals do recognize that an insurrection occurred. They can't ignore the shattered glass in the streets of Seattle yesterday. What they want is to downplay the significance of these events that mean so much to us, and that we are continually trying to push forward. They want to reassert and reaffirm them, but in a different direction. Ultimately, what they want is to block the possibilities that the revolt has opened up, to dissuade us from going further in this uprising. As with all democratic liberal reformists, what they're trying to do is exploit the outburst to make it so that things change, but only *a little*—which is to say, not at all.

There's a moral component to this as well, a deep ethical problem. This wing of the counterinsurgency is just one more way that those in line with the system have found to manage and to exploit Black death. It must be recalled (and I will return to this below) that there are scores of young Black children who lost their lives in the uprising, and that activists, "woke" journalists, progressive politicians of all stripes, and even so-called BLM activists are profiting off their deaths. This is a continuous narrative in American society, and it will not stop now unless we do something about it.

By denying the event, they seek to obscure the revolutionary truth that was ushered in through the streets. They want to extinguish the present that we brought about. They want to sap our energy while they propose superficial palliative adjustments to preserve the system. The history of America is the history of attempts to reform race relations. If they haven't gotten it right by now, they never will.

Whatever they do, whatever slight changes they make, there will always remain an insatiable drive to brutalize and kill Black people. Anyone who profits off this change is complicit in that murder. If you block the revolutionary trajectory of the rebellion, you have blood on your hands. Anyone who remains complicit with the system is the enemy, tout court.

By contrast, the right has adopted the opposite approach to the event. Besides us revolutionaries, they are the only voices today that acknowledge that the rebellion occurred. There's an illuminating honesty to what William Barr says. Think of it this way: before he can forcefully smash and eventually suppress an insurrection, he must first acknowledge that one did, in fact, occur. In this way, there's an honesty to Trump's words. Trump and his entire Fox News crowd, all those who are calling for law and order, have no choice but to acknowledge the existence of the uprising, precisely because they want to crush it. Just today, Trump declared on the news that he intends to send federal stormtroopers not only to Portland but to New York, Philadelphia, and Chicago.[5] To justify such a decision, he must acknowledge that the uprising did, in fact, happen. These are the two sides into which our opponents may be divided, the Janus face of the state we confront today.

What is more, the rebellion shows the liberals what it means to defund the police *halfway*, instead of abolishing and outright destroying them. If anyone thinks it suffices to undertake a series of small measures and quick fixes, or that they can reform and preserve the police as a force, while simply shrinking it—well, the result is what is happening right now in Portland. Let that be an example to liberals. On the other hand, those who recognize that a change really did occur, and who now seek to stomp it out, are typically more aligned with fascist trajectories and politics, since they are typically the same people who feel the need to dream up and defend a sort of immutable, eternal, and transcendental idea of law, order, and white supremacy. Whatever deviates from the ideal, this fascist side of order will seek to annihilate. For this reason, it is compelled to refuse those same reforms that the liberals attempt to push through. For instance, this is why Trump is so upset about changing the names of military bases. The issue itself doesn't actually matter, but the sort of power he represents cannot stand such changes and seeks instead to crush and flatten the event itself in its tracks.

There's only one way to deal with this fascist wing of the state: it operates with violence, and we return with violence that's more powerful. However, as concerns the other, more reformist side that aims to deny the event in order to incorporate it into their own objectives, we need to be a little bit sharper in how we handle them. We need to be deceptive, like Machiavelli's fox. Honesty isn't their mode of operating. They have always sought to deny what lies right before our eyes. Deception and subversion are how we are going to have to play them; we need to deceive them twice over.

When it comes to these two sides of state, I do not wish to claim that either one is any more nefarious than the other, but simply that these are the two sides that we have to contend with and ultimately defeat.

2. While spearheaded by a Black avant-garde, this largely multiethnic rebellion managed to spontaneously overcome codified racial divisions. The containment of the revolt aims at reinstating these rigid lines of separation and policing their boundaries.

To begin with, it must be said that former African slaves and their ancestors have been the avant-garde of *everything* in this country. There's no culture in America, in this American wasteland, without us. There's no classical music; there's jazz, and that was invented by us. Besides that, America has nothing to offer the world, and it never has.

However, I used the term *avant-garde* in a more specific sense. There were no leaders. We were not leaders of the revolt. We were the avant-garde who spearheaded it, who set it off, who initiated it. What ensued was a wildly multiethnic uprising, and the reformists will do everything in their power to make it so that this truth is erased. If you were out on the streets, you know you saw people of all different kinds. Different bodies, different shapes, different genders manifested themselves in the streets together.

There's a lot of talk about how to end racism, especially within corporate and academic circles. We saw how to end racism in the streets the first weeks after George Floyd was murdered.

It was only after the uprising began to slow down and exhaust itself that the gravediggers and vampires of the revolution began to reinstate racial lines and impose a new order on the uprising. The subtlest version of this comes from the activists themselves. Our worst enemies are always closest to us. You've all been in these marches, these ridiculous marches, where it's, "white people to the front, Black people to the center"—this is just another way of reimposing these lines in a more sophisticated way. What we should be aiming for is what we saw in the first days, when these very boundaries began to dissolve.

The most devastating example of how the racial lines and boundaries are reimposed comes from the example of Rayshard Brooks's long-time partner, Natalie White, who offers the most blatant example of this racial policing seen so far. White was called out by so-called "woke" Twitter activists for her involvement in the protests in Atlanta over her dead partner. Eventually, they implicated her in the burning of the Wendy's where Rayshard was killed. It is up to us to never reinforce these sort of bourgeois constructs of guilt or innocence. Whether she had a hand in the destruction or not, I don't judge her. That is not up to us; we stand in solidarity no matter what. But I *do* hold accountable, I do place blame on, the wannabe do-gooders, these "woke" Twitter activists who implicated her in what occurred. I lay the blame solely on those activists, and Rayshard Brooks lays the blame on them from the grave.

Order neatly defines collections of people—these are the prerogatives of prison guards, of the police. We should remember the example of John Brown, who was often criticized by his so-called allies and friends for relating to Black people in a way that they deemed unacceptable. If you saw the way John Brown related to Black people in his time, you might think he was being criticized for relating to Black people as human beings. Every time we cross over those racial boundaries and meet each other as human beings, this is when we will be criticized, especially by the most advanced parts of the counterinsurgency. John Brown was heavily criticized for his advocacy of militant tactics, and Frederick Douglass was among the most vocal critics of his advocacy for insurrection. Douglass would come around later, but history would prove Brown right: *the only way to abolish slavery is through violent insurrection.* History has now redeemed him to some extent. What I want us to think about is this: If John Brown were alive today, what would he be like? How would he behave? John Brown would be in jail alongside Natalie White for crossing over those boundaries.

3. By avoiding the morbid libidinal core of white supremacy, identity politics, intersectionality, and social privilege discourse comprise the most sophisticated sector of this police apparatus.

We've all come in contact with it at some point, particularly if we have been involved in politics for some time. We all know that identity politics, this talk about "white privilege" and what people call "intersectionality"—all it does is reinforce the racial lines that we're trying to overcome. If it ever had any use or goal, the uprising has superseded it at this point. Let me work through these ideas one by one.

Privilege: I think we all know, or we can all admit, or we *should* admit, that *privilege has become a purely psychological concept.* There's a long history to the notion of white privilege. It dates back to W.E.B. Du Bois, to Theodore Allen, to Noel Ignatiev, to Harry Haywood. For each of these authors, what was in question was a theoretical construct whose aim was to incite white workers to strike alongside Black workers. Somehow in the twists and turns that are American politics, the notion became psychological, a way to make white people feel good about their guilt. If you look at, for instance, Peggy McIntosh's definitive text on white privilege, she talks about the privilege of being able to chew with your mouth closed. I don't give a fuck about chewing with my mouth closed.[6]

As for intersectionality: I did a talk at Red May, so I won't go into this too deeply here, but, as John Clegg and I tried to show, the presuppositions that intersectionality holds are becoming empirically false.[7] What the data is beginning to show is that, for instance, there are more Black women prison guards than there are those going into prison. This doesn't discredit the struggle and plight of Black women, but, as a construct, intersectionality is showing its limits. In fact, there are more white women being incarcerated today than Black women, oddly enough. As for Black men, we all know they just sit in jail and stay in jail.

Whatever intersectionality once wanted to do is no longer feasible or viable as a guide for us. In my talk with Red May, I suggest that we get back to the roots of Black feminism. We need categories that understand the Black feminist struggle beyond the oppression that the system inflicts upon them. I cited Toni Cade Bambara's book called *The Black Woman.*[8] In her excellent preface, she refuses to define what a "Black woman" is. She does not say that a Black woman is the intersection of two oppressions; she does not say that Black women are in the margins of two different systems of hierarchy. What she argues, rather, is that Black women are an open possibility to be further understood through their revolutionary activity. In place of intersectionality as a discourse of systemic oppression, what we need to do is to bring back the idea of Black feminism as *a discourse of struggle.*

Finally, by opening up this definition of what and who Black women are, what Toni Cade Bambara was saying was that Black women cannot be tied down by any static identity imposed upon them. Of course, they are something *more.* If we look at the history of Black folks in this country, *we're always something more than what has been foisted upon us.*

Identity politics, intersectionality, and social privilege discourse: all are modalities of the police.

What's more, above all, is that each of these discourses ignore the morbid and terrifying libidinal politics that undergirds race in this country. It took someone as courageous as James Baldwin to say this, and everyone is still afraid to repeat it. If you read his phenomenal short story "Going to Meet the Man," you can see the dynamics of racism in this country acutely. To briefly summarize the story: it starts in the bedroom of a white heterosexual couple.[9] The white man is struggling with impotence. How does he get over his impotence? He remembers back to a time as a child where he was brought to a lynching. At that lynching the corpse was not only mutilated, it was sexually mutilated, and he was given the genitalia. Once he remembers being handed the genitalia, he is able to become erect.

This is deep stuff. No one likes talking about it. But this is the core of racism that we need to reach. What's more, I think no one wants to touch this part of the race problem, because we are all implicated in it. It is obvious that white liberals get off on videos of Black murder. It is even more obvious that there are Black liberals who are more than happy to sell these videos of Black death for their own careerist goals. So long as we fail to take into account these libidinal drives within racism, we will not be able to explain how and why Ahmaud Arbery was killed. It had nothing to do with the police. It had to do with what is driving American society as such.

4. The insurgency cannot be confined within any well-circumscribed sociological category. By necessarily exceeding all classification, it is an excluded remnant detaching itself from all that binds together the American wasteland. Consequently, this combatant formation

can only be defined in terms of its movement and its development, as that which emerged during the first weeks of the revolt and which will dissolve itself upon the full completion of the revolutionary project.

As I said earlier, every conceivable kind of person participated in the revolt. This can be confirmed by any participant. There is no category that can sum up everyone who was there. The best we can say is that what we saw was the inclusively excluded, or the part of America that has no part in it, and that wants nothing to do with this place. Such a formation can only be grasped by how it is moving outside and against the current state of things that can only be traced by way of its trajectory: against the state and capital, against American society. What is now up to us is to deepen and strengthen this spontaneous organization, so that we come up with something together that is even more terrible, even more powerful, than what we saw last night. Something that splits American society in half.

5. The so-called Black leadership, therefore, cannot and does not exist. It is a chimera to be found exclusively in the white liberal imagination.

You hear it everywhere. I've heard it from every city, every friend who texted me. If I called a friend and said, "Hey, what happened in NOLA?" or "What happened in Chicago?" If there were riots, if people got busy, there was no mention of a Black leadership. If things stopped, if things were stultified, all we heard about was a Black leadership.

The thing is, I have never in my life actually seen a Black leader. Why? Because they don't exist. If there are Black leaders, they're dead like Martin and Malcolm. If you're worth your salt, you will be killed. If there are Black leaders, they are in jail with Mumia and Sundiata.[10] If there are Black leaders, they are on the run with Assata.

There is only one category of people who speak of Black leaders, and we know them as white liberals. The Black leadership is nothing other than a figment and hallucination that exists solely in the imagination of the white liberal's mind. The odd thing about it is that somehow white liberals have more contact with Black leaders than I have ever come across in my entire life. It is as if a channel extends from the Black leadership directly into their head.

There have been reasons proposed as to why the classical formation of Black leadership no longer exists. One argument, which can be derived from many of the new sociological studies (there was a big report about this in the *New York Times* as well), asserts that to develop a firm hegemonic leadership of the sort we saw in the past typically requires a substantial middle class. But if you look at the data from the last forty years, the Black middle class has been under constant threat. Hopefully it stays like that, honestly. It is very hard to define what exactly the Black middle class is. If you do say there is this well-defined group, and if you're able to circumscribe this well-defined group, they typically exist within the white community. Just to speak a little bit more personally from my experience in New York, I am hard pressed to think of ever meeting a Black middle-class person growing up or of ever even hearing their rhetoric and their nonsense. But it's not really a thing anymore.

Why does the white liberal need to hallucinate and invent a Black leadership for him or herself? Ultimately, it is because whitey loves property. Property enjoys a special prestige in American life; it has a special kind of sanctity. We always get these calls for the Black leadership from white liberals whenever the windows start to crack. There is a very important reason that property has this particular kind of sanctity in America, as many historians are starting to confirm and argue.[11] For most of its history, the most important property in America was human property, shackled and chained. We need to weaponize this argument and say that whenever property is protected, it is protected for white supremacist ends. If property is truly the pursuit of happiness in that trifecta of life, liberty, and the pursuit of happiness, the existence of that happiness and property is premised upon the negation of Black life and Black liberty. So the protection of property is something that we need to attack explicitly.

6. The current crisis derives from a contradiction that proceeds from the two Janus-faced sides of post–Cold War American governance: an inconsistency between the demands of the sovereign imperial state and globalized biopolitical security. As a result, the metropolitan center has begun to experience the sort of chaos and instability that it has classically sewn within the colonial periphery.

This dynamic captures the situation that we are living in today, and which we have been experiencing acutely over the past few months.

On the one side, we have state sovereignty, the classical notion of the state. Following Schmitt, but most importantly following Agamben, the paradoxical foundation of the state proves to be important to the way it operates. To define the state, the state must employ extralegal and extrajudicial measures to found itself. Every time the state founds itself, it must go outside the law that it seeks to create. What has occurred classically, and we have a lot of historical examples of this in America, is that whenever there's a crisis the state imposes some sort of state of exception to create the order that it needs to reassert itself.

As we saw, for example, in the American Civil War, in the two Red Scares, and most recently in the War on Terror, the executive branch of the government has continually mobilized itself beyond its formal legal parameters and confines.

We see this today especially with Trump. Trump is using and abusing his executive powers, but it is better to say that he is using them in the way that they were set out to be used. What was originally the province of the legislative branch has now been taken over by Trump himself.

This component of the US asserting itself has also been seen in its foreign wars. We need to keep in mind, and I will come back to this, that—and for some reason this fact has been downplayed in the past twenty or thirty years—America is the one imperial power on the globe, and it serves itself aggressively around the world. After the collapse of the Soviet Union and the Cold War, we have seen the United States become the police officer, or the storm trooper, of the entire earth. This is one side of governance.

It is important to contrast this with another form of governance, which is typically called biopolitical discipline or biopolitical security. The latter differs from the enforcement of the law carried out by the classic state. Rather, it names the management of lives. If the state kills, biopolitics is concerned with the protection of those lives—for its own ends, of course.

The most recent regime of biopolitical control is what is known as "security." What "security" does is it allows an event to happen, so as to then manage that event. These events are varied. They can be something like pandemics, like the COVID-19 pandemic we're going through today, they could be famines or disasters like Katrina, and they could also be insurrections like the one we are hopefully fomenting right now. What the state does in these instances is to make a statistical calculation and try to find acceptable terms within which it can allow events such as pandemics to occur, while keeping them within neatly circumscribed boundaries.

In addition to the paradox of the state that we see in the state of exception, there is also a strange biopolitical paradox of preparedness that we are experiencing right now. The paradox typically goes like this: after a disaster—say, a pandemic or a famine—there is a drive within the security apparatus to begin preparing for the next disaster. After SARS in the 2000s, there was a big push to be prepared for the next pandemic. This over-preparedness then is put on the back burner when it comes to light that the next disease is not going to appear when we expect it to. The famed medical anthropologist Andrew Lakoff drew attention to this paradox, which we have seen again recently. There has been preparedness for pandemics, but the preparedness was then put on the back burner, so that when the COVID-19 pandemic came we were still not ready for it. We are dealing with two different types of paradox at once here: one that must venture outside of itself in order to found itself, and the other a cycle of preparedness that consistently generates unpreparedness.

There is the legal side and the statistical side of the state, the nation-state in its classic form and this more global operation of security. I would like to argue that these two directives are colliding with each other and forming some sort of crisis.

Legal means to an end have been in a constant state of crisis: *Trump just can't do anything right.* Whatever he does seems to backfire, and that does not seem to always be the worst thing. Trump, with his deluded mind, has become an agent of anarchy.[12] Now, of course, he doesn't *think* he is—it is up to us, when this chaos reigns, to utilize this for our own ends. What I'm saying is that we need to inhabit this chaos that the state is inflicting upon itself.

Unlike liberals and reformists, we are not here to reaffirm and reassert law and order. We are not here to transform America into one big safe space. *We are here to make the chaos and the disorder more terrible than it has ever been.*

We must do what revolutionaries have always done: we must make the contradiction intolerable.

7. As the rebel slaves did with the periodic outbreaks of yellow fever in Haiti, there is a hidden partisan knowledge to be uncovered surrounding the novel coronavirus pandemic that also can be exploited and weaponized against established power.

In the Imaginary Party's best book, titled *To Our Friends*,[13] the authors mention a pamphlet issued by the CDC in 2012 on the subject of disaster preparedness.[14] It is a part American Tiqqunists tend not to mention. To make disaster preparedness pertinent and hip to the youngsters, the CDC invokes the example of preparing for a zombie apocalypse. Their basic argument was that if people can prepare for a zombie apocalypse, they will be able to prepare for a natural disaster, such as a flood, a storm, a pandemic, or even an insurrection.

The Invisible Committee argue in their book that this fear of zombies has a long and racialized history, linked in no uncertain terms to the fear of the Black proletariat. The other side of this fear that doesn't want to be mentioned, that refuses to be mentioned or is repressed, resides in the paranoia of the white middle class over its own worthlessness.

If we look back over the history of zombies, the figure of the zombie appeared within the voodoo utilized during the Haitian Revolution. There was a person by the name of Jean Zombi who ended up taking the name because he participated in the massacre of slave owners. What I think is particularly instructive for our purposes today is that the Haitian insurgents were perfectly aware that they could use the yellow fever pandemic against their former masters and against the army, whether Napoleon's army or the party of order more generally. The insurgents waited until the yellow fever outbreak took hold. They knew that their former slave masters' army would be devoured by the pandemic, and they also knew that they had built up an immunity to that pandemic. So they waited until the army had been decimated by yellow fever, and *then* they launched their guerilla attacks.

What I am arguing for here is something very similar. We all know that Black people and brown people are disproportionately affected by the COVID pandemic. This is a medical problem. But it is much more than a mere medical-scientific problem, it is a political problem. We must reject the sort of sanitized liberal politics of safety that is afraid of the pandemic, that is largely a sanitary discourse around masks, distancing, etc. I know this is a political issue now. On the flip side, I'm not defending right-wing conspiracy theorist ideas that the pandemic does not exist or that it is just a flu, etc. What I'm proposing here is that we develop a kind of partisan knowledge—our own knowledge about the pandemic—to exploit the pandemic for our own good and to use the knowledge of the pandemic as a weapon against our enemies.

8. The insurrection will involve precise coordination from within the constellation of riots: the paradoxical organization of disorder beyond any measure of control. Accordingly, the problem of insurrection has equal parts social and technical dimensions.

What I am advocating is a paradoxical ordering of disorder, an Organized Konfusion (for those who remember the rap group). To do this, we must read up on tactics; we must look into what exactly was smashed, what exactly was looted, and how and why the occupations were effective or ineffective. We need to think *strategically* about the chaos that we inflict in the streets.

What is more, we also need to anticipate new tactics, struggles, and strategies that will emerge, so as to intensify these struggles and tactics. We can anticipate that occupations and rent strikes are going to take place in the near future due to the looming threat of eviction that is occurring in all of our heavily gentrified cities. But I think we need to go beyond these defensive struggles, be more creative, and initiate tactics that go on the offensive. In fact, what I am advocating here is employing the whole arsenal of proletarian strategies and tactics—from riots through strikes to blockades.

We need to be creative in our tactics and strategies. As we have seen in the recent Twitter hacks, these are just as important. What's important is that we be creative in how we deploy these strategies and tactics.

What is the modern equivalent of the telephone exchange in Barcelona that was so savagely fought over during the May Days in 1937? What is the modern equivalent of the St. Petersburg rail line that the insurgent workers fought so hard over in revolutionary Russia? We have a unique problem, in that we live in a huge country. We need to figure out creative ways to break this distance and utilize it for our own ends, i.e., as pure means.

9. Materialize the ever-present specter of a second, more balkanized civil war by fragmenting the fragments of a crumbling empire.

At least since Trump was elected and took office, the archetype of civil war has been looming over this country. There are historical reasons for this. Since the American Civil War was for some the most traumatic experience this country has ever collectively undergone and for others the most liberating, it stands as a figure that is continually recalled within the collective imaginary, but I think there are also structural reasons. The fundamental operation of the state works by warding off the ubiquitous threat of civil war. The state, as such, can be thought of as that which blocks and inhibits civil war. What is unique about this country is our singular emancipatory tradition, which is itself bound up with our understanding of civil war.

I would otherwise cite Kenneth Rexroth's excellent autobiography, where he explains that the radical abolitionists who took part in the Civil War gave birth to children who became the first era of the American socialist, anarchist, and communist labor movement.[15] But I think the best example comes from Du Bois's classic book *Black Reconstruction*.[16] It was the proletarian general strike of the ex-slaves that truly put the final nail in the coffin of slavery. It is precisely this lineage of an emancipatory, liberatory, but nonetheless violent civil war that needs to be updated for its second coming. Another important precedent is Harry Haywood's "Black-Belt" thesis. As a member of the central committee of the Communist Party USA, Haywood argued that revolution in the United States of America would involve an independent Black state in the South. I think this is no longer feasible, but I think what he was grasping at and trying to deal with was the problem of revolution in a country that is simply massive.

The revolution here presents a problem of sheer scale for us. This is, I think, why Haywood argued for the breaking apart of America. We have no historical precedent for a revolution in such a large, industrialized, and modern state, so we have a unique problem to grapple with.

I do not know exactly what this looks like. What is certain is that this country is already beginning to break and fracture, and it is up to us to break and fracture it further, into so many pieces that it can never be put back together again.

Revolution, here more than anywhere else, will involve the messy task of division. Here too, we have a unique problem, for we must avoid the rather aggressive, ugly, and dangerous nationalism that occurred in other cases of civil war that we have seen over the past forty years. I am not advocating another series of Yugoslav wars, nor am I advocating what has occurred in Syria. Nonetheless, we must harness civil war as an emancipatory liberatory power. The fundamental goal is to break America apart into a constellation of federated communes.

10. The fulfillment of the revolutionary project is ultimately an inescapable ethical obligation that each of us have to the dead and the exploited.

At the risk of sounding naive, I sincerely believe that the riots that we have all witnessed and hopefully participated in this summer have opened the window to insurrection and even a full-blown revolution. It is possible that I may be miscalculating the potentialities that have emerged. Still, it is entirely impossible for anyone to have participated in the current uprising without having the fundamental core of their being unalterably changed. For me, and I know for many of you, we feel the revolution deeply within our souls, and it changes our very outlook and our approach to how we live our lives. All the pervasive cynicism, all the rational self-interest, all the nihilism, *all that is constitutive of the typical American citizen is slowly being worn away by the insurrection and the uprising.*

What this shows us is that the revolution is truly beyond us, truly beyond each and every one of us here. It surpasses all the boundaries thrown up by American individualism. It forces us to finally look beyond ourselves and recognize that America has wreaked havoc as an imperial power around the globe for a century.

The fight is not only for the living but also for the dead. We owe the revolution to the millions of slaves who never knew a second of freedom. What the long list of martyrs who have fallen during this uprising deserve from us is nothing other than the completion of the revolution.

Pasolini wrote an essay about a trip to America. What really took him was one of the phrases that no one says anymore but was a big part of the Civil Rights Movement: "we need to throw our entire bodies into the struggle."[17]

The dead of the struggle scream out for vengeance, and we must avenge their deaths. As Walter Benjamin famously put it, "not even the dead will be safe from the enemy if he is victorious."[18] Tonight is the night to begin to settle accounts once and for all, to end their victorious reign upon the globe, and to allow the dead to finally rest.

August 2020

PART II

REPORT BACKS

Welcome to the Party

New York Post-Left

Since early March, New York has been in quarantine paralysis. Over twenty thousand have died in New York City alone, disproportionately working-class brown and Black people. Hundreds of thousands more lost their livelihoods. This shocking new reality left many wondering if the pandemic would be the final nail in the coffin for a city where, for decades, the economy has so brutally triumphed over people.

Then, in an instant, we all marched outdoors together, inspired by images of the first days of revolt in Minneapolis, its fearless crowds looting a Target and setting the Third Precinct on fire. Some of us in the crowd were essential workers, forced to risk exposure to the virus to make ends meet. Some of us chose to face those risks for the sake of mutual aid projects. Others had been isolated inside for months. All knew breaking "shelter in place" orders to gather in a crowd spelled potential disaster for a city already at the epicenter of the epidemic. With infections declining, it seemed worth the risk.

The first solidarity demonstration, held Thursday night, May 28, in Union Square, was contained with the same policing techniques that had been effective in tamping down the momentum of the disruptive Black Lives Matter marches in 2015. A demonstration was called for the next night at the Barclays Center in downtown Brooklyn. There police surrounded the square, pepper-spraying the crowd and making seemingly arbitrary arrests. Soon barricades were built on a nearby avenue, and a police car was set on fire, while others marched to reconvene at nearby Fort Greene Park.

That night a young multiracial group of protesters attempted to storm the 88th Precinct in Brooklyn, followed by hours of street fighting, in which the crowd hurled bottles and bricks and damaged every police vehicle in sight, eventually setting a van on fire—acts of resistance virtually unheard of in New York. The police fought back with baton and pepper spray charges, ultimately repelling the crowd from the doors of the precinct, but not before their desperate message rang out through the city: *they were losing control.*

The next day, mass marches took place in all five boroughs, producing a nearly endless stream of images of the NYPD's violent desperation. In broad daylight, in front of the media, police responded to the ongoing vandalism of their vehicles by pepper-spraying, penning, and shoving protesters. In at least one incident in Brooklyn, they drove a car into dozens of protesters to break a road blockade. These tactics were intended to disperse, divide, or at least paralyze the march, but people fought back and continued over the bridge to lower Manhattan. As night fell, the crowd built barricades and clashed with the police as it marched toward SoHo, the downtown neighborhood lined with luxury boutique stores, looting streetwear brands and burning police vehicles along the way. As was the case in much of the country that night, the spell of police control had been broken. No amount of force seemed capable of stopping the joyous crowds smashing their way into luxury shops and freely distributing the clothes, shoes, phones, jewelry, liquor, and skateboards among the crowd and to passersby.

On Sunday night, May 31, the police attempted to block a large march in Brooklyn from crossing the Manhattan Bridge at dusk but, worried about the optics of violently confronting an orderly crowd, they let them through. Once in Manhattan, the crowd began to build barricades, break windows, and clash with the police, just as on the previous night. Only this time the city had taken care to clear the streets of trash cans and other potential projectiles. While a segment of the crowd stood-off against lines of riot cops in Chinatown, others marched freely through SoHo to Union Square for hours. Taking and doing what they pleased, while defending each other, they loudly chanted the slogans: No Justice, No Peace; Fuck the Police; Fuck 12; George Floyd; NYPD Suck My Dick.

Outside the Strand Bookstore, flaming barricades and volleys of bricks and bottles held back a small detachment of riot police while hundreds danced in the street and shared looted bottles of whiskey. With the police spread thin, hundreds of mostly Black youth, organized in crews and dressed in all black, began quietly making their way downtown. Over the course of that night, the luxury stores of SoHo were systematically looted. The cycle of rioting, dispersing, and reconvening went on until early in the morning.

What to make of the looting from a pro-revolutionary perspective emerged as a key question during these nights. Often the looting followed patterns familiar to us from the descriptions of Minneapolis, or even the Watts riots in 1965. Everything taken was freely shared among those present in a festive atmosphere, the looters seemingly intent on calling into question the value of commodities and the world that upholds that value. They often seemed as interested in the novelty of what they were doing as in the objects they were taking. These looters emerged from crowds that seemed to shapeshift between peaceful protests and riots, kneeling with police one minute and running down an avenue smashing windows and starting trash fires the next.

By Sunday and Monday, it became clear that the police were not seriously confronting the looters, having been repelled by "airmail" from disorderly groups and even shot at or run over by vehicles coming into Manhattan to loot. Spanning from SoHo to the Upper East Side, as well as pockets of the Bronx and Queens, organized crews began to methodically clean out shops, carrying away as much as they possibly could, either for themselves and their friends or to sell. Images spreading in the news and on social media of organized looters and the scale of destruction they left in their wake seemed to lend itself to the notion that there were "professional looters" opportunistically using the protests as a cover.

On the ground, this distinction felt much less clear-cut. Some of what appeared methodical could best be described as *social looting*. It was done in fairly dense crowds and maintained a festive air. Throughout the weekend one could see scenes of people tossing out boxes of iPhones to anyone passing by, distributing twenties from looted cash registers, and leaving jewelry on the sidewalk. But one could also catch glimpses of crews fighting one another for turf or looted goods. While it may be tempting to draw a line between political and opportunist looters, we are unable to draw any strong conclusions without intimate knowledge of the origins and dynamics of these crews.

By Tuesday the distinction between protesters and looters had really taken hold in the media. Just as the narrative around outside agitators had succeeded in creating conspiratorial hysteria throughout the nationwide rebellion, de Blasio and NYPD advanced a narrative that distinguished orderly from disorderly, peaceful from riotous, good from bad, with a distinction as clear as night and day: the curfew. The police would be hands-off in the daylight, keeping the bulk of their forces two blocks away from the marches. At night they would come out swinging and make arbitrary arrests, with the Manhattan district attorney promising to keep suspected rioters in jail indefinitely. Few were willing to either publicly support the "bad protesters" or criticize the professional activists who appeared out of nowhere, asserting themselves as "movement leaders," providing justification to the violence used against anyone willing to continue the momentum of the weekend's street fights.

With an 8:00 p.m. curfew and the doubling of the number of police forces, beginning on Tuesday night, the peaceful protesters and would-be rioters were forced to collide back into one another. Now unable to take territory on their own, well-masked crews of Black youth could be seen dotting the sides of marches in Manhattan, waiting for their moment. As each night went on, they would break off from the larger marches, along with their accomplices, for smaller-scale roving riots, often targeting the same stores as previous nights, but each night they found themselves more isolated.

A well-publicized militant action in the South Bronx on the night of Thursday, June 4, the fourth in a series of Fuck the Police (FTP) protests against Metropolitan Transportation Authority police, was kettled the minute curfew began. Almost the entire crowd was arrested. The NYPD was no longer allowing marches to cross the bridges, and snatching bikes from protesters created an aura of fear. Although the movement was still massive, popular, and willing to break curfew, its weight tilted heavily toward the "good protesters," bathed in the sunlight of the mayor's praise. By Friday, one week after the first clashes, the "bad protesters" largely stopped coming out.

They will be missed. The hundreds of Black proletarian youth and their accomplices who swarmed through lower Manhattan or Midtown each night provided the struggle with a dynamic spark to the soundtrack of Pop Smoke. They had no interest in formulating demands aside from "suck my dick." Rather than being stuck in clashes with the police, their goal became to evade them through the shopping districts that have become most alienated to life in New York City. Decades of leftist street slogans like "Demand nothing," "Diversity of tactics," "Be water," and "An injury to one is an injury to all" came to them organically.

The constant return to downtown Manhattan illustrated a certain strategic deliberateness. Few were willing to defend the luxury stores in that black hole of alienation. Only the politicians fretted about keeping up appearances that Manhattan is anything but a luxury gated community for an increasingly terrified bourgeois bohemian elite. Despite speculation that the NYPD have some sort of blackmail gun to de Blasio's back, this is the real reason he tolerates their brutality—they are the army defending the world of the rich, but now that world is dying from factors both objective and subjective.

By Saturday, June 6, it was clear the riots would not return. Nonetheless, New York City maintained daily mass marches and rallies distributed across the five boroughs in almost every neighborhood with almost every kind of activity: meditation, bike marches, street parties. The sound of fireworks could be heard throughout the city every single night. In many working-class neighborhoods, a different pyrotechnic display could be seen every couple blocks. A recent *New York Times* investigation confirmed what anyone could have guessed: the city's proletarians are celebrating the riots and having survived the pandemic and are self-consciously exhibiting their defiance.[1]

While energy has remained high, the movement's sharpest edges have been dulled by police violence or captured by the progressive ideology of the neoliberal city government. Unable to develop new tactics in order to stay dynamic, the movement has found itself at something of an impasse and currently lacks direction. Whether this holding pattern will be disrupted by unexpected turbulence or a gentle landing awaits us is yet to be seen.

Are we to keep attempting to voluntaristically push it forward forever, or must we wait for the next atrocity? Between these poles, it may be possible for pro-revolutionaries to find a new rhythm and way of relating to the still vibrant mass movement, even if it no longer seems to hold an immediate insurrectionary potential. At the same time, pro-revolutionaries need to be durably organized to sustain their capacity through the valley to prepare for the next peak—which we will know from the smoke rising from a precinct.

It is unlikely we will have very long to wait, even if the four Minneapolis police officers are not acquitted. The situation in America, and in New York especially, is particularly combustible. With the massive rates of unemployment brought on by the pandemic and tens of thousands actively on rent strike, there are already millions who feel they have little left to lose. What will happen this summer if there isn't a new stimulus package and people begin to lose their unemployment boost?

It is no coincidence that this uprising took place at the tail end of mandated social distancing as an epochal economic crisis takes shape and the only solution of the neoliberal order is to discipline restless "essential workers" by pauperizing an underclass into a desperate reserve army of labor. The refusal of politicians to cancel rent, end mass incarceration, or stop prosecuting crimes of poverty are a clear sign of this strategy of reifying the hierarchies that turn the working class against itself: citizens against immigrants, white workers against Black workers, and Black workers against the Black underclass. At the heart of the movement for Black lives, lurking beneath its most lauded petty bourgeois reformist figureheads, is a profound recognition of the superficial nature of these antagonisms.

Like the initial revolts that spread from Ferguson, this rebellion was at a scale and intensity unseen in the US since the Sixties. It is evidence that we are in a cycle of escalating struggles, each picking up where the last one left off. The occupation of university campuses in 2009 inspired Occupy in 2011. The killings of Trayvon Martin in 2013, and Mike Brown and Eric Garner in 2014, inspired weeks of marches and blockades across the country, but aside from the antifascist mobilizations of 2017 and brief occupations outside ICE facilities, the Trump era had been relatively quiet until late 2019. When struggles against authoritarian neoliberalism spread across the globe, from Sudan to Chile and from Haiti to Hong Kong, such rebellions inspired New York City's FTP marches against the rising cost, declining quality, and racialized policing of the subways. These marches helped cohere a layer of militants oriented toward, and now experienced in, direct action.

Even as those FTP marches got progressively more intense, they never broke out of the activist demographic. This latest wave was the first to involve a much wider cross section of the city and to bring to the fore a faction that understands that Black lives will never matter so long as we live in a society defined by white supremacy and capitalism and was willing to joyfully and fearlessly subvert that society night after night.

For now, we may be entering a phase of stabilization, in which liberals will redouble their commitment to empty reforms. To support the bravery of the insurgents, certain types of rhetoric should be overcome:

- *The dichotomy of "good" and "bad" protesters.* Although they are imagined opposites, one provided the bark of mass movement, while the other offered the bite of direct action. They are strongest when they exist together in the streets. If any side is to be critiqued, it is those elements that seek to tear the unity apart for the sake of their careers.

- *Conspiratorial thinking.* The idea of singular groups of bad actors, whether they be a global satanic pedophile elite, outside agitators, police infiltrators, or "bad apples" of any variety, chokes the expansion of solidarity needed for the movement to continue building power. The sides are most clear in the moments of frontal confrontation: rebels on one side, police and property on the other.

- *Abolition as the end goal.* The abolition of the bourgeois institutions of police, prisons, and borders is certainly a revolutionary goal, but it can only be achieved by a social revolution that abolishes class society, the economy, and the bourgeois state. The implications of looting can be defended as a coherent gesture of this core mission: the expropriation of the wealth of society and the world alienated from us. The "bad protesters" hate the police and say so but only burn police cars or destroy precincts at their convenience. The logic of attacking police and looting shops is not based on some illusion that the number of cops or quantity of commodities will be diminished, but on the idea that the struggle against them is moving toward a situation where they will be made irrelevant.

- *Leadership.* Our acknowledgment that Black proletarian youth acted as a vanguard in this movement is not meant to imply that one should seek a young Black leader and follow them, or that the Black and brown proletariat are the only class fraction with revolutionary potential. In each wave of struggle, different layers of the class serve this vanguard function, pushing the moment to its limits through recognition of their own interests, self-organization, and bravery. Historically, though, Black proletarians have tended to provide the detonation for much wider social unrest. Rebels not from this background will be stronger comrades in future struggles, whatever form they take, by developing their own confidence, goals, and organizations. As much as possible, however, revolutionaries should try to make and keep contact with those George Floyd insurgents who trashed Manhattan for three nights straight, while resisting a cross-class alliance with professional activists.

June 2020

Frontliners to the Front, Part I

Anonymous

It is necessary to describe, with intimate knowledge, the collapse of respectability politics, the unraveling of compulsory nonviolence, in the symbolic center of American pacifism. At the end of May, following the murder of George Floyd by Minneapolis police, angry people across Metro Atlanta burned cruisers, smashed storefronts, looted shops, and threw bricks at the police. For nearly two weeks, dozens of autonomous and leaderless groups descended on the city and its suburbs, sometimes blocking traffic and other times simply holding signs. Every night of the first weeks of June, crowds descended on Centennial Olympic Park to violate the curfew. Pitched battles with the National Guard gripped the area, as rowdy clusters of people built barricades, de-arrested one another, and slowly developed a tactical intelligence appropriate for the times. Every day, more people arrived with helmets, goggles, gloves, shields, respirators, and more. Every day, the tear gas seemed to work less and less.

Regardless, hundreds were arrested, some of them brutalized by Atlanta police, the National Guard, Fulton County Sheriffs, the Department of Natural Resources, and other police forces conscripted by the city government to clear the streets. As the revolt blinks, entering its second month now, a window opens for repressive counterrevolutionary forces. Black youth will overwhelmingly pay the price if we fail to advance new perspectives, openings, and practices capable of subverting the machinations of the colonial state and its white supremacist auxiliaries.

From Open Rebellion to Unruly Protest

In the first two weeks of events, from May 29 until the second week of

June, more or less, crowds gathered across Atlanta every afternoon and evening and clashed with police. When it was possible, smaller crews looted stores around downtown, in Buckhead, and even farther into the suburbs. We have heard reports of scattered looting as far as Johns Creek. In Lawrenceville and in Gainesville, some kids are being charged with following police officers to their homes and throwing Molotov cocktails at their vehicles.

In any case, following weeks of disorder and the militarization of the city by the National Guard, the crowds slowly shrank in size, if not in determination. It was not uncommon during this phase to hear people bemoan the ritualized events at Centennial, as arrests became more prominent features of the night, and the possibilities of open contestation seemed repeatedly frustrated by self-appointed "organizers" and "Black leadership" voices—all of whom suspiciously seemed to echo the commandments of the police.

In this context, protests were organized in other areas of town, including in Midtown, and at strange hours. On one occasion, nearly five hundred people, nearly all punks, skaters, queers, and other alternative youth, met at midnight in Little 5 Points. This crowd managed to repel police with fireworks, making space for the vandalism of the Savi grocery store (a business infamous for giving free food to police officers), while winding around the neighborhoods east of the city for hours, listening to loud music and generally breaking the formula of contained revolt.

Killing of Rayshard Brooks

On June 12, Atlanta police officers Garrett Rolfe and Devin Brosnan killed twenty-seven-year-old Rayshard Brooks in the parking lot of a Wendy's in South Atlanta. The officers shot him in the back as he attempted to flee. Within an hour, around seventy-five neighbors were gathered at the scene, demanding answers and cursing at police officers.

The next day, hundreds gathered at University Avenue and Pryor Road, outside of the Wendy's. Many people wore ski masks, hoodies, respirators, helmets, gloves, goggles, and more, as the crowd repeatedly surrounded police officers and forced them to retreat. When self-described "organizers" commanded the crowd to their knees, a small group of Nuwaubians exclaimed, "Kings don't kneel," and ordered everyone to stand. Eventually, a police cruiser had its windows smashed in the parking lot of a liquor store. Cops from the infamous APEX Unit fired bean bag rounds and tear gas into the crowd, which failed to discourage those gathered, many of whom threw the canisters back.

Within thirty minutes, hundreds of protesters were blocking southbound traffic on I-75/85. Others began laying siege to the Wendy's, which had reportedly called the cops on Rayshard Brooks. Hundreds cheered as the windows were smashed and fireworks were shot into the building. When police arrived, driving recklessly into the crowd in hopes of dispersing it, their vehicles were smashed with hammers and bricks, while some individuals shined green and blue lasers into the windows of the car, ostensibly obstructing the vision of the officers inside and their cameras. The fire truck was also blocked by protesters, while the building was engulfed in flames.

Frontliners to the Front

Following the mass torching of the Wendy's, a large crowd marched to the Zone 3 precinct located at Cherokee Avenue near Atlanta Avenue. Officers Rolfe and Brosnan both worked out of Zone 3, which is located nearby, in Grant Park, an affluent and predominantly white neighborhood.

From this night on, a larger section of the movement—the abolitionist currents, broadly speaking—began adopting tactics proportionate to the demands of the situation. When the crowd arrived at the precinct, individuals began throwing rocks, bottles, and fireworks at the police, who busied themselves erecting barricades. When the conflict stabilized, dozens of umbrellas emerged from within the crowd, and were used to block police visuals, as the frontliners repeatedly attempted to break the police defenses. Before long, tear gas canisters were being fired in Grant Park for the first time in decades, possibly ever. On social media and text threads, fliers and infographics from recent Hong Kong and Chile protests circulated, translated into English, allowing some people to study the tactics utilized by others in circumstances like these. The methods developed by anarchists and their fellow travelers over the last twenty years seemed to suddenly gain widespread purchase among anyone seeking out mass, participatory, anonymous subversive strategies.

Every few days, more and more determined crowds, with less news coverage and sometimes lower numbers, attempted to storm the Zone 3 precinct. One night, an individual threw a Molotov cocktail at the police lines, although it failed to explode. The general style and composition of the protests at the Zone 3 precinct did not swallow the movement, as other events and crowds continued to mobilize daily across town and in the nearby suburbs. Still, it is undeniable that we have entered a higher phase of subjectivation, in which new combative protest cultures, aesthetics, crews, cliques, and methods are developing within the framework of the ongoing revolt against anti-Blackness and police violence.

As the participants and curators of the new front-line protest culture continue to refine their own needs and methods, it is becoming less common to hear individuals default to identity-based pseudo strategies ("white people to the front") and more common to see multiethnic crowds of young people work together in a chaotic tactical storm to accomplish shared goals with practical means. Instead of asking for those perceived to benefit from relative privileges to sacrifice themselves at the front—a demand that can only be embraced by weak-willed and inexperienced white students who, regretfully, will be smashed in a second, without putting up a fight—it is slowly becoming normal for people to address one another on the basis of shared ethical understandings and intentions: "frontliners to the front, lasers on the cameras, barricaders to the back, cameras film the cops, not the bloc."

Only this kind of intelligence can help us move to the next phase of struggle. If it is necessary to question the role of white people in the movement, it will have to occur with deference to the capacities and power that each individual is capable of bringing to the table with tact and enthusiasm, not shame, virtue signaling, or acquiescence.

No Justice, No Peace Center

In the days following the killing of Rayshard, community members of all ages and backgrounds gathered at the ruins of the Wendy's to pay homage, to light candles, and to talk with their neighbors. The building, now covered in graffiti, became a kind of locus of Black communal joy, as some chose to bring smokers and grills to the site, to give sparklers to children, and to commune with whoever gathered. It is outside the scope of this article to discuss the self-organized encampment built at the Wendy's—renamed the "Rayshard Brooks Peace Center" by its inhabitants. Reflections and perspectives on the three-week-running "autonomous zone" will have to emerge from those who dedicated themselves to its development and maintenance, which the author of this text can hardly claim to have done.

In the aftermath of the June 13 revolt in Peoplestown, South Atlanta, the chief of police resigned, and the city government worked overtime to discredit and obscure the realities of the situation on the ground, finding themselves unable to establish a desirable balance of force with increasingly hostile and prepared crowds. To make matters worse for the mayor, officers across the city began calling in "sick" in the hours and days following the indictment of the two cops who killed Brooks.

Police morale was at an all-time low, as officers felt unwilling to work with the district attorney's office, with the mayor, with the National Guard, with the state patrol. The only strategy the government retained was spreading gossip, rumors, and false narratives about gun violence, increased crime, and "unprecedented disorder" engulfing the city. In reality, the phase of open insurrection had long passed, and any increase in violent acts could just as easily be attributed to the spike in unemployment related to the ongoing COVID-19 pandemic.

The Fourth of July

On the Fourth of July, a large contingent of police encircled the Rayshard Brooks Peace Center/Wendy's, threatening to evict those encamped. Simultaneously, around midnight, a crowd of just over one hundred people descended on the Zone 3 precinct, now scarcely guarded by more than a dozen officers left with no anti-riot gear. The crowd did not miss a moment to erect barricades, with those inclined to break up and throw bricks doing so. Some shined lasers at cameras, while others tossed massive firework mortars at officers and the building. When police reinforcements arrived, the crowd fled the scene.

Marching through the residential streets of Grant Park, it was not long before the group, seemingly well-prepared despite being an informally organized crowd composed of small crews and individuals, descended on the Georgia State Patrol headquarters. Immediately, individuals in the crowd went to work destroying a police vehicle, while many cheered, and others began throwing rocks at the windows of the facility. Many, many windows were smashed, and the exterior of the building was painted with abolitionist and anti-nationalist slogans. Some enterprising young people began shooting fireworks into the smashed windows and quickly set about using lit objects to start a fire in one of the offices. Having smashed nearly every street-facing window and seemingly set the building alight, the crowd continued to march into the neighborhood and managed to disperse with no arrests.

While the fire inside the building was extinguished, the flames nonetheless terrified the ruling class and political elites, who rushed to call in the National Guard again. They are continuing to blame a surge of gun violence on the protests, with the repressive operations of the extreme right, the Trump administration, the moderate left, and self-styled "progressives" seeming to come from the same playbook. Counterrevolutionaries are prepared to use any methods—from tear gas through curfews to identity politics—to crush what is underway.

Whether or not the emerging combative subjectivities can retain the initiative is to be seen. In any case, it seems unlikely that the countless people who have participated in the clashes and have gone through the same experiences of development and evolution as we have will simply return to respectable and tame protest cultures soon. As for us, we will continue to fight, to think, and to develop. We are not afraid to pause and catch our breath, because we know that even if we do not win, we will never be defeated.

Black Lives Matter
RIP George Floyd
RIP Rayshard Brooks

July 2020

Frontliners to the Front, Part II: Between Politics and Rebellion in Atlanta

Anonymous

In my last article, "Frontliners to the Front, Part I," released on July 8, I cataloged the overarching structure of the George Floyd Rebellion in Atlanta, Georgia, from May 29 through July 4, 2020. From the fiery afternoon of May 29, when thousands burned police cruisers and looted stores downtown, through the pitched battles of early June to the killing of Rayshard Brooks and the subsequent minoritarian actions taken in its wake, it seemed clear that the period of open insurrection had ended by mid- or late June, but that new front-line protesters might be able to retain the conflictual initiative for a bit longer. I believe that hypothesis was correct. At the time of writing, October 15, it seems clear to me that this new period has ended.

For posterity's sake, so that emancipatory movements in the near or distant future may act with greater understanding, what follows is an imperfect account of some general dynamics of the second half of the George Floyd Rebellion in Atlanta. Countless protests, actions, events, fundraisers, and meetings have occurred within the context of the rebellion, far more than is within the scope of this article to address. I do not believe it is preemptive to say that the rebellion of this summer has ended, nor that it is a contradiction to insist that large waves of autonomous resistance and mobilization are coming in the near term as a direct result of the sequence set in motion this June. What follows, I humbly dedicate to everyone who threw back tear gas canisters, who stayed up all night making sure people were getting bailed out, who offered first aid or emotional support to those wounded by police, and who physically attacked storefronts, police cars, and carceral and bureaucratic infrastructure or cheered heartily for those who did.

"Enough Is Enough"—The Counterinsurgency Refrain

Following the tragic death of Secoriea Turner on the night of July 4, on University Avenue, Atlanta Mayor Keisha Lance Bottoms held a press conference at which she audaciously claimed that "these aren't police officers shooting people on the streets of Atlanta, these are members of the community shooting each other." Having failed to adequately advance this narrative—essentially the "Black on Black crime" myth—in the previous two weeks, despite daily attempts involving Killer Mike and other cultural icons of the Black bourgeoisie, the killing on the night of July 4 seemed to be a tipping point in the eyes of the public, marking the definitive end of mass mobilizations in the context of the George Floyd Rebellion or the local killing of Rayshard Brooks by the Atlanta Police Department. Every few days, television news coverage, especially aimed at white suburbanites, demonized teenagers selling water bottles on the sidewalk, young people racing cars and dirt bikes, and protesters all in the same breath. After the mayor's press conference, Governor Brian Kemp wasted no time extending the deployment of one thousand National Guardsmen indefinitely to the Georgia State Patrol (GSP) headquarters, the governor's mansion—where protests occurred regularly late at night for several weeks—and the capitol building.

The trashing and partial burning of the GSP headquarters on the July 4, detailed at greater length later in this essay, shocked the authorities. Georgia Bureau of Investigations; Georgia Bureau of Alcohol, Tobacco, and Firearms (ATF); Atlanta police; and other law enforcement agencies fanned out across the state, knocking on doors and approaching people for information on the protest. No public statement was made by any participant, and no formal section of the movement denounced the action, a sign of the maturity, horizontalism, and informal self-organization widespread in the rebellion. (Note: to date, there have been no arrests associated with the vandalism of the GSP headquarters.)

As the days went by, center-left and right-wing pundits and social media personalities initiated a phase of advanced misinformation, simultaneously claiming the movement had been "hijacked" by white people, "antifa," and "insurrectionary anarchists," as well as by undercover white supremacists. NBC News began publishing delusional historical revisions, claiming that the protests in Minneapolis began "peacefully," and that "public support had waned after protests became violent." The idea that a rupture catalyzed by Black youth could become a vortex for every disaffection scandalized the political and professional classes across the country. The received intelligence coming from the universities (as "anti-oppression politics") is that non-Black people can participate in struggles alongside Black people, but only passively or only as "supporters." In other words, the revolts of Black people should be kept in an ahistorical container, and others should not seek to advance adjacent or overlapping aims for their own reasons within the general crisis of governance initiated by the Black working class. Fortunately, the movement retained its hyper-diverse character, catalyzing rebellious and self-directed participation among the (non-Black) Indigenous, immigrant, and white working classes. The revolt continued to race ahead of all commentary, laying radical and reformist ideologies to waste, week after week.

July 25: National Day of Action in Solidarity with Portland Protesters

In Portland, Oregon, taking advantage of the growing discourse around "agitators," the Trump administration deployed a new federal police force composed chiefly of Border Patrol officers to crush the nightly resistance taking place there. This failed utterly, as thousands of protesters surged into the streets, and public sympathy once again seemed to support militant direct action against the police, the government, and the stagnant economy—still completely closed in most cities because of COVID-19 restrictions. After viral footage circulated showing unmarked officers snatching protesters off of the streets and shoving them into vehicles, autonomous groups in the Pacific Northwest called for a national day of solidarity to take place on July 25.

In Atlanta, around two hundred protesters, nearly all of them in frontline gear, converged on the joint Department of Homeland Security (DHS)/Immigration and Customs Enforcement (ICE) headquarters, located on Ted Turner Drive downtown. Catching police completely off-guard, the crowd utilized nearby equipment and barriers to construct a large barricade in the road. When a single officer approached the crowd, people began to heckle him and throw objects, forcing him to retreat. For the next hour, at the very least, protesters smashed windows and shot fireworks into the headquarters. The officers inside fled the building, which incurred heavy damage. Police claim vandalism costs to the building alone were at least $200,000. The facility was boarded up for several weeks. No arrests were made. Anonymous participants sent the following statement to local news, which published the statement:

> In solidarity with Portland, a crowd gathered in Atlanta outside the DHS/ICE office. These agencies are directly responsible for ruining untold numbers of lives, and for the violent policing of the Portland protests. We will fight with everything we've got against Trump's private police force, against authoritarian and despotic governance. What the police produce, above all, are their own grave-diggers. Their fall and the victory of the ungovernable are equally inevitable.

Media coverage of this and similar solidarity actions across the country—including bold actions in Seattle; Oakland; Aurora, Colorado; Richmond, Virginia; and elsewhere—was surprisingly minimal, as the corporate press focused endlessly on Trump's Twitter account, and election coverage was beginning to eclipse everything else. In Austin, Texas, Garrett Foster was shot and killed by a far-right extremist during the solidarity protest, a signal of the grassroots counterinsurgency in embryo.

Kenosha, Wisconsin, and the Shifting Balance of Forces

On June 16, just after the murder of Rayshard Brooks and the subsequent torching of the Wendy's on University Avenue, Georgia Governor Brian Kemp lifted nearly all restrictions on businesses aimed at reducing the transmission of COVID-19. As bars, restaurants, and worksites of all kinds began to slowly reopen, the protests began to shrink, with many workers kicked off Pandemic Unemployment Assistance and forced to work with no guarantee of their well-being. By mid-July, nearly eight hundred people had been arrested at protests in Atlanta and its surrounding suburbs, including several dozen for serious felonies. Many more had been injured or traumatized by the wanton use of tear gas, flash-bang grenades, rubber bullets, and other "less-lethal" munitions utilized by the National Guard and the Metro Atlanta police forces in the preceding weeks and months.

In early August, a new myth advanced by the Democratic Party and its NGO hydra that the George Floyd Rebellion and all subsequent Black Lives Matter protests actually served the interests of Donald Trump more than anyone else began to spread! According to this line of reasoning, Trump was using the unrest as an "excuse" to blame the Democratic Party for not suppressing the riots and to deploy his new federal troops. The protests, so the narrative goes, were "helpful" at first but were now turning (white) people against the movement. The Democrats were already blaming Black people for their possible electoral loss. Many leftists fell for this deceitful and disgusting talking point, just as they had naively fallen for previous myths and tropes over the summer: that "piles of bricks" were being staged by police to provoke rioters; that arson and looting was being coordinated by white supremacists and Boogaloo Bois; that outside agitators were traveling across state lines in large numbers, endangering local communities and leaving before the repression came crashing down. If you believed all of the tropes, myths, half-truths, and lies rolled out in the context of the rebellion, you would have a hard time believing there had even been a rebellion at all! This new myth couldn't have appeared at a worse time.

On August 23, the Kenosha Police Department shot twenty-nine-year-old Jacob Blake in the back seven times in broad daylight as he was getting into his car, where his children were sitting in the back seat. Impossibly, he survived. By nightfall, residents were throwing bricks and Molotov cocktails at police, looting stores, and smashing their way into the courthouse. By the second night of rioting, the Department of Corrections building was ablaze. Spontaneous protests in Madison, Wisconsin, descended on downtown, smashing storefronts and erecting burning barricades. On the third night of the unrest, Joseph Rosenbaum and Anthony Huber were shot and killed by seventeen-year-old Kyle Rittenhouse. Rittenhouse was a part of a semi-organized network of white vigilantes and militiamen who had descended on Kenosha and other cities to curtail protests and to act as a paramilitary auxiliary of the local police. In the days that followed, professional sports teams from multiple leagues went on strike, refusing to play, as a sign of direct sympathy and solidarity with Jacob Blake and the Kenosha protesters.

On August 25, 300 to 400 people gathered at Woodruff Park in Atlanta for an emergency solidarity demonstration. Around 150 people donned all-black clothing and made some other material preparations. The crowd marched directly toward the Zone 5 precinct downtown and began constructing barricades in the road, using police barriers and newsstands. A window of the precinct was smashed, and a dramatic de-arrest of a protester radically escalated conflict with the police, who rushed out of the precinct deploying pepper spray in every direction. The crowd began to scatter, especially those who had not arrived prepared for this possibility.

As police began to throw flash-bang grenades, frontliners regrouped and began shooting firework mortars and throwing stones back at them, which, in turn, sent the officers running for cover. Now on Peachtree Street, a crowd of around 100 people, nearly all dressed in black, continued marching north together, as police were seemingly mobilizing to trap everyone in the downtown corridor before they could safely disperse. While Atlanta police were being pummeled with bricks, the Georgia State Patrol (GSP) deployed a BearCat—an armored, tank-like vehicle. The GSP seemingly has a larger budget than local police and seemed anxious to avenge the vandalism of their headquarters. The remaining crowd turned onto West Peachtree Street, but the BearCat followed. Several Molotov cocktails were reportedly thrown at the vehicle, and while journalists were present for this, they failed to report it. We can, however, be certain that every police officer in Atlanta was debriefed on this development.

A helmeted officer quickly emerged from the top hatch of the BearCat and began shooting marker rounds at protesters from close range. Failing to regain the initiative or to turn around to confront its enemy, the shrinking crowd was forced to turn east on Pine, hoping to escape downtown as quickly as possible. At the intersection with Piedmont Avenue, Georgia State Patrol deployed tear gas, splitting the crowd in two. Demonstrators trapped downtown were demoralized and forced to walk alongside the so-called "Black Revolutionaries," a group of paid actors who pretend to be an armed militia and who indulge in photo opportunities for local police. Several people in this crowd were snatched off the sidewalk as they walked back to their cars. The other crowd, continuing east into Old Fourth Ward, repeatedly engaged in determined clashes with police, who were attempting to enclose them on every block. Nearly all of them managed to escape the area without being detained.

Movement Deceleration

Now that police had finally regained the definitive upper hand for the first time since early June, they were determined to keep it. Protests and marches continued almost daily for the rest of August, many of them brutalized by APD. As activists and community groups continue their fight to open the Rayshard Brooks Community Center on the site of the University Avenue location where Rayshard died, police officers often mobilize disproportionate force to intimidate those gathered to hear speeches and promote reasonable demands. On several occasions,

National Guardsmen and officers in riot gear mobilized for crowds of seniors, parents with their children, and other unassuming demonstrators holding sidewalk vigils or simple protests. Local police deployed the same overwhelming force in the final weeks of the Occupy Atlanta protests nine years ago, as mayors across the country coordinated simultaneous attacks on encampments and the marches and protests that followed those evictions. A similar dynamic was emerging across the country once again. As the crowds continued to shrink, for all of the reasons I have laid out and more, police did not miss the opportunity to reestablish their preferred position of tactical and logistical dominance. Amid all of this, people of conscience continued to quit local police forces in droves, while others began blowing the whistle on department-wide corruption. We can only hope this continues and accelerates.

Justice for Breonna Taylor?

On September 23, the Kentucky attorney general announced that no officers would be brought up on charges for the murder of Breonna Taylor, but that one officer would be charged for missing her and recklessly endangering her neighbors with his stray bullet. The Taylor case had become a cause célèbre for the movement over the summer. An emergency action was announced that night, once again meeting at Woodruff Park.

Around three to four hundred people gathered on short notice, many dressed all in black and wearing helmets, with some also wearing bullet-proof vests and carrying single-person medical packs. The events in Portland and Kenosha, where armed counterprotesters have increasingly attacked protesters, seemed to have an impact on the general atmosphere within the movement. Protest organizers announced that there would be no formal speeches, and that the crowd should resist any attempts by activists or bad actors to utilize a megaphone or adopt an authoritarian posture to control the crowd. This did not work. In a short time, a semi-formal coalition of protesters arrived who seemed determined to lure everyone to the capitol building, an ideal terrain for the police who were already stationed there with support from the National Guard.

Upon arrival, police immediately began shooting frontliners with marker rounds, as they had previously done at the Kenosha solidarity event. Lacking shields or projectiles, and with the area surrounding the capitol in a state of constant architectural control, the crowd was forced to retreat north, back onto Peachtree Street. Within a few blocks, individuals wielding a megaphone entreated the crowd to stop. Lacking a spontaneous or obvious objective and being composed of more tame people and students than the previous few months of protests, most participants seemed willing to listen to the self-appointed leaders. What exactly they planned remained completely unclear. The crowd sheepishly returned to the capitol and was swiftly tear-gassed and shot at with rubber bullets. As the movement has lost the tactical initiative, and actions have tended toward less ambitious aims, identity-based pseudo-interventions previously discarded seemed to be reembraced, especially by the college students in the crowd. "White people to the front," screamed the people holding placards and signs, seeking comforting assurance in a night with seemingly no clear direction or opportunities. Everyone wearing helmets and hoodies seemed to ignore them, perhaps with a tinge of annoyance. Police and National Guardsmen encircled most of the remaining protesters and slowly formed a kettle on terrain designed exactly for that. While some people escaped, and many left early, a few dozen people were detained and/or arrested.

One More Attempt

Several weeks prior, a dance party was supposed to take place at midnight in the Little 5 Points plaza. The event was called off when organizers realized police had already encircled the entire neighborhood and had spread rumors to business owners that "antifa" were coming to burn down all of the bohemian shops.

On September 26, a protest of around 120 people, nearly all dressed in black, met at Freedom Park in Little 5 Points. This crowd marched immediately to the Little 5 Points mini-precinct, which had temporarily covered its sign with a piece of paper to obscure its true operations. Sparing the precinct, the crowd continued to march into Inman Park, cheering the individuals smashing ATMs and graffitiing and receiving applause from the overwhelmingly white restaurant patrons on North Highland. Just a few blocks west of the restaurants, on the bridge passing over the Beltline, dozens of officers left their cars, which flanked the crowd on the bridge, and charged into the crowd, arresting anyone they could. Had protesters observed the advice of activists operating a police scanner Twitter, they would have known that this was exactly what the police had hoped for. Had protesters stopped at the first parked police vehicle, instead of advancing parallel to a line of seven or eight of them, they could have provoked officers into tear-gassing the crowd in full view of the hundreds of wealthy bystanders cheering them on. This alone could have opened a new sequence of revolt in Atlanta. Having missed this opportunity, the situation reached a stalemate.

The Return of Politics Is the Death of the Movement

"For millions of people, life itself depends on the speediest possible demolition of this history, even if it means levelling, or the destruction of its heirs. And whatever this history may have given to the subjugated is of absolutely no value, since they have never been free to reject it; they will never even be able to access it until they are free to take from it what they need, and to add to history the monumental fact of their presence."

—James Baldwin, *No Name in the Street*

The situation still teeters on the edge. The edge of what? Of civil war, of insurrection, of a constitutional crisis, of the collapse of an age? It seems like an entire world is burning up in flames of rebellion and climate decay alike. There's no guarantee about the future, except for what force we can bring to bear on the situation ourselves. Nearly a thousand people are dying of COVID-19 every day in this country. As the Senate hesitates to pass another stimulus package, nearly half of all US renters are on the cusp of eviction. Students and teachers have been forced to return to dangerous in-class schedules. On television, the president gives a nod to the Proud Boys, while his opponent says he "supports the police," when asked if he supports Black Lives Matter.

Will the next sequence of rebellion emerge from the prisons or camps, from renters or those forced from their ancestral homes? Perhaps it will be students and teachers taking joint action to defend themselves from a highly contagious disease. It could be regular people joining in the streets to oppose far-right extremists or to respond to the failure of the courts to convict killer cops. It could be a confusing array of forces acting in an uncomfortable alliance to oppose a constitutional crisis initiated by Trumpist forces within the state on election day or in the following months. It's almost useless to calculate the likelihood that unrest will continue or to waste precious time modeling the future in order to more clearly glimpse the uncertainties of the mass disaffection underway.

What's important is to give up waiting, *to give up politics*. Prepare yourself, prepare your team, prepare your neighbors to bring the situation to a higher level of tranquil ungovernability. Give yourself the means to win, whether that's food and health autonomy, a rapid response network, a bulletproof vest, or a stack of cash. What comes next is anyone's guess, but there are certainties that we can move on immediately.

- *Study the revolt.* What methods did people use most effectively, and why didn't other methods catch on? Could discarded attempts spread at a later date, or should they be put aside? Where did people fail to initiate riots in June, and why? What limits did the revolt encounter that it was unable to overcome or, perhaps, was even unable to recognize? Get together with your roommates or a small group to discuss how you see these and other pressing questions. Develop measurable and actionable hypotheses for yourself and your team.
- *Prepare the world.* Be accountable to the entire world, not just to your own community. Wherever you are in real life, ask questions. More than twenty million people participated in protests this June and July, and they all had unique experiences.[1] The way forward is hidden in small fragments within each of those experiences. Nurture every section of the movement (even the people you don't know) with ideas, attention, resourcefulness, financial aid, and whatever else is needed. Build networks, squash beefs, skill up. Cultivate a combustible and resilient environment.
- *Be ready to move.* When the moment comes, don't hesitate. Hesitation is as contagious as courage but twice as lethal.

Rest in Peace
George Floyd
Breonna Taylor
Sarah Grossman
David McAtee
Rayshard Brooks
Sean Monterossa
Luwatoyin Salau
Garrett Foster
Joseph Rosenbaum

Anthony Huber
Michael Reinoehl
and all of those who died fighting for Black lives.

Rest in peace little Secoriea Turner, eight years old; this world is not good enough for you.

October 2020

Imaginary Enemies: Myth and Abolition in the Minneapolis Rebellion

Nevada

This past summer, I sat down to write a letter to my friends in the international collective Liaisons about the uprising in my city of Minneapolis.[1] This letter was inspired by news of police in Richmond, Virginia, accusing the participants of a July Black Lives Matter demonstration of being white supremacist agitators in disguise intent on causing destruction—accusations that we had already seen here at the end of May. More recently, rumors to this effect have circulated online about the unrest in Philadelphia after the police murdered Walter Wallace Jr. at the end of October. My letter attempted to illuminate how the state used the fictional or exaggerated figure of the "white supremacist agitator" to perpetuate anti-Blackness and capitalist property relations, by facilitating the mass organization of auxiliary policing groups. Minnesota governor Tim Walz and Minneapolis mayor Jacob Frey led an effort to cast rioters as white supremacists coming from outside of Minnesota to destroy our cities. This precipitated the mass independent organization of auxiliary law enforcement in the form of neighborhood watches and community patrols to stop these supposed white supremacists.

As revolutionaries, we must ask ourselves why, at the height of what was easily the largest rebellion in over half a century, much of the city organized to assist the police in crushing it, often in the name of the very anti-racism at its heart? My aim here is to assess the role of the *"white supremacist outside agitator"* as a discursive figure in the state's counterinsurgent strategy, so that partisans may more effectively counter it in the next uprising.

In what follows, I will analyze three elements that, although they arose organically from the rebellion itself, nonetheless laid the groundwork for the state's white supremacist agitation narrative. These three elements are: first, the visible presence of the far right in the first days of the uprising; second, white participation in the revolt; third, the way the revolt quickly assumed a geographic and political scale that was beyond the comprehension of both observers and participants. Together, these elements undermined the traditional political narratives that framed what people expected to see from a rebellion against racism and the police. This opened the situation to competing narratives by which to make sense of white participation and the presence of white supremacists, including one that held white supremacists responsible for the violence of the rebellion. I will explain how this narrative divided much of the sympathetic base of the uprising, which deprived rebels of popular support and allowed them to be crushed by the National Guard, thereby preserving the very order that was the enemy of the revolt.

Speculation on white supremacist involvement began already on the first night of the uprising. A handful of Boogaloo Bois drove down from suburbs like New Brighton to join the clashes that had been taking place all evening on May 26 outside the Third Precinct. This is not the place to examine their ideology in detail. Suffice it to say that, despite their far-right positions, some of them saw the murder of George Floyd as the unjust action of a corrupt police department and affirmed the uprising as a valid response to it. They photographed themselves with their flag in the streets (their images were widely circulated online) and then left soon afterward. In the next few days, this group of Boogaloo Bois received an upsurge of attention, starting with antifascist activists who attempted to alert demonstrators of their presence, marginal though it was.[2]

Regardless of whether the Boogaloo Bois did, in fact, view the escalating conflict in the streets of Minneapolis as a righteous cause or merely as a means to bringing about their "civil war" with the government, the revolt exploded far beyond their narrow vision. Just as with the Yellow Vests of France, the mass looting of shopping districts pushed the movement tactically beyond where the far right was willing to go. They were thus given two options: to participate in an uprising that centers Black liberation (and thus decenters their own ideology) *or* to let themselves be sidelined and left behind by the uprising.[3]

By the second day of the revolt, many Boogaloo Bois had already relegated themselves to defending private property in response to the widespread looting. A video that circulated on social media from the second day shows a group of them outside of GM Tobacco between the Target and the Cub Foods, walking a tightrope on which they try to balance "supporting the uprising" with protecting the store *from* the uprising. A week later, the narrative of white supremacist rioters allowed social justice groups seeking to defend private property to more easily navigate a similar tightrope. This led to an ironic turn of events in the case of Minnesota Freedom Fighters (also known as the Northside Patrol, made up of groups like the NAACP and city councilor Jeremiah Ellison), which collaborated with these *same* Boogaloo Bois to protect stores from vague threats of white supremacists—despite themselves being the only group visible on the ground associated with these threats. Just as this irony was lost on most, so too was the contradiction between the narrative of white supremacist rioters and the facts of the matter, namely, that the most prominent far-right presence in the uprising was engaged in the *defense* of capitalist property, not its destruction.

Despite the centrality of Black liberation in the George Floyd Rebellion, it cannot be said that the uprising was entirely Black. People from every conceivable demographic and identity participated in it. In his piece "How It Might Should Be Done" (see this volume, pages 61–76), Idris Robinson uses the metaphor of an avant-garde to describe Black participation in the revolt. He states, "We were the avant-garde who spearheaded it, we set it off, we initiated it. What ensued was a wildly multiethnic uprising." Skepticism or suspicion of white participants is understandable yet was relatively uncommon during the first few days of the revolt. However, by the fifth night, it had become a dominant reflex, due to the emerging paranoia around white supremacist involvement. White participants in the streets who broke the law were assumed to be outside agitators—if not white supremacists—without any other evidence than their skin tone. In the midst of tear gas, shattered windows, and hails of rocks, people were pressed to identify themselves and, in some cases, to give their street addresses. Those who refused were sometimes attacked.

As has been discussed elsewhere, to blame what happened on outsiders or provocateurs robs the rebellion of its power, by delegitimizing it along with its participants. We should not forget the racist history of the "outside agitator" as a tool of counterinsurgency, which was a narrative originally used to explain slave revolts, as enslaved Blacks were said to be docile until stirred up by white abolitionists from the North.[4] Beyond disempowering rebels and reproducing racist tropes, however, I want to insist on the legitimacy of white abolitionists who decide to join the front lines. The truth is that we *all* have a stake in Black liberation. As Fred Moten once said, "I just need you to recognize that this shit is killing you, too, however much more softly, you stupid motherfucker."[5]

The revolt in May occurred on an unprecedented scale. As we know, the Third Precinct was the epicenter of the first three days of unrest, before the police inside were forced to flee, before the precinct was burned, and before the focus of the crowds moved on to other targets, including the Fifth Precinct, which very nearly fell as well. However, even before the burning of the Third Precinct, crowds flowed outward from the epicenter and brought unrest across the city, into St. Paul, and even into the suburbs. While the first crowds kept many officers pinned down at the precinct, swarms would assemble in other areas to loot and burn stores—generally with the assistance of cars, where a group of people would pull up, break in, grab what they could, and peel out before police could respond. In other words, from the very start, the rebellion was also a mass phenomenon of smash-and-grabs.

In attempting to make sense of the early stages of the rebellion, inherited logics of both representative protest *and* militant protest fail us. From the perspective of representational politics, those who were swarming and looting stores across the city were not "protesting," as their actions did not present a grievance for which they sought recognition. That is, these actions were not only deviations from "legitimate political protest," they opportunistically took advantage of such protests for private gain. In reality, however, the looters were *directly abolishing property relations*, which are inextricable from the violence of anti-Blackness. Let us recall that the order of private property is what killed George Floyd in the first place. It is one thing to hold a sign that says, "Redistribute the Wealth"; it is another to decide that all that shit on the store shelves is ours for the taking—and take it.[6]

While it is commonplace to adopt the frame of representational politics and to dismiss looting as opportunistic, when such looting and destruction turned to stores that ostensibly identified with the cause of social justice—primarily Black and other minority-owned businesses—they were often deemed malicious, or worse. The crudest form of identity politics involved postulating that these stores could not have been targeted for any other reason than racist motivations. There was often no evidence for this speculation; it was posited as self-evident. In the most absurd of cases, corporate stores falsely labeled themselves as "Black-owned," either by writing it on plywood boards like modern-day lamb's blood or by those protecting them to legitimate their defense of property. If we cease to view every act of property destruction or looting as an expression of a grievance, this logic begins to erode. It is not my intention to argue that minority-owned stores should be targeted, but that such incidents do not offer any insight into participants' racial or ideological backgrounds.

Instead, I argue that this created a new division within the uprising that helped to transform it into a "militant" protest movement. Here, the classic dichotomy between the "good protester" and the "bad protester" was replaced by the dichotomy between the "good rioter" and the "bad rioter." In other words, rioters were now divided into those whose militant action can still be understood within the grammar of protest (fighting the police or attacking a corporate department store) and those whose actions exceed and escape this traditional understanding.

After four days, the upheaval had spread far beyond what anyone could have anticipated. Refusing to play by the rules of nonviolence, it escaped the trap of representational protest. Its composition was too diverse to be neatly categorized by any demographic or political affiliation. Then, on the morning of May 30, Governor Walz hosted a press conference describing the rioters as white supremacist outsiders who were out to destroy the city. He was followed by both Minneapolis and St. Paul mayors, who fabricated statistics to back up those claims—only to quietly retract them days later. Online rumors were amplified and misinformation was circulated at a truly dizzying speed. In the midst of the chaos, they offered a legible and understandable enemy to all of those who were searching for stability but could not be mobilized by the explicitly racist rhetoric of "Black looters" or the right wing's fear-mongering about "antifa." This fear would instead be ascribed to the face of evil par excellence: the white supremacist.

Blaming the violence of the uprising on "white supremacists" allowed the state to undermine the anti-police rage of the rebellion and resume its prior role of protecting citizens against extremism. The state intentionally shifted the target of people's anger from the systemic racism that murdered George Floyd (and countless others) to relatively marginal actors. In my letter to Liaisons, I identified this as the rhetorical figure of synecdoche, a movement from part to whole or whole to part. The location of white supremacy and anti-Blackness is displaced onto an *extremist part*—a small assortment of bad actors—which only serves to mask their true whereabouts in the heart of civil society as a whole.

This displacement made room for a new alliance between social justice advocates and antifascists, on the one hand, and vigilante law enforcement, on the other. While police were forced to retreat, this alliance was forged with new neighborhood watch groups and citizen patrols protecting against the lawlessness of the riots. Armed patrols guarded businesses, while smaller roads were blocked by citizens who performed ID checks. After curfew, citizens' checkpoints allowed only residents and police to pass, while many more stayed home in fear of vague threats of indiscriminate violence. Frightened citizens called the FBI to report out-of-state license plates, while others preferred taking to social media to spread rumors and report "sketchy activity." Meanwhile, the National Guard had little trouble arresting the few who dared to continue defying the curfew.

These patrols varied from neighborhood to neighborhood, block to block. They were also ideologically diverse, and, while they might not have directly collaborated with one another, they all effectively accomplished the same goals. In some areas, white homeowners sat on their porches and called the police on neighbors they'd never met, whom they deemed to be suspicious. There were, of course, many small business owners who armed themselves to protect their stores, such as the owner of Cadillac Pawn on Lake Street, who murdered Calvin Horton Jr. Majority–Black and Native American neighborhoods also set up their own armed patrols, often with the help of nonprofits that considered themselves an extension of the protests (or at least in support of them). Examples include the Minnesota Freedom Fighters mentioned above (who collaborated with the armed far right) and the American Indian Movement (AIM) patrol near Little Earth, a majority-Native neighborhood. The AIM patrol was celebrated for its role in protecting property, including the apprehension of some white teenagers for looting a liquor store that had been broken into two nights before.

Patrols like these justified their actions along racial lines. However, like AIM, they consistently helped protect white-owned businesses, corporations, and banks. In some cases, these patrols inadvertently ended up protecting racist property owners who just happened to be located on their "beat," but even in cases where businesses were owned by racial or ethnic minority groups, these patrols and their valorization of property *structurally* aligned them with the forces of civil order. As Idris Robinson observed, "whenever property is protected, it is protected for white supremacist ends."[7]

The formation and alignment of racially diverse neighborhood patrols in defense of private property was only possible by way of a counterinsurgent, synecdochal displacement that identified violence with white supremacy. This is the only way that such a massive project could emerge so quickly and with such popular support. This counterinsurgent initiative even cloaked itself in the language of police abolition, with neighbors suggesting that they were "prefiguring" what would replace the Minneapolis Police Department when it was abolished, with no concern for the fact that they were assuming the enforcement of the very same legal order here and now. Truth be told, they are not wrong. The type of police abolition that has gripped the city's imagination *is* merely the same regime of law, only upheld by nicer faces. Instead of police, there are to be "community security forces"—or the "office of violence prevention" (which has recently emerged here in Minneapolis). The only effect such institutions could ever have would be to integrate the population even more profoundly into the police operations that already govern their lives.

The figure of the white supremacist agitator does not simply tarnish the memory and legacy of the revolt. It also illuminates the very stakes of the movement itself and its call for abolition. It must be said that revolutionary abolition does not simply mean the defunding of any specific department, as many activists advocate today. Nor does revolutionary abolition simply mean doing away with the brutality that police use to enforce the law, as offered by restorative justice.[8] Instead, revolutionary abolition must mean *the abolition of law itself*, along with the property relations that the law upholds.

In May, we witnessed a revolt of such magnitude and ferocity that it has no equal in this country for at least half a century. We can see the rubble from it still, all around us. To be sure, revolution consists of so much more than merely burning and fighting, but it *does* involve these actions, which were at the very heart of the uprising this summer. To condemn them is to condemn the uprising.

Just as we approached the precipice of total insurrection, stability and order were reintroduced to the city, when nothing seemed less likely. The next time revolt erupts in our streets, let us be prepared to resist the reimposition of law and order, no matter how "radical" it presents itself to be.

October 2020

In the Eye of the Storm: A Report from Kenosha

Fran, JF, and Lane

"What's so simple in the moonlight by the morning never is."
—Bright Eyes

The night of the shooting, bands of armed white men dotted the landscape before we even arrived in Kenosha. Police roadblocks along I-94 barred easy access to the small Wisconsin city and forced us off the highway early, to hack it through backroads. Passing through sleepy, darkened suburbs miles from any sign of protest or rebellion, we were struck by the silhouettes of men armed and outfitted for combat, alongside makeshift checkpoints and roadblocks, and an otherwise eerie quiet. These would-be vigilantes were in for a boring night. By the time ours was over, though, we'd have seen comrades gunned down in the street by an armed vigilante operating with the explicit approval of the local police and the Midwestern city of Kenosha become a fierce political battleground for the unfolding political crisis in the United States.

For the two evenings before Kyle Rittenhouse murdered two demonstrators and injured a third, Kenosha had been something entirely different. Immediately following the barbaric shooting of Jacob Blake, locals quickly took the streets. After initially gathering around the location of the shooting, a crowd formed in Civic Center Park in front of the Kenosha County Courthouse. A video from earlier in the day showed an officer getting a brick to the head. When we arrived, this antagonistic tone and the willingness to fight back had only grown. It was a tribute to summer's enduring spirit of open revolt. What began with the mass response to the murder of George Floyd would not be ending any time soon.

As in Portland, the downtown courthouse became the central focus of anger. As centers of white supremacist "justice" and punishment of the poor, where extortionate fines and fees are collected, callous sentences meted out, and lives destroyed to nourish a class of parasites who live off the so-called "justice system," courthouses are obvious targets in themselves. Before the rebellion, Kenosha was perhaps most famous for the 2004 murder of Michael Bell, a white man, which brought considerable public attention to the Kenosha Police Department's internal culture of covering up for cops who kill, and even led to a bipartisan bill requiring outside agencies to review police killings in Wisconsin. Another scandal a decade later furnished an inside look at the rotten business of "justice" in the lakeside city, when, in a rare move, Wisconsin's Supreme Court investigated Kenosha district attorney Robert Zapf for withholding evidence that Kenosha PD officer Kyle Baars had planted evidence on one of the defendants in a murder trial, including a bullet. The final report of the court's investigator depicts in stark language a police department covering up evidence planting all the way up the chain of command, with the chief and a district attorney playing along. Similarly, a 2015 scandal surrounding Officer Pablo Torres shooting two people in ten days under suspicious circumstances—the latter, fatally, on his first day back after going on leave for the former—ended with Torres being exonerated by none other than DA Zapf and being promoted to detective. These are only the stories that grabbed headlines; there must be countless more. While it's unlikely these insults were needed—on top of the injury of daily violence and degradation under American policing and courts—to single out the courthouse for attack following the shooting of Jacob Blake, they provide all the more evidence that we shouldn't ask why Kenosha and places like it go up in flames but should wonder instead what took so long.

Approaching the courthouse, we saw sanitation trucks engulfed in flames, galvanizing and exciting the crowd. The police's attempt to block the roads by commandeering the city's infrastructural resources had backfired. Instead, it later proved a strategic asset as an appropriated barricade for the protesters. People graffitied the walls of the courthouse and were met with cheers of encouragement. Minutes later the building was covered in slogans, including "Be water, spread fire" and "They kill us because they fear us, honor the dead." We then watched as the courthouse windows were smashed, and someone threw a large cement brick through the door. These acts enlivened the crowd, and if any voices called for "peace," "nonviolence," or "de-escalation," we didn't hear them over the clamor for vengeance.

More and more people were showing up at the park. Some went right to the courthouse, where protesters passed out surgical masks to protect the participants from COVID and identification. Others posted up in the windowsills of the high school across from the courthouse, taking part by being present. Passengers hung out of windows of passing cars bumping music, providing a soundtrack for the frenzy. People were filling in the nearby streets. No age or race monopolized the gathering's composition.

Back at the courthouse, the escalation continued. Molotov cocktails exploded around the building. While the crowd loved this, the police did not. A small band of cops emerged to extinguish the flames, while others approached, clad in riot gear, firing "less-than-lethal" munitions, such as tear gas, rubber bullets, and flash-bang grenades. Like many sleepy towns across the US, Kenosha revealed an astonishing supply of military equipment, including multiple armored military vehicles, commonly known as BearCats.

Two armed protesters stood directly in front of the first BearCat to arrive until it backed away. Approaching again, the police fired on the crowd. The protesters responded with rocks and fireworks from behind the torched sanitation trucks. As the night wore on, it became clear that the police could do little more than protect the courthouse. Sensing this, the crowd directed its attention to the property in the immediate vicinity. To the west of the courthouse, protesters took down the Dinosaur Discovery Museum's large outdoor dinosaur statue, amid the kind of debate and ad hoc deliberation that would recur at many sites of destruction. The high school's windows were smashed and graffitied. The used car lot to the southeast then went up in flames. It was almost 3:00 a.m. when we left the crowd that had gathered to watch the blaze. A fire like that acts as a smoke signal; we knew there would be more tomorrow.

By the second night, Kenosha was national news and the National Guard had been called in amid great fanfare. But the people were undeterred. The crowd returned to the courthouse, now protected by a line of combative riot police and BearCats. The protesters were also prepared. There were significantly more masks in the crowd, but this was only the minimum preparedness. We saw shields and umbrellas, along with helmets, goggles, and other protective gear. Laser pointers menaced the band of cops guarding the courthouse. We even saw Portland-inspired leaf blowers to combat the tear gas. The global crowdsourcing of essential protest gear—from Hong Kong to Santiago and countless places in between—allowed many of us to protect ourselves and those around us from police violence.

It seemed at first like the night was going to be a long battle at the courthouse. The police repeatedly fired rubber bullets and tear gas and made near constant use of the LRAD. One of us took a rubber bullet directly to the torso from point blank range, and nearly two weeks later, a sizable bruise remains, along with lingering pain. Volunteers ferried chunks of concrete and brick back and forth from the ruins of a nearby church, and eager revelers broke large pieces into small ones to hurl at the police line, but this band of well-equipped police was able to hold a large angry crowd at bay and spare the courthouse the fate that befell Minneapolis's Third Precinct three months ago. Thus repelled, however, the crowd hit the streets.

The courthouse may have been the real prize, but, like the night before, the large multiracial crowd was willing to settle. It dispersed from the courthouse and unleashed on the city the fury it was unable to visit upon the police and courts. The few cars that survived at the nearby used car lot torched the night before were immediately smashed to bits and set afire, as if it were unfinished business. Businesses were smashed open and their shelves emptied. The atmosphere was positively carnivalesque and almost wholesome. One woman walking by with an armful of stuff said, "I don't even know what I took!" Much ink his been spilled drawing upon abstruse philosophy and political theory to justify looting, but we find it an act that speaks for itself and doesn't need us to chase after and rationalize it. As looting spread, along with arson and general mayhem, groups of teenagers knocked over lampposts along the route of a jovial yet ferocious riot. The sound of glass breaking was ubiquitous. "Some people can sound like cars," writes Kuwasi Balagoon. "Some can imitate a fire engine. But to hear the sound of glass breaking, glass must be broken."

It was somewhat bittersweet to see businesses like low-end used car lots and small boutiques smashed up and set on fire. Alfredo Bonanno likens the earliest eruptions of insurrectionary violence to "a blow of the tiger's claws that rips and does not distinguish"—while leaving the task of distinguishing to organized revolutionaries. But even making such allowances, we must ask ourselves: What was being smashed and looted? Knowing what we do about America's fucked-up justice system and suffocating structural racism, it's tempting to imagine many of the revelers were smashing up nothing less than an open air prison patrolled by the pigs who shot Jacob Blake, administered by the rotten court system that wastes the lives of young people of color with no hesitation, and defined by the kind of stupid everyday interpersonal violence that accompanies life under such a tyrannical regime.

Accordingly, the flame that burned the hottest was the Department of Correction's probation and parole office, which went up in a great plume of smoke that was like perfume to our nostrils. "Get the PO building!" someone called out as the crowd approached. The mood was exuberant. Graffiti scrawled on the building rhetorically calling to "abolish" it was superseded in short order by an act of proactive abolition. We can only imagine how many hours of people's lives have been wasted by this probation and parole office, with its sadistic punishment thinly veiled by the trappings of humanist "rehabilitation." Perhaps with this in mind, revelers wasted no time in reducing it to a smoldering pile of rubble. Good fucking riddance!

From the outside, these scenes must have seemed dreadfully dangerous to anyone living nearby, not to mention those out on the street. This relies on two common misconceptions about riots. The first is that rioters often target the personal residences so cherished by working white people whose entire lives are sunk into their homes—hence, the brave sentinels we beheld outside town standing guard against a largely imaginary threat. The second is that riots are pure lawlessness and, hence, dangerous to be in or around, perhaps especially—in the imagination of the average Fox News viewer—for white people. This could not have been further from the reality we experienced in the eye of the storm. The mood was festive, and people worked together across the lines of race, gender, and age. There was a kind of overriding ethics. Imperatives issued from all sides: "Stop filming!" and "Don't burn that one, there's an apartment above!" At one store a group of armed men told the crowd to keep moving: "Not this store ... but I don't care if you hit the one down the street!" For the most part, these instructions were obeyed, and the only interpersonal violence we saw involved people unwilling to stop taking incriminating photographs.

Requests rang out—"Someone burn this one! Someone better burn this one!"—as locals found a more direct means of settling grievances than leaving a bad Yelp review. In this vein, among the places that elicited excitement was a predatory paycheck loan office. Similarly, revelers smashed open a bank with great enthusiasm but, finding no money, contented themselves with setting a fire inside. Outside, the crowd attempted to break open an ATM. A few helpful volunteers emptied the clips of their guns onto it from close range, but no money was found. Cars driven by revelers snarled traffic, with one brave driver refusing to budge for a police BearCat, instead driving as slow as possible to allow a crowd to escape a hail of pepper balls (paintballs filled with pepper spray) that ricocheted off apartment buildings—the only attack on residential property we saw that night!

The rioting Monday night ended when the crowd ran out of city to ransack and allowed itself to grow thin enough that the police felt comfortable moving in, firing pepper balls and forcing the crowd to scatter down alleys and into backyards. As small groups took off in every direction, we forfeited the advantages of numbers that had kept the police at bay for hours, the power of the collectivity degenerating into the curse of the monadic individual. From there, the evening became a dispiriting game of cat and mouse between heavily armored police vehicles and small bands of retreating revelers on foot. Hotly pursued by a BearCat, we ducked behind a house near the courthouse to change our clothes. The house's owner, a younger Black man, emerged to see what we were doing—armed with an AR-15 and pistol strapped to his leg, clad in a bulletproof vest. When we told him what we were doing, he relaxed and told us we were welcome. He watched out for us while we changed and told us when the coast was clear. Despite this oasis in a fraught terrain, we were nonetheless isolated and vulnerable. The magic spell of the riot was broken, but, almost unbelievably, when the smoke from dozens of structure fires had cleared, there had only been six arrests. It's amazing the shit people can get away with when you roll with a big enough crowd!

The following night, the night of the shooting, a call had gone out on Facebook for wannabe militia types to play "Call of Duty" in real life. We witnessed tense standoffs all night, with an ad hoc militia a few dozen strong pointing their weapons at protesters. The scene immediately preceding the shooting was a three-way showdown between police BearCats trying to clear the street, militia clustered around a gas station, and a crowd, smaller than the previous night but nonetheless dedicated, testing the limits of the possible against the threat of live fire. We saw incredible courage on the part of a multiracial crowd staring down and even clashing with armed paramilitary who were pointing guns at all of us, with great fear in their eyes. It must have been the first time many of them tried this kind of shit on American soil, but we don't doubt that some, like the police clad in their military costumes, brought with them experience terrorizing poor people of color abroad.

Ironically, the militia types tended to function as an armed version of the liberal "peace police" you meet at many leftist demonstrations. They rhetorically presented themselves as allies of the movement but defenders of private property and were willing to intercede forcibly on the behalf of objects, even if it put human lives at risk. They stood guard over piles of rubble, extinguished dumpster fires, and guarded businesses they had no connection to. Interestingly enough, one of them told us to "go burn down the police station; we'd be fine with that." We didn't get a chance to find out if this was a bluff. After a series of tense skirmishes in which their weapons were pointed at unarmed people, with threats exchanged from both sides, the militia's zealous protection of others' businesses proved, as many of us had guessed, to be a pretext for opening fire. The story of the shooting is well documented and has since been dissected from every angle, but in the heat of the moment we had no idea what was going on. Shots echoed—lots of them. A seemingly unrelated motorist pulled up and sprayed some of us in the face with a fire extinguisher. A crowd gathered around the body of Joseph Rosenbaum, attempting to provide first aid, as a group of young Black women cried that he was already dead. We heard other shots, which turned out to be the shooting death of Anthony Huber and the wounding of Gaige Grosskreutz. At the time, it sounded like an all-out attack from all sides.

While the right-wingers had been the only ones flaunting their weapons during skirmishes throughout the night, once the shooting began, guns appeared in the hands of many of the young locals. It's unclear if any of them shot back. The small crowd of heroes who chased down the gunman or provided emergency care to the victims were in the minority, however. Most folks either pulled out guns for self-defense, retreated and scattered down side streets, or both.

The journey back to the car was far more terrifying than any of the BearCat chases from the previous nights. We didn't have that far to go, but the echoes of gunshots ringing from who knows where made every space of open terrain feel like unwelcomed exposure. After crossing an empty lot, we hid behind the side of a car only to see a lone white man driver spot us, pull his car around, and stop right by the car we were hiding behind. To our left an armed Black man was walking toward us with a determined gait. We kept moving. We didn't feel any kind of fight or flight response—we felt present, alert. Thinking was for later; movement was for now.

We tried to drive away from all the gunfire, but even this proved difficult. When we finally found a way out, we pulled over to rest by a park. We were about to head out when a bunch of cars turned down the street ahead of us. They just kept coming. We thought maybe traffic was being diverted down this street, but that didn't make any sense. One car turned around and the Black driver yelled something at us. Though we were unable to make out what it was he said, it was enough for us to know we were unwanted. We turned around so as to not disturb what we were now terming a caravan. We'd gone a few blocks and were stopped at a red light when an SUV with multiple Black passengers approached us. "What were you doing back there?" the driver asked us through the window. "What are you trying to do?" We let them know we were just trying to head out of town, that we had gotten lost. "We're on your side," we added. Just then a big truck with two huge flags—"Join or Die" and the thin blue line—drove up to the light and took a right. "Like, we are not with them," we told the driver. After quickly eyeing us one last time, the SUV ran the red and sped off to the right in what seemed to be a hot pursuit.

In hindsight, there was a stark difference between how the police and the militia managed the crowd. The police, largely hanging back in their BearCats and episodically firing tear gas, flash-bang grenades, and pepper balls, rallied the crowd à la Portland to hurl objects, shout taunts, fortify behind dumpsters and other tactical barricades found in the street, and otherwise hold its terrain. By contrast, one militiaman opening fire accomplished what the police could not, dispersing a large crowd and initiating a game of cat and mouse like the night before, only with far more police and National Guard troops posted in the dark and fewer of us. Since the rebellion kicked off in late May, we have witnessed a tactical maturation in the streets, especially around the need to "stick together!"—a command that often echoed across crowds thinning and becoming vulnerable to police assault. However, the shooting served to disperse much of the crowd. It's up for debate whether that is a good thing or if we need to socialize a collective practice of holding ground amid gunfire. This will be a difficult discussion between cities facing these questions and will require most of all that bravado be left at the door.

We returned the following night. We had to. Kenosha was on edge.

The crowd was the smallest yet and heavy with press, who flocked like vultures to the scene of carnage. There were at least thirty cameras in a crowd of roughly one hundred. Two groups of inexperienced organizers feuded for the direction of the march and led the same chants we've heard for countless hours all summer in marches that drag on uneventfully for hours until all but the most dedicated slink off and go to bed. The previous nights' tactical militancy seemed a million miles away. Sensing no threat to order, the cops and National Guard troops stayed out of the streets and staged in the dark nearby. The energy was gone. We paused at the spots of each murder for a moment of silence and heard from Anthony Huber's grieving partner. Her words were a powerful homage to a man we had walked alongside the night before, and who died facing down a mass shooter, armed only with a skateboard.

After some disagreement over where to march, we set off for "where the rich white people live, to wake them up!" At roughly midnight, we undertook an impromptu noise demo in a wealthy Kenosha neighborhood, shining lights in windows, with a few brave young men even knocking on doors. The mournful vibe became festive, and the procession wound up feeling cathartic. Most interestingly, the militia were nowhere to be seen. While many of our comrades imagined this to be a great victory for them, it's possible to imagine the opposite. Had the soldier boys gotten more than they bargained for? Still, the energy was much different. We chanted the same leftist chants over and over again, led by the two groups of organizers who vied for leadership over the dwindling march. When we stopped at an intersection, a now ubiquitous ritual of formulaic BLM protest marches, one of the groups yelled at us to let the cars pass.

A subsequent shooting in Portland has raised the specter of recurrent gun violence between tiny groups on both sides, sure to skew toward young men free of pressing financial and familial commitments and alienating to just about everyone else. Having seen the carnage in Kenosha up close, we are convinced this is the wrong path. But what is the alternative? How can we build active self-defense against armed fascists and the state, without falling into the trap of making our primary political activity an engagement with these forces of repression on their preferred terrain? The issue cannot be resolved on paper, but we can say for sure it will be guided not by what we want to destroy but what we want to build: communities of solidarity, inclusivity, and radical equality, based on human needs, and not the dictates of profit.

This is not to say violence is not necessary. Americans can scarcely resolve disputes over parking spaces without resorting to violence, never mind a radical reconfiguration of society from the bottom up. We, therefore, solemnly renounce nonviolence. But we hold that the very humanist tendencies that make many of us useless with guns and ammo are our real weapon and must be used to formulate an alternative vision of sociality that we both espouse and practice, as we help usher in the new world growing within the shell of the old. This is, of course, an abstraction and can only be made concrete in practice. Only consistent engagement in the moment on its own terms, coupled with ruthless critique, can orient our steps through the fraught terrain ahead, where the fog of war hangs heavy and low.

For better or worse, however, we found no such ambiguity in the revelry of the Kenosha Rebellion. In it we beheld the simple beauty of people standing up for themselves, taking great risks in common, caring for one another, and developing a shared ethics in the streets and on the fly. The new world seemed so close, if only we could keep it going long enough to progress from destruction to creation. Driving out of Kenosha, all was still, save for the occasional silhouette of a rifleman ready to mete out deadly violence against the specter of Black and white revolt now broadcast into living rooms across white-flight America. What remains of the unity we experienced on the streets? Is it lying in wait for its next opportunity to pop up, like the proverbial old mole burrowing deep below our feet? Or will it, devoid of conscious human will acting to forge coherence and consistency over time, linger on in memory like a pleasant dream shared by so many who nonetheless awoke condemned to the state of powerless alienation our society calls individuality? If this is so, what forms of organization can sustain the dynamic development of a full-fledged insurrection over time, without becoming a fetter to its unfolding?

In the proverbial morning after, it has been surreal and disorienting to behold the Kenosha Rebellion, extracted from its familiar context on dimly lit streets we came to know so intimately and spread across headlines and cable news the world over. Seeing Trump's ghoulish figure cutting shadows across the terrain that belonged so totally to the people in the throes of righteous revolt seems like nothing short of the desecration of a sacred space. Looking back to an experience increasingly convoluted by all that has happened since, our experiences in Kenosha increasingly appear like a distant memory, a jumble of exhilaration and heartbreak. Accordingly, we find it ever more difficult to know how to feel in its wake, much less to feel it. Perhaps euphoria and trepidation countervail to produce a dull flatness of affect in which we have been mired since the flames went out. More likely, the profound and radical ambivalence that characterizes the present conjuncture is expressing itself through us. It's hard to know quite what to make of what happened there and what it portends for the months and years ahead. Far from the eye of the storm, where all was so clear, the chaos of American life makes less and less sense with each passing day.

Dedicated to the memories of Joseph "JoJo" Rosenbaum and Anthony Huber. Rest in power, comrades.

September 2020

Rhythm and Ritual: Composing Movement in Portland's 2020

Anonymous

While Portland's uprising has been part of the general US #BLM movement, it has also been singular in many respects. Among its distinctive features are its continuing commitment to nightly action; the degree of popular support it enjoys from regular Portlanders; the rich new ecosystem of movement groups that provide it with its various functions; and the emergence of a popular, confrontational, and fiery but limited set of tactics. In spite of these impressive strengths, the uprising has struggled to develop a clear abolitionist vision or practice of community security, a fact that has generated a number of problems. To address this limitation, we look to the fabric of experiences that have become common in the streets, which already hint at a way forward. Beyond the more basic "diversity of tactics" framework, we encourage the growth of a more robust model for composing popular power capable of amplifying our decisiveness and increasing our capacity for practical coordination across differences. The path toward an autonomy-supporting culture is framed by a shared goal, namely, to grow the uprising's power to change life. It is this more general commitment that allows us to navigate many of the false oppositions the movement throws up at us.

•

Morning arrives. The sky is a looming golden red, dull with murk. Movement outside means using the gas masks originally acquired for tear gas—as long as they're also rated for particulates. It's hard to breathe, so Portland's taking a breather. But Portland's uprising is also already pivoting to mutual aid, refitting protest practices to support evacuees and houseless folks wracked by wildfire smoke.

When the rain comes and the smoke clears, the street actions will return, but for a moment, a reflective mood sets in. What has happened? What have we learned? What might we try to improve?

This document shares one such set of reflections. It has been shared widely to solicit feedback, but it does not pretend to capture every aspect of what has happened—and, of course, many will diverge on exactly what to do next. The goal here is to model an open-handed, non-purist, and practical mode of thinking seriously about our situation.

•

First, a sobering thought: *this is for real.* The continual stacking of ruptures in 2020—COVID, the uprising, fires, Trumpism: we live in deeply unpredictable conditions, and we all know it. It's scary. It's also an environment in which, at the very moment that impending doom feels like it's pounding toward us, actions matter more than they ever have before. *Our* actions in particular, i.e., the actions linking each of us into practices of revolt, all of which are rooted in one way or another in the illegitimacy of existing forms of power. This is an expansive "we," made up of the many different kinds of people moving in different directions in response to this moment, but this "we" is also specific: it's a fabric of living relationships, here and now. It's fuzzy at its edges, overlapping and linking with many who don't see themselves as radical, which is one of its strengths. What brought us together is "fuck the police," but from there we have continued in many directions. Our intention in what follows is to explore this "we" and how we can embrace the complexity of its power.

A Rapid Newsreel of Portland's Uprising

A black-and-white flickering countdown, then the title screen: Portland's Uprising!

In the first days after George Floyd's murder, small protests morph into a massive march into downtown. Seething anger concentrates outside the Justice Center, whose doors are forced open and a small fire lit inside, followed by a night of rioting and window smashing. City officials react on Twitter with outrage, imposing curfews. This emboldens us, as we commit by the thousands to defying them every night. Eventually, officials give way, but the chronically excessive violence of the police radicalizes a large proportion of the crowd, many of whom are experiencing it for the first time. This results in a growing commitment to stay in the streets.

Over the following days and weeks, multiple actions take place daily all around town. A pattern emerges: on the east side, large rallies and marches led by a well-defined group that controls the mic—an agenda of reform; on the west side, downtown, a much more dynamic, decentralized, action-oriented crowd, apt to pull down any fence the city throws up. Both are Black-led, albeit in quite different ways.

Time moves on.

Rose City Justice, the leading group for the now-waning east side rallies, collapses under internal and external tensions. The Portland Protest Bureau, frequenting the west side, absorbs some of their number. "Swooping" (i.e., showing up to a radical-organized event, taking over its direction using megaphones, denouncing and diverting from direct action, leveraging white guilt) is born, quickly followed by swoop resistance.

By July, the west siders are a smaller but hardened crew. The cat-and-mouse with cops through downtown becomes a familiar routine. People know each other not by face (masks) or dress (black) but by idiosyncrasies.

Then Trump's ALL CAPS pronouncements lead to a heavy-handed public invasion by federal forces, which generates a massive influx of resistance—thousands upon thousands, more every night, enraged at the sight of undercover van abductions and munition headshots.

A new pattern emerges downtown: the dance of the two demos. The Portland Protest Bureau corrals a crowd in front of the Justice Center with high-powered mics, while others wait next door at the Hatfield federal courthouse for the action to start: fireworks, fence-pulling, trash fires; barrage after barrage of munitions and tear gas; leaf blowers and shields, retreats and advances. We win. The feds withdraw.

In a matter of a week the infrastructure of the uprising has grown by leaps: new groups provide on the ground resources, new "identity blocs" emerge within the crowd, including the Wall of Moms, Wall of Dads, vets, clergy, teachers, and more. While our crowds slim down when the feds move out of sight, thousands remain involved. The pattern now becomes a cycle of actions in a different part of town every night: the North Precinct, the Multnomah County Sheriff's Office (also used by Portland police), the police union office, and others.

As Portland becomes a national meme for the right, we get acceler-
ating harassment and assault by "chuds" coming in from the suburbs or
across the country: driving at/through marchers, throwing pipe bombs
and firecrackers, beating up on isolated protesters walking home, stalking
people, and the like. Bulletproof vests emerge. Street medics start focusing
on how to stanch blood loss. At one of the Trump-rally invasions, a right-
winger is killed. Tensions, stress, and fear are high.

Still, we persist. The hundredth day of action arrives. During the day,
hundreds join three highly successful celebrations of Black lives and
mutual aid in public parks, with scouts patrolling the peripheries. At
night, and despite heavy police presence reinforced by the state patrol, a
thousand people contest the streets of East Portland.

Then, with bizarre heat and windstorms, the smoke rolls in from
fires burning right outside the city. Tens of thousands are evacuated. An
uprising rooted in care for Black lives pivots its infrastructure to care for
evacuees, the unhoused, and the displaced too.

Fade to black. This is not the end.

Black Lives

Portland is notoriously the big city in America with the smallest Black
population, just 6 percent. At its inception Oregon excluded Black immigration to the state by law. While World War II brought large numbers
of industrial workers to Vanport shipyards, resulting in the growth of a
thriving Black community, that community has been disrupted repeatedly
by city planning: freeways, stadiums, convention centers, gentrification.
And by police violence.

There is a continuous history of Black struggle in Portland, since
at least the 1960s. Mayoral candidate Teressa Raiford is not only the
founder of the city's long-term street activist organization confronting
police violence (Don't Shoot PDX), she's also the granddaughter of the
targets of infamous race-baiting during the major surge of resistance
in the 1970s and 1980s against cops killing Black men. Original Portland
Black Panthers like Kent Ford have been on the streets regularly these
last months. Another, Lorenzo, started Riot Ribs.

On the other hand, relative to other cities, the established Black
middle-class establishment is fairly conservative. In fact, it's conservative relative to most of Portland, even on issues like police. This means
that Black organizations like the Albina Ministerial Alliance, which has

shepherded incremental police reform efforts for decades, have been sidelined by the uprising. When Rev. Mondainé of the local NAACP chapter tried to hold an event to announce his July *Washington Post* article denouncing the protests as a "white spectacle," few showed up. The article was trumpeted nationally by appreciative right-wingers and centrists, but it fell flat locally. Why? Because while protesters are certainly majority non-Black (probably more or less in proportion with the population of the city), and "spectacle" is not a bad word to describe how Portland's uprising has been used by national media, the experience in the streets is something different.

Portland is small enough, and the movement is big enough, that a significant proportion of residents either have personal experience of the streets or know someone who does, and the street actions demonstrate a remarkable, complex, imperfect, but very tangible experience of Black leadership.

In particular, competing Black leaderships often disagree very palpably. Like most of the organizing in this period, virtually all of the key street-relevant Black organizing teams have emerged since George Floyd: Rose City Justice, the Portland Protest Bureau (which rebranded as Black Unity, following its mentors from Eugene), Fridays 4 Freedom, the Black Youth Movement, and others. In the spaces that organize without visible leadership teams, like the direct-action events, individual Black leadership is similarly new, is at least as strong, and has become more and more visible.

Many cities report rapid and successful clampdowns against confrontational tactics, with well-established and well-resourced liberal middle-class Black organizations co-opting the narrative in the early phases of the uprising. We escaped that outcome, likely because Portland's version was less organized at the outset. By the time "swooping" became a honed technique, a large core of people had already developed a strong sense of solidarity with each other in their practical opposition to a police force that had abused all of them in the days and weeks before. This became the basis for the "counter-swooping" culture that consciously follows street-level Black leadership in more abolitionist directions.

It's been a rocky journey, of course. Many non-Black participants in the streets no doubt began as stereotypical progressives with more "Black Lives Matter" signs than Black friends, more familiar with college-style anti-oppression language than with the Black radical tradition. Mistakes have been made, big ones, messy ones, sometimes on a national stage (see Wall of Moms). Nonetheless, over time, those holding down the streets have grown a committed practice of foregrounding Black voices and the message of Black liberation (see Moms 4 Black Lives).

This means that many white Portlanders have learned in quite practical terms that following Black leadership requires making choices. Black perspectives are profoundly varied. Those that speak loudest in the media and from podiums are generally amplified by collaboration with established interests, but in the street actions can be found a deep Black rage, dedication, and love that fuels a commitment to abolishing the forces that keep us bound—and ideas for how to do it, ourselves.

How do those seeking to act in solidarity decide what to do? Through this uprising, non-Black Portlanders have discovered they must by necessity make their own decisions. How? Based on their own experiences, needs, and desires. The motive force must come from *their own* lives but be linked with Black lives in struggle.

Those who join together in the nightly direct actions do so because those Black feelings in the streets resonate with their own. Those interests and ideas align with their own. Along with Indigenous and Latinx and other people of color, white people in their thousands are beginning to act as coconspirators on the long journey toward undoing the power of empire. While structural racism means that much remains very different among us, and mistakes continue to be made, the shared collective experience of repeated brutality on the part of the police, night after night, deepens our relations.

All this places us, knowingly or not, within the frame of the generational lineage of the Black radical tradition. Among the many inspiring practices tellers of that tradition emphasize is the attention to culture, dignity, relationships, and practical experience at the heart of political struggle. In the Portland story that follows, we discern ways in which those features are present here and now as well. This too deepens our relations.

Where such connections lead remains to be seen. Developing a robust, resilient complicity against racism is very much an unfinished business, and a much longer story. Whatever else it has been, Portland's uprising (as elsewhere) has been composed of regular folk of many races, mostly working-class and poor, led by Black radicals into direct confrontation with the pointy end of state repression, together. That's something.

We Got Us

These new movements in the streets gather a wide variety of people. The experience of a hundred days and more of intense action together is frightening and exhausting, yet many people remain committed and engaged. Why is that?

We see two patterns at the heart of it. First, not only are most of those involved newcomers to street action, but most of the key crews and collectives are new as well. Second, the emphasis on practical care for each other is present in an especially deep way.

The newness of the organizing means that people are much less encumbered by the successes and many failures of the long-term Portland radical scene. This allows people to be more open to each other and to new ideas and practices. In this way, through the dynamism and intensity of an extended moment of rupture, ideological or identity differences have caused less antagonism than in "normal" radical subcultures. Because people don't arrive already highly identified with specific groupings or with intergroup baggage, the profound bonding via traumatic and exhilarating experiences in the streets connects people generally to all the others present.

The openness and connectedness have been complemented by an organized attention to caring for each other. Some of this attention does descend from earlier waves of Portland's radical movement, such as the street medic infrastructure (in which old-school crews have been joined, sometimes uncomfortably, by many new groups and individuals) and the teams providing snacks (SnackBloc, joined by Snack Van, etc.). For the most part, however, heroically popular groups like the Witches (providing PPE, munitions protection, and other gear) and Riot Ribs (a free grilling phenomenon with a meteoric rise and fall) each emerged during the course of the current uprising, providing a bit of carnivalesque feeling during events, until the police arrive. Even familiar activist functions such as scouting, communications, traffic control, and the like have been subsumed under the mantle of creating more safety for participants (SafePDXProtest), rather than the "protest marshal" language that might have been used before.

In turn, this culture of care is more inviting to newcomers. For most of this time, in fact, people have been largely generous and forgiving with each other. (This, in contrast with a preexisting radical scene that has torn itself apart for years over ideological and personal rifts.) In fact, there's a specific group (PDX Comrade Collective) focused on holding a space for people to meet, make friends, and form affinity groups—every night. It can't be emphasized enough how important this openness has been for maintaining ongoing turnout in the hundreds, night after night after night. As some people are caught up in the court system or pull back due to trauma, others take their place.

This tenor of generosity is under threat, of course. Issues of patriarchal and racist behaviors are ongoing and must be addressed, and we don't have widely shared, successful models to draw from. Inevitable infiltration always stokes antagonisms, while exhaustion, fear, and loss come out in hurtful ways too.

After all, we are under pressure from racist assault and a staggering load of state repression. Wise practices through which to care for each other must be our first line of defense. This means growing our agreements around how we behave together and making them stick. It means knowing all of us will make mistakes, and that those most likely to stumble are those most recently arrived, who are also those we must most welcome and whose growth we must most support.

We got us.

Popular Support

Despite concerted efforts from the mainstream media, the conservative middle-class Black establishment, and the parodic national discourse, the protests in the streets remain broadly popular in Portland—far more popular than the police or the mayor. This is borne out by polls, as well as by the experience of walking down streets while chanting (or running back through those streets, chased by cops, tear gas, and flash-bangs) and having neighbors cheer us on from doorways and windows.

Such popular support is by no means a given. In Portland, as elsewhere, black-clad anarchist actions with broken windows, graffiti, etc., are often disdained by nonactivists. Something is different about this time around.

Part of it has been the Portland Press Corps. This is the crew of journalists that has run in the streets with the actions, night after night after night. They began as a hodgepodge of freelancers, young stringers for the local weeklies, a few actual press employees, and a much larger pool of amateurs and livestreamers. Unlike almost all mainstream press covering protests past, these reporters have experienced much of the violence the protesters receive (if somewhat less targeted, and that only after repeated court injunctions). This means that they developed a sense of camaraderie not only with each other but also with the uprising. As a result, they have both the capacity and the motivation to tell a deeper story than the simple "police press release + sign slogans + flashy photo" that too often comprises media narratives. At least in part due to the corporate-driven hollowing-out of newsroom careerists, they became the essential source of copy for local, and then national, outlets wanting to cover what soon became a very big story.

There has been legitimate debate about the tactical dangers of broadcasting images that identify people to fascists and cops. Even as many reporters have become much better at protecting their sources by avoiding faces, generalized "anti-media" sentiment persists among some crews on the ground, but there should be little doubt that the uprising would be far more isolated if not for the clear, consistent (and remarkably accurate) story that the Press Corps has managed to insert into otherwise antagonistic platforms.

Yet even the Press Corps is swimming against the current of corporate media. For this reason, it's been even more important that a wide range of "regular folk" (i.e., those outside self-isolated activist milieus) were radicalized by the experience of getting beat on by the Portland Police Bureau in the early days. Because of this, an even wider range of people linked by their networks have been exposed to an insider, personal view of what has happened.

Added to this has been the ongoing efforts to canvass neighborhoods impacted by protests, to do clean-up, to expand mutual aid to other communities, etc. While this has not been a centrally coordinated effort, and many individual actions have undermined it, we remain surprisingly *not yet* detached from the fabric of the city.

Breaking Police

Police are given license by the state to control, beat, and kill, but they cannot control, beat, and kill an entire population, as there's nowhere near enough of them. So they depend on the "cop in the head," the deference we concede, most of the time, to what we believe is likely to spare us from harm. If we are to "destroy cops," by which we mean, undo the system of policing, we need to develop practices that degrade the police's capacity to maintain this violent order.

Over the period of the uprising, through street actions, Portland's confidence and skill at countering the cops has consistently grown. At one level, we can see this in group responses to police orders: we are more resilient when attacked, don't pull back until forced, and return as immediately as possible. We use shield walls and fireworks to contest space, and sometimes just sheer numbers. Contesting physical space in this way also contests the legitimacy of the police to use violence to force their will. It contests the "cop in the head"—for those choosing to act directly in the moment but also for those who are in the crowd or watching from their porch or on livestream, or even TV. This is a start, but what does it look like to actually interrupt the function of the police more generally?

One approach has been to "poke the bear," i.e., to provoke police actions by means of graffiti, small fires, throwing water bottles, and the like, night after night, even if it seems like they might otherwise ignore us. Why? To prompt as large a response as possible, as many hours of overtime, as many separate riot vans and dismounting and bullrushes as possible. The aim is to physically and financially exhaust the police. Police have repaid us for this in beatings, chemical poison, and countless arrests, but it has also cost the police, dearly. Like a form of industrial action that interrupts the "factory" of policing, it has forced the city to consider whether it wants to entertain serious concessions or else double down on repression.

It's important to note that our successes have depended on clearly limited terms of engagement: no live fire, first of all, and some constraints on utter brutality. These constraints are not a given, of course. They result from a structural fear on the part of city officials and the police leadership that increased brutality against resistance will cost them more than they gain. To maintain limits on repression, we must make that fear real and make both individual cops and the larger structure pay for their "excesses."

We've had some success at this. We've seen political officeholders ordering limits on tear gas and reassigning officers, we've seen the district attorney drop charges, etc., but as the stakes have risen, and as it has become increasingly clear that this uprising will not fade without a fight, both the mayor and the governor have risked antagonizing their progressive base by giving both tacit and visible signals that fewer holds are to be barred. The cops have amped up the raw violence of their arrests, targeting people more randomly, intimidating and harassing even in the absence of anything remotely illegal, and with the recent long-term federal deputizing of state (and now city) police, they are giving free rein to Trump's US attorney to throw the book at the dozens arrested every night. This approach represents a risk for the ruling order. Will they succeed in crushing the uprising before an even larger one rises in its place, one radicalized by the vicarious experience of the raw fist of illegitimate power? This is something we have influence over.

Abolition

Police abolition has transitioned over the last six months from a fringe topic of debate to the center. Slogans like "Fuck the police," "No good cops in a racist system," and "Disband the PPB" can now be heard every day in the street. Various municipal legislatures (Minneapolis, among them) have stated their intention to disband their local police force. Far more than ever before, the topic is on the table. Now we face the challenge: What can abolition mean in concrete terms?

Obviously, some of the techniques for achieving this goal are more or less clear: not only general moves like the overturning of economic injustices that drive most crime but also some that are more specific, such as new kinds of crisis teams to handle 911 calls that don't pose the threat of violence, which is the majority. But what do we do with violent, aggressive behavior? How do we address it? What does winning abolition look like?

Whether the city council enacts it or not, "we" as movements or as communities will need to create community security by direct action. Yet in Portland's uprising (and in many other contexts), our movements have displayed significant weaknesses in doing so, even when we have "control" over the situation. A few notable local examples illustrate both the challenge and the opportunity this entails.

By early August, Riot Ribs, an extraordinary practice of defiant food-borne radical love, was undone by an armed takeover led by a disgruntled participant. Many challenges contributed: the takeover was led by a Black man calling out relatively privileged activists who held the purse strings, while houseless folks worked for free. But the takeover was itself called out by Black radicals, for making a buck out of the movement and turning violence on comrades. Many newly woke folks lacked clarity on how to follow Black voices, while still making critical choices among them. Others, clear on who to listen to, still had little idea what to do.

What *do* we do? Despite arguments on Twitter and the fact that the police had largely abandoned downtown Portland to us, we were unable to solve the problem well. In the end, most of the Riot Ribs crew skipped town, leaving the rest of us to awkwardly avoid the "usurpers." A couple of weeks later, this failure came home to roost. One of the crew of aggressive young folks who congregated around the new occupiers of what had been Riot Ribs, someone who assaulted people regularly, kicked an intervening bystander unconscious in a late-night attack that went viral, damaging our credibility both to ourselves and in the eyes of others.

Shortly thereafter, Michael Reinoehl shot a right-winger, and then five days later was himself killed by a federal task force. His is a complex story, but the various emergent narratives since his death share key elements. We all knew right-wingers were gunning for us, awaiting an excuse to attack and kill, but we hadn't worked out a clear, collectively shared response to the threat. Instead, an ad hoc mix of self-protective measures emerged, into which Michael stepped early on as a self-designated "security" agent. Individuals had concerns about some of his erratic or patriarchal behaviors, but there was no context in which to address them. By his own account, Michael found himself arriving at the tail end of a tense situation with little information and no support from a wider security infrastructure. He apparently felt that the pressure of "security" was on him and made a choice that escalated the situation, not only for himself but for everyone.

What happened was tragic, not least because our confusion over how to relate to Michael undermined our ability to grieve and organize around his assassination by cops. He was part of our movement and was also a flawed human taking actions impacted by our movement's flaws. His actions were outside the implicit parameters most people in the movement act within, but we also have had no shared way to know what those are, no collective way to practice them. Remembering Michael, we are left with a gap, a missing piece, an unease. Because while we may not align with his actions, we share his fear of looming threat. We need to defend ourselves, our communities, our movements. To do so, we cannot rely on police, and we should not become police. Another way must be found.

"What does abolition look like?" is not an abstract problem. It is visceral, right here and right now. We have made progress on this problem, here and there, in different ways, but it is not yet enough. How can our commitment to autonomy and community security be woven together? Perhaps we begin by reflecting on how to address the sorts of immediate challenges above. Perhaps new practices emerge in the streets or in occupied encampments. Perhaps we organize door-to-door in a likely neighborhood and take over "first-responder" status ourselves, forcing the cops out block by block.

Whatever it looks like, it will be hard, full of contradictions, full of mistakes and learning from mistakes, and then making mistakes again. But it's worth it.

In the remainder of this document, we use details of Portland's experience to trace a possible way forward.

A Framework: Us

How do we undo the police? How do we wrench space for community security out of the fabric of violent control as part of a larger momentum to change social relations? How do we not get crushed?

We suggest: by focusing on us. If we can continue to grow and spread tendrils of relation throughout the broader society, while also crafting stronger practices that grow our power to act in more encompassing and coordinated ways, then we are succeeding. On the other hand, no matter how exciting or glossy they are in the moment, if our actions diminish us, if they attenuate our coordination and power, then we are losing and need to change course or direction. This distinction, which assesses the "utility" of an act in a practical way, based on specific circumstances, rather than in an ideological way, based on abstractions, allows us to sidestep and deactivate many of the false oppositions that often plague strategic reasoning.

For example, consider the familiar dichotomy of pressure politics versus direct action. On the one side, there are those who relate to their actions as techniques designed to push politicians or other decision makers within the system to change something; on the other, there are those who see action as a way of taking matters into their own hands. Is there a hard opposition here? If we consider the impacts of our actions over time on our own power, we see that sometimes forcing decision makers to change policy can give us breathing room to grow, rather than be crushed; it can build the confidence of newcomers that meaningful change is on the way, while avoiding the pitfall of reinforcing the legitimacy of those same elites. (Of course, it's more common for such actions to serve as a prelude to co-opting us, demobilizing our support, and getting things "back to normal," but which outcome prevails has a lot to do with us.) On the other hand, when taking matters into our own hands, if we do so in such a way that a small group of "radicals" becomes alienated or disconnected from the thousands of others in the city currently participating in the uprising, we make ourselves easier to crush. That's not powerful.

This framework suggests that when struggling over tactics, priorities, and alliances, we focus on what, in a very specific situation, will most grow our power to act. Since the growth of collective power proceeds by qualitative leaps, it's not an algorithmic problem; there is no simple calculus to follow. It's never a straight line from action to outcome. However, we can make guesses and wagers mid-course about what makes most sense, without having an abstract plan in advance. It's about remaining "alert" and staying connected or in contact with the dynamic.

This is what it takes to become strong enough to create security without oppression—to abolish police.

Composing Movement

"Composition" is a recently evolving term for understanding how we grow our power to act and how this becomes linked with other formations around us. Wherever a struggle draws all different sorts of people in, "composition" refers to the sensitivity, modesty, and tactical intelligence that can allow various segments, functions, and participant groups to articulate and coordinate well enough to act together without a single leadership, line, or identity.

For instance, in this uprising Portland's ideological, generational, and subcultural scenes—usually self-segregating—have been drawn closer together in mutually supportive ways. What makes this possible? While there is no fixed form to follow, a diffuse yet rich conversation has begun circulating in recent years over what works and what doesn't.

One contributing factor has been the flexible use of slogans, which helps weave people together, even as they may be quite differently interpreted. "Black lives matter" itself is a supreme example. "Say his name! Say her name!" is at once a grieving cry, an educational tool, and a marker of solidarity. Shouting together puts our bodies in resonance. Nearly all of the distinctive slogans of this moment revolve around protecting each other, bringing us together. "What did you see? I didn't see shit"—"Stay together, stay tight; we do this every night"—"We got us." Yet newcomers will experience these phrases completely differently than veterans; for some, they are a promise, while, for others, a reminder, or even nostalgia.

As for what "this" is that we do each night, what "shit" we don't see, and how exactly we "got" each other—each person will invoke their own referents.

Another factor is the density of shared daily experience. From *within* a shared context of action, choices that otherwise might seem aligned with this or that "ideology" or "subculture" become eminently practical and useful in ways that anyone on the ground can see. These days, it's blatantly obvious why the black bloc is useful. Moreover, this need not result in uniformity; at various points other formations have adopted other approaches (such as the mom, dad, vet, teachers, doctors, clergy blocs using other-colored outerwear) that interplay with the black bloc, without negating it either symbolically or in practice. Instead, they become part of an ecosystem of support.

Our practical learning around composition has been perhaps most clear in regards to that hoariest of obstacles, the so-called "violence/nonviolence" debate. Here too, the debate has been largely superseded in the streets. This is not to say that it's been replaced by a simple, clear unison about burning everything down all the time. There have been contested moments, over and over, typically over fires. Was the fire at Mid-K Beauty Supply legit? What about at the Elk? What about at the Justice Center, where people were inside? Obviously, burning an empty precinct is fine. *Right?* Some people start a fire. Others discuss it and yell about it. Sometimes, a group tries to put it out, maybe successfully. This is a much messier process than a definitive "yes" or "no" appropriate for all cases, which would then be enforced by a class of protest police or an anti-protest police squad. In the streets, people change their minds. Practices evolve. What made no sense last week, seems eminently reasonable today.

While these practical contestations of tactics in the streets may lead to individual tensions, our sense is that they tend more generally to bring people together. Groups are not developing in isolated self-righteous echo chambers; they are struggling outwardly and inwardly, while remaining in active *contact*.

Limited Terms of Engagement

Out of this street-level process, and without much real space for generalized debate about it, a specific repertoire of tactics developed in the first hundred days. We may refer to it as the "Portland model" of contesting space with the police. Broadly speaking, it includes: shields, umbrellas, gas masks; graffiti, smashing cameras, smashing windows (of "appropriate" targets); throwing water bottles and fireworks; lighting trash fires, but not actually trying to burn down buildings (or even burn out cars); offensive and defensive use of lasers; throwing paint balloons, not Molotov cocktails.

Overall, the principle of selection consists in those things one can do that are unlikely to produce grievous bodily harm to humans. At one level, this is a limitation. Once any such limits are put in place, it becomes harder to suddenly shift the repertoire to accommodate deeper forms of insurrection. On the other hand, insurrections that don't generalize and spread to other segments of society tend to fail sooner or later anyway.

In all likelihood, what makes the difference is *how much* of the broader support of people you need to keep with you at each phase, as well as what reactions this or that tactic will generate in the security forces and how these will impact us. There's no universal rubric, and we can't know what impact this or that action will have in advance with any certainty. Still, the closer you are to things, the better you can guess. For now, the "limited terms" of the Portland repertoire have allowed us to push through the artificial wall of the "violence/nonviolence" stalemate. Despite chronic messaging from elites, most Portlanders do not appear to consider night-time protesters to be illegitimate, as they probably would if they were actively hurting people.

Community Security

The way we approach such tactical questions has an analogous bearing upon how we think about developing community security. In each case, we are dealing with a process whereby street conflicts preside over the emergence of a *shared sensibility* regarding what is acceptable and what is unacceptable, which establishes agreements by identifying appropriate behaviors and maintaining these criteria in practice over a sustained time.

We have had some successes in developing such security norms, but they are fragile. Why? In general, we have been hamstrung by a lack of imagination regarding what "protest community security" (as opposed to protest policing) could mean—even *as* we practice it! We lacked a language through which to frame what we were doing, leaving us without any sense of how to reinforce our shared sensibilities when they came under sustained challenge. This explains in part why the more challenging experiences involving allegations of abusive behavior, such as Riot Ribs and Reinoehl, have been so hard for us to navigate.

The upshot of this weakness is that we need to take abolition more seriously than we have so far. We need to start practicing it now. Because abolitionist community security protects our movement from internal threats as much as from external threats: not only from infiltration but also from rape and racism. Such practices demonstrate to others that there's actually a path forward, something we could draw on in dangerous situations, and not just hot air. Most importantly, it increases our collective power: the more people we organize into community security structures, the more space we seize from the police. In fact, these structures provide a template for "reforms" that we can pressure politicians into, which (with work) result in actual long-term de facto Capitol Hill Organized Protest (CHOP)–like liberated zones, even if these are noncontiguous and porous at first. In other words, if done effectively, addressing our internal shit could propel us toward an "endgame" with the city, in which we are able to defeat the PPB and begin laying the seeds of its demise. We might fail at this, but it's at least worth trying on what it would look like to win. We've become used to failing, being crushed, then licking our wounds until next time, but there are other options. Our actions actually do change the fabric of social reality. Especially now.

Caveats

At this point, an understandable objection might arise: Does it even make sense to discuss abolitionist frameworks for community protection in isolation from all the other dynamics that attend a revolution or insurrection, such as mental health, housing, supply chains, and the like? After all, without the interruption and redefinition of the structures of capitalism that crush us daily, won't the chronic problems of our society doom any efforts to create a "revolution in one sector"?

Yes, full success will require larger, more fundamental changes. But abolition in particular cannot merely be an idea that recedes beyond an ever-deferred horizon of the "revolution to come," while remaining inactionable in the present; it must also be an experimental practical force, here and now. In Portland, people are coming out every night and reappropriating the basics of life; they are answering the practical tasks that any insurrectional sequence will bring with it, including mental health and well-being, and they are doing so in a context of (limited) "war." This means we are already responsible for addressing security needs, as detailed above.

How can we avoid ending up like those establishment nonprofits in Minneapolis, where "community security" is wielded as a means for elites to quash insurrection? The difference is that it is *we* who develop a community security approach for ourselves. When the problem is addressed *autonomously* in ways that build upon the complexities we frontliners have already developed with the broader community, including the agreements regarding our tactical repertoire noted above, we may still make mistakes, but when *we* do the "deciding," we can change our minds, if we discover that the choices we previously made have undermined our power. "Security" as a problem functions as a *tactic* within the context of an imminent, experimental, local *strategy* oriented around the growth of collective power and action. It is not a value system imposed from outside by those who claim to "know better."

How can we make decisions and enforce them, without reproducing the oppressions of the state?

Here too, we should bear in mind how the limited tactical repertoire emerged, since it testifies to a form of imminent "decisiveness" that emerged without ever being formally "decided." But, as we also noted, such a process is of limited utility if it remains unspoken. For example, how do we ensure newcomers learn about it? How does this sort of decentralized consensus on practices interact with hostile newcomers, infiltrators, or organized groups arriving with their own agenda?

As shared practices emerge, we should develop a pattern of noticing them and making this fact explicit to one another. The more that shared affirmations and cultures can be communicated explicitly, even when they remain quasi-generalities, the better.

Difference and Decisiveness

The method of composition responds to a basic feature of our chaotic times, namely, the implosion of mediating social institutions. For us, embracing a model of decentralization is a necessary reckoning with our times. Beyond the organizational considerations related to security culture or the dangers of political representation, we must recognize that, at a deeper level, the very meaning of struggle and revolution today is decentralized in itself.

Contemporary movements are not coalitions between preexisting political interest groups or organizations. Rather, today's movements gather singular individuals *in* their singularity, without fusing them into a formal whole. While the crucible of the streets will always produce new practical formations, which could (we pray) seed crucial new lifeways over the long emergencies to come, it is useless to ask our movements to fuse them into homogeneity here and now. For the foreseeable future, strength will come not by unity but as agility amid chaos. We must acclimate to a situation in which diverse people share common experiences in the streets while assigning very different meanings to them. The problem is not to gather all the atomic particles into a new mass subject but how to develop a permeable and flexible space of action in which diverse bodies and desires can coordinate across their separation.

From this perspective, difference and disagreement is not inherently an obstacle but can be a resource and a source of strength. Diverse attitudes or positions not only create different pathways for newcomers to connect, they can also imbue our actions with a broader range of wisdom by providing experimental evidence and feedback as to what's working and what isn't. The question is not: How do we sustain collective consensus across the whole movement? It is: How do we cultivate the structures, attitudes, skills, and relationships that deepen our capacity to act in coordinated ways, even if we do so for different reasons?

Where consensus would otherwise fail us, rhythm and ritual can help shore up consistency. "Stay together, stay tight" is a ritual, emphasized by the follow-up phrase: "we do this every night." We know it is a ritual when we see it bellowed full strength even by those that are new or who cannot come every night, because they have a different mode of life. We must create spaces in which such patterned relations can grow. We must notice them, cultivate them. Snacks, medics, and self-care are important for nourishing individual bodies—but how do we nourish relations within and between groups?

Last, the model of the "spokescouncil" that has been in use in Portland in various ways since the alter-globalization movement is emerging again today. We encourage such a council, not merely to coordinate the familiar "affinity groups," which assumes that everyone organizes in more or less the same way, but also as a way to make space for very different modes of organizing. This requires skilled design and diplomatic renegotiation. To that end, such a spokescouncil can also choose not to make the need for "100 percent consensus" a stumbling block but can draw upon "open-decision" frameworks, whose goal is to strengthen various forms of decisiveness and the deepened capacity of people to act together with power. This approach allows groups to see who agrees on a proposal and to work to refine and broaden it but also, in parallel, to support those who are already prepared to act on their agreement immediately, even if others disagree. This increases the value for marginal groups to join, reduces the drag of debate over minutiae, and de-emphasizes the importance of controlling the stage.

However, a spokescouncil is not a magic wand; not only might there need to be different types of councils, but not every movement function demands such mediations, since many can often be resolved through more organic forms of relationship building. The aim here is to weave together not just "identities," "sectors," or "proto-sovereignties," but the seeds of "kinships" that keep power close to home and rooted in the land people share with each other and the rest of life. Throughout the entire process, we must pay attention to more than just words, ideas, formalities; we should, rather, remain on the lookout for ways to honor and grow the links that engage convivial hearts and spirits.

Enforcement

When no one has the monopoly on violence, but everyone is responsible to address harm, then "community security" is about people taking responsibility for their understanding of shared practices and gathering support for enacting them. This can be a profoundly autonomous process. As we noted above in the example of fires set and put out, it's something that is already happening in practice that would benefit from becoming a more explicit process. Doing so would allow for greater clarity as to how much support exists or is needed, making it easier to decide whether and how to intervene in this or that situation. What we are proposing goes well beyond the limited tolerance of "diversity of tactics," which often reinforces the separation of the parties involved. Our movement forms should not be like oil and water slipping past each other but need to be coordinated and linked. The goal is not just to tolerate differences provided they take place in different places or at different times but to develop intelligent ways to *compose a bloc* that draws upon the strengths of its various singular pieces. In this way our tactics do not simply *coexist* but actively complement each other. People will absolutely base their choices on their values and the kinships they are a part of, but discussions about best tactics should be as tangible as possible, rooted in a shared attention to the growth of our collective power and capacity, toward more care and not simply in abstractions.

Freedom

One objection to this approach to composition is the worry that it might constrain our individual freedom. We see this as a misunderstanding—and a dangerous one—of the kind of freedom we really want and need. "Freedom" understood as unrestrained individual choice maintains its primarily virtual coherence only by virtue of the structures of capitalism and empire. Modern "freedom" is an ideal tailored to the experience of the supermarket, of subcultural branding, of media on demand. Its perpetual transience—between cities, identities, occupations—has its purview exclusively within this highly restricted, palpably spectacular, and increasingly digital realm. Even as it "feels" itself to be infinite, it remains entirely dependent on the invisible horizon of this political economic substructure.

This limited conception infects too much of our understanding of "radical" freedom. Dropping out, being in motion against the state, refusing identities or ideologies: as far as they go, they are all framed as being *against* the existing regime, tied to its limitations. By contrast, we say that the freedom to become something new, to travel beyond horizons and not simply between increasingly interchangeable versions of sameness, requires our participation in collective existence. At one level, this is just a recognition that the "individuality" constructed by liberal capitalism is a mirage; things never actually work that way. We are relational beings through and through. Now more than ever, we are called to activate our capacities for creative collective being. To face down security forces, to sustain mutual aid, to abolish police, we need deeply coordinated action. Such coordinated action demands new forms of motivation, new sources of resilience and strength—at least as much as it demands tactics and communications. We need to become new kinds of people, related as kin in new ways, with new cultures of being. How we do so is a matter (a "materiality") of political economy, considered deeply enough to include the spirits that animate our collectivities. It is we, though there are many of us, and this "us" is not one but is itself many—it is not "I."

This is something we have explored in these last months of struggle in Portland. We have formed new ways of being related, not uniform but interconnected. This has been a source of our power.

A Test Case

The first Molotov cocktail was thrown on the hundredth night. From the perspective we've been developing, it was a total flop. A small group had decided that it was, or should be, part of the repertoire. The moment we arrived near the cops, it was thrown with no warning. It landed short, burning two comrades and startling the crowd, whose panic was made worse by the massive police barrage that immediately followed. The tear gas caught many off guard, as the escalation had hastened what normally was a fairly incremental process.

What could have happened instead? Let's imagine a sequence: People see someone preparing to escalate the repertoire in a qualitative way. Someone says, "Hey, that's not part of our menu here, what are you doing?" The person explains their intentions, if they want to. People at least check in with the crowd nearby, so they're ready, etc. Ideally, part of this would involve ensuring the safety of comrades.

There are obvious concerns with this approach. Firstly, it runs security risks: people don't want to be talking in a big group about this sort of stuff. Moreover, what happens if people in the crowd don't want it to happen?

We need to imagine a culture of debate about potential tactical choices that would not simply leave everyone to automatically default to personal preference. In such a hypothetical debate among groups and between them (e.g., in a spokescouncil, but other modes can also be imagined), the issue can be addressed: When/how is a given tactic considered appropriate? Such discussions would then inform both those considering using them and those considering intervening. After this sort of open discussion, even if the escalation in question does take place against the will of others, at least they are less likely to be shocked. Moreover, this is a process that can test at least a part of how a tactic will impact the group's power of action—if it will turn off a lot of people, that might be foreseen.

No doubt there will be disagreements. Some may well say: "You disagree now, but once you see how beautiful it is in person and how the images of it circulate the globe over, you'll want to try it too!" Others may disagree strongly enough to keep an eye out in the streets and intervene. It will be a contest of wills, of power, in the streets themselves, where the consequences can be more clearly seen. It has pitfalls, but it is better than refusing to address such disagreements at all.

Looking Ahead

There are no crystal balls. We don't know what is to come, how Portland's summer will evolve into the fall and the winter, given the instability underlying everything right now. This moment of reflection has deepened our awareness that what matters most is us. Led by the Black radical tradition, may we pay attention to the weave that composes us. May our care for each other make the promise of "we got us" into community security, something we can rely on when danger lurks—fuck the police. May we welcome newcomers, even as they stumble. May we reach beyond the usual suspects, even when it's awkward. May we grow.

Stay together. Stay tight. We do this every night.

Soon, the smoke will be washed away. Proud Boys will be back in town, the damp squibs. Friends and kin will have to make more decisions about how to support our Black friends and neighbors, how to cultivate shared protocols, how to be decisive. Historical conditions continue to evolve. Perhaps, in a few weeks, thousands, and then thousands more, outraged and frightened Americans will be flooding the streets. They will be asking themselves, asking each other, asking us: What can it look like to contest control of the streets—and win?

Let's see. Let's see together.

October 2020

At the Wendy's: Armed Struggle at the End of the World

Anonymous

For Rayshard Brooks, for Natalie White, for Secoriea Turner

Atlanta, June 12, 2020. It was just before midnight on a Friday night when we got the news. I was sitting out front of a house with everybody else at a party. Most of us were fucked up—intoxicated by a mixture of adrenaline from seventeen days straight of rioting, a months-long supply of looted liquor, MDMA, and everything else you could put in your body to help it shed its old skin and take on new shapes in the collective body of the revolt. The carnivalesque atmosphere deflates instantly.

Someone came out of the house in distress. "The police just shot a man at the Wendy's. B [a close friend of hers] saw the whole thing. He was in the parking lot filming and is being held as a witness." A shot of panic dulled the mood. We all knew what happened to the person who filmed Alton Sterling's murder, just like what happened to the person who filmed Eric Garner's murder. We had to get him out of there quick. Wendy's?! At University and Pryor? The building was right down the street.

Eventually, we decided to head to the scene. A small but angry crowd was facing off with a police line. The crowd was mostly Black, reflecting the neighborhood where the killing took place. People screamed at the cops and the Black district attorney who came out to calm people down. No one was having it. They talked among themselves about what had happened, made no secret of the guns they were carrying, and held the streets until late. We exchanged glances with comrades and residents in the crowd. It was too early to tell what would happen, too late in the night to expect a crowd to form.

•

We struggle to think of the George Floyd Rebellion as a single movement, and even to make transregional claims about its political content. We can only speak of the events that unfolded in different places—we speak of Kenosha, of Portland, Minneapolis, Chicago, New York City, Los Angeles, Richmond, Atlanta, the Capitol Hill Autonomous Zone (CHAZ) in Seattle, each with its own dynamics. What the rebellion has made clear is that we are living through the ongoing and uneven fragmentation of the United States of America as we know it.

I have spent the last ten years trying to imagine what something like the George Floyd Rebellion would look like—debating what would set it off, how people would fight, what stores they would loot, how it would all be coordinated. Never in my wildest imagination could I have pictured this.

•

On the day the Wendy's burned down, alien peace police were left to shout through their bullhorns at a local crowd that ignored and moved past them without the slightest regard. Attempts to organize the crowd along racial lines— "White people to the front!" and so on—were almost entirely ineffective. While a few people were duped into standing on the highway to mimic the effects of traffic, down on the road below, the bulk of the crowd was able to collaborate and coordinate ballistics and weapons across racial lines. The myth of the "outside agitator" sounded like a sick joke in the ears of everyone on the ground.[1]

The first days of the occupation were a free-for-all. Every night, teenagers came out to block the roads with flamethrowers, guns, swords, and cars. Sideshows took over adjacent intersections, and by nightfall caravans had formed to loot the rich parts of the city. The occupation of space wasn't limited to the parking lot. It was porous and diffuse, mobile rather than fortified.

We showed up at the Wendy's almost every single day, enjoying the distinctly anti-political feel of the space. But as time went on, we were unsure as to the endgame of the occupation. We had been busy building infrastructure and forming alliances with some of the security team but hadn't had much conversation with anyone about what would happen next.

Fast forward a couple weeks. On June 29, a comrade sent us a message over text from the Wendy's leadership, addressed "to whom it may concern." The authors of the message called the occupation a "private protest" before going on to say, "We have a detailed plan, and we do not want our wants to be confused with other community wants." This was the first we had heard of a "detailed plan." They continued: "As of now we have broken no laws." They "want[ed] community politicians to sit down with [them]" to organize the construction of a peace center and a national monument, among other things. The rest of the letter listed demands for police abolition. We had to laugh at the idea of calling it a "private protest," and especially at the part where they said "we have broken no laws." Somebody had burned that building down, and that sure as hell wasn't legal. Plenty of people are facing charges for that. The self-appointed leadership clearly hadn't been there from the beginning. They had no more right to ownership over the space than anyone else. This was the first time we had heard that anyone wanted to transform the Wendy's into a "peace center." It was unclear to us exactly how that was supposed to happen. Just sit in the parking lot long enough with guns, and the city will give it to you? Only once the strategy was announced did we realize the utter absence of a strategy.

On (Militant) Black Leadership

The group that built a permanent occupation at the Wendy's was not in any way affiliated with official Black Lives Matter or any other preexisting activist group, and for this reason we cannot describe it as a political leadership in a traditional sense. The occupation's atmosphere was remarkable in its absence of leftist or activist roles, such as people proselytizing, giving orders through megaphones, calling general assemblies, or making attempts to "organize" others. While a visible and traditional activist leadership was nowhere to be seen, what emerged instead was more along the lines of a silent and informal leadership.

The roles at the Wendy's can be understood through three clearly defined categories: a council of leaders, a gang leadership element, and a security team made up of largely younger men whose role was to guard the entrance to the parking lot of the Wendy's, do nightly patrols to watch for signs of police raids, and from time to time block the roads and control traffic. Overall, the leadership presented many obstacles to unleashing the full potential of the occupation, making it more of a cop-free zone than an autonomous zone.

Contemporary movements are constitutively leaderless. This is not a moral choice—a decision to oppose any command issued from on high— but a condition of our epoch. As the We Still Outside Collective recently wrote, "What they call 'the Black leadership' *does not exist*." This is to say neither that nobody takes initiative nor that no one tells people what to do. Far from it. The point, again, is epochal. In the 1960s, there was NAACP, SNCC, Revolutionary Action Movement, Black Panthers, Weather Underground, SDS, BLA with their concomitant figures—Martin Luther King Jr., Huey Newton, Assata Shakur. Who are these figures today? If there are plenty of martyrs from the struggles of the past several years, there are no leaders. Even if some chapters of the formal Black Lives Matter organization have survived the previous BLM cycle, they have largely played a pacifying role in the current uprising, have advocated for reforms, or at best have been reduced to voicing support for more militant actions that they had nothing to do with. Black Lives Matter survives not as an organization but as a meme, that is to say, a slogan at best. When leaders do emerge, they are unlikely to have any impactful engagement with the struggle—leaders today only lead struggles one place: to their end.

The leadership at the Wendy's chose the goal of creating the Rayshard Brooks Peace Center, which was intended as a place to set up services of care and healing for Black people. This goal seemed appropriate for the situation, and even potentially achievable, and as an idea it won the support of many participants at the occupation.

But the strategy was confused in that it attempted to combine elements from a confrontational and militant occupation with the ultimate goal of having a chat with city politicians. In this way, the conflict over the occupation's outcome has an unsuspected analogy to the conflict over the ZAD.[2] Would it be better to maintain a militant space that refused to negotiate with the city, but which would ultimately be crushed militarily? Or did it make more sense to engage in negotiations to score more permanent victories that, while potentially recuperative, might ultimately empower those involved? (On this note, it is interesting that recent reports from Portland have tried to call the same dichotomy of "pressure politics versus direct action" into question.)

The problem of leadership at the Wendy's exceeded traditional critiques of movement leadership. Such critiques tend to focus on actors who attempt to circumscribe the limits of action to largely symbolic gestures, while neutralizing or denouncing any forces that attempt to exceed this framework. In the text "On Black Leadership and Other White Myths,"[3] for example, the particular problem attributed to the Black leadership is its pacifying attempt to stifle unmediated Black rage in a bid to appeal to the white imaginary. While such a critique captures the problem of Black leaders like Atlanta mayor Keisha Lance Bottoms, this narrative doesn't effectively describe what happened at the Wendy's. Specifically, while the leadership there dictated what forms of action were and were not legitimate, they did not pacify the movement, nor did they make any attempts to present a more palatable version of Black rage that would gain widespread symbolic support from white civil society. Instead, the opaque leadership accelerated a militant stance toward conflict to a point that, as I will describe below, contributed to the occupation's eventual downfall. The problem of leadership combined with the armed nature of the occupation consolidated power in a manner that overdetermined the rest of the situation.

From a pragmatic perspective, the main obstacle presented by these more militant attempts at leadership is that our organizational systems were incompatible, which prevented communication between them almost entirely. It was almost impossible for a group operating with a closed leadership and a clear sense of internal constitution to interact and engage with chaotic, leaderless swarms. The hierarchical form of command of the pseudo-leaders at the Wendy's occupation could not interact with those accustomed to operating on principles of autonomy. With regard to its own organizational system, the leadership at Wendy's had a clear sense of who was who, and as a result it was able to clearly distribute tasks and delineate a structure of command within its own ranks. But this model of organization belongs to a bygone era, in which participants of a movement might seek coherence by forcing everything into alignment or expecting ideology or identity to provide a practical unity.

In contemporary insurrections, this hierarchical structure of command and its concomitant drive toward unity is being replaced by a form of immanent collective intelligence. Gestures and communication spread across an increasingly fragmented *socius*, without consolidating any coherent organizational body or identity. Actions and tactics shared on Telegram or social media and *détourned* to fit the needs of specific locales spread in a memetic fashion. Our organizational task, therefore, has more to do with mediating differences than with overcoming separation. Facing the organizational problem with an understanding of fragmentation as a condition rather than a shortcoming will be crucial to allowing our movements to flourish—rather than decay—under the mark of leaderlessness.

•

It's Juneteenth. The mood is vibrant. We're in the middle of a revolution. We're on a porch getting high again, seven or eight of us in full gear, about to head down to the Wendy's for the night. All of the sudden we hear gunshots. Now, this is Lakewood Heights; people shoot guns off every night in this neighborhood. But I've never heard anything like this in my life. In total, over one hundred rounds were fired off. The gunfire continued on and off for about thirty minutes. We get the news that someone we know got hit by a ricocheted bullet. They tourniqueted their own leg and sat there calmly, waiting to be driven off. Luckily, they make it out without any severe injuries. Later, we learn that the initial gunfire came from white people who drove up and opened fire on the Wendy's.

Juneteenth marks the first day that we weren't at the Wendy's. We take a breather the next day as well and gear up to do a big barbeque on the day after. It seems that people don't really know what's going on at the Wendy's, so we try to open it up to the community and try to attract some new people to the space. We need the space to grow. We need more people to come with their own initiatives and help build the space up.

We put out a call for donations and receive plenty of funding. We prepare an exorbitant feast. I'm not talking about hot dogs but several different kinds of meat and fish and a giant pot of chili. We spend the better part of a day preparing. We take two cars down to the Wendy's around one in the afternoon. The first car gets in fine, with the barbecue in the back. I'm in the second car; we roll up and try to enter the parking lot, car packed full of food. We're greeted by a strange man holding a laminated sheet of paper when we approach the driveway. We crack the window, and he says, "Have you been to the Peace Center before?" "Sir, this is a Wendy's," I didn't say. Rather, "I've been here every day, and I've never seen you here. Who are you?" The man gets heated, tells us we need to pull over and listen to his speech before entering. We ignore him and signal to some of the people we knew from days prior and try to get our comrades to come help us out. The man grows impatient and starts yelling, "Pull away! Move to the other side of the road!" At this point, things get really tense. All of a sudden, our car is surrounded by people with guns, so we comply. The car turns around, and we're stuck up through the window as we drive the car across the street. Well, now it's a bit stressful. We get escorted across the street, where we park. Our car is still surrounded. "Y'all got any bombs in this car, IEDs," someone says to us. I'm, like, "No, I've been here every day. You've seen us here. We came to cook for y'all, and the car is full of food." They search the car; I hide the knife I brought to cut food under my seat as discreetly as possible. Back in the Wendy's parking lot, deliberations are underway. We chain smoke cigarettes to pass what feels like an eternity. Our friends are still behind the armed checkpoint. All we can do is wait. Finally, we get through to them that we're there to grill. An older dude comes up to us: "I know that you all are here to do good things for us, but do not do harm to this community. I promise you, if you do harm to this community, we have snipers on you, there's over fifty guns in that parking lot right now. If you misstep, you won't make it out alive." We assure them we mean no harm, and then we receive an armed caravan back across the road. One of the members of the security team tells us, "It's good that you're out here with us. Everybody who's not with us is gonna die."

Once we reach the opposite shore of the Wendy's parking lot, we begin to unload. Shortly thereafter, a disagreement ensues in the parking lot, and then finally someone comes up and tells us to get the hell out before we get chased out, at which point we head out and set up around the corner and deliver trays of food to the space from afar.

The shooting on Juneteenth turned the unbounded protest into a defined and limited occupation, and white people were temporarily banned from the space. It made sense for them to tighten up security after a shooting, but the ultimate result of this was a sharp increase of militarization of the space combined with a suspicion of everyone who hadn't been there before. As time went on, visitors were told they could come observe the monument to Rayshard, but that after paying their respects they would have to leave. At its worst, anyone who wanted to stay longer would have to sign in with the security, report which tasks they wanted to complete and how long they expected to be there, and get out after they had finished what they came to do. In a notable instance, a young kid who had volunteered to set up a media strategy for the occupation was permanently banned for cutting a hole in the fence of the parking lot into the neighboring lot, a giant open space filled with plenty of barricade materials and plenty of hiding spaces, as well as a hidden exit. It was no longer a space to vibe as it had been in the early days, and certainly no longer a place for experimentation.

Paranoia and Fatalism

Paranoia and the proliferation of conspiracy theories are integral parts of our contemporary political atmosphere. If police and politicians cannot repress a movement beforehand or in the moment, they are likely to try to divide it after the fact, seeding mistrust among actors by attributing malicious intentions to those responsible. The police in Minneapolis have pursued this strategy, attempting time and time again to pin the most significant acts of the revolt on "white supremacists."

Participants at Wendy's were not immune to these kinds of conspiracy theories. Thus, at one point, people agreed that the shooters attacking the camp on July 5 were "Russians" sent in to derail the movement. For much of the time, many people thought we were outside agitators as well. It is to be expected that Black people distrust the intentions of a group with several white people who came to the Wendy's. We don't expect this mistrust to be overcome immediately, but as the leadership became more and more paranoid it became increasingly difficult for our group to do anything. Thus, the food we brought to the occupation in an attempt to add a reproductive element to the struggle was deemed "poisoned" and not to be eaten. In another instance, a bamboo structure was built to create a makeshift rain cover, since there was little to nothing in terms of reliable protection from summer rain. After completing the structure, it was (almost certainly intentionally) broken out of a mistrust of our intentions. Finally, the higher-ups were absolutely certain that the KKK was going to come to the Wendy's on the Fourth of July and start shooting people. Some participants had asked us if we would volunteer to infiltrate the KKK. We assured them that if it were actually true they were coming, we would likely know about it. Alas, they didn't really hear us. As a result, on Fourth of July they decided to call in support from NFAC (Not Fucking Around Coalition), a Black militia.

While paranoia stems from an inability to trust the good intentions of other ("outside") actors, fatalism is caused by an inability to trust in a desirable outcome of the struggle overall. Simply put, by fatalism I mean the condition of fighting with a lot of determination but no hope. Keeping track of all the movements that come and go, one cannot help but get concerned hearing young people say, "I'm ready to die for this shit." It was the kind of things we heard often from the mouths of these young Black men, armed to the teeth and talking about defending a parking lot containing little more than a burned-out building. Of course, in some respects the space is sacred, since it was the site of a police murder. On the other hand, the inability to detach from this sentiment is itself lethal. Fatalism is not a mistake on anyone's behalf. Rather, it seems more to be a condition of emergent revolts induced by a lack of clarity around the ultimate political horizon of revolutionary movements in general and, beyond that, the gloomy horizon of our species as a whole. If we are not merely fighting for negotiations (and I expect a large portion of the movement wants much more than this), and if there is no shared perception of what revolution means anymore, then it's also not clear what victory could look like aside from burning down police precincts. I am not saying that brazen militancy is something in need of strategic correction by more "rational" revolutionary experts. Indeed, it almost seems as if it is precisely these sorts of strategic expectations inherited from the twentieth century that cause dysphoria among more seasoned experts. However, the problem remains: without a shared sensibility around their ultimate revolutionary objectives, revolts risk adopting a strategy of exponential escalation, which can lead only to repression or to burnout.

This fatalistic mindset is recognizable to anyone familiar with the problem of the warrior or the militant subject, both of whom undertake ever-increasing exploits with diminishing returns. Many frontliners faced this problem as well: they continued protest after protest after protest, never satisfied with what they had achieved, since it hadn't resulted in the burning of a police precinct or something like revolution. This not only opened them up to being targets of repression but lent their activities a sense of desperation, meaning they don't know when it is time to disengage from street battles, which in turn makes them feel disappointed or jaded with the struggle. If we're unable to detach from a specific mode of conflict in a timely manner, we risk being trapped in symmetrical battles with the state that are largely reactive or vindictive. In his autobiography *Bad*, James Carr, a legendary outlaw and prison rebel known for his camaraderie with George Jackson, famously criticized the guerilla ideology that was a part of both prison organizing and Black radicalism in the early 1960s: "I realized that as a militant I would always be at the mercy of arbitrary acts. The militants and the Tactical Squad [riot force] live symbiotically since the leftists speak in the language the goons can understand: the purely military resolution of power relations." He continued, "I saw that all the alternatives I'd set for myself were reactionary in that they were merely direct responses to crimes committed by the state. The terms, the terrain, and the weapons of my past struggle had all been dictated by my enemy. This had increased my rage, but also increased my willingness to enter into combat in such a way that I couldn't win."[4]

Political action in our present will be characterized by paranoia and fatalism—and a revolutionary strategy must find a way beyond these limitations. Both paranoia and fatalism are born of a paradoxical situation of being incapable of finding meaningful action outside the current conflict *and* an inability to place faith in a collective process of empowerment. The essential question remains how to cut through the confusion caused by misinformation, paranoia, and fatalism and prevent the struggle from exhausting itself internally. On the one hand, partisans must actively combat the spread of misinformation by being the first to set up communications infrastructure that allows people to fact-check information and discuss plans and ideas in a decentralized fashion. Beyond that, they must figure out meaningful ways to provide clarity around revolutionary goals that are immanent to the movement itself, which will help prevent people fighting in desperate battles they cannot win.

How are we to engage in conflicts in which participants so easily lose contact with the reality of the situation yet are, at the same time, willing to put their lives on the line, all without the possibility of victory? The problem of fatalism goes back to the question of leadership: it has historically been the role of the party to intervene and lead proletarians out of desperate, dead-end struggles and onto a historical trajectory that ends in victory. Today, we cannot point to any group, party, organization, tendency, or anything similar that would provide cohesion to the movement, even after the fact.

●

It's the Fourth of July. A block party is organized at the Wendy's. For the first time since the shooting on Juneteenth, the space is open. That means anyone is welcome to come. This was what we had been thinking needed to happen all along. Hundreds of people that hadn't been there before enter the space. There's old folks and children, and people who have been traveling all over the country to protests come out. There's tons of food, a DJ tent with people dancing, people drinking all day long, and blunts are being passed around. It's the high point of the movement; everything comes together. A few activists set up some circus of a "political education training"; luckily, they were quickly moved to the back of the parking lot where nobody could hear or see them, since they couldn't have been more out of touch with the vibe if they had tried. Despite that, I'm glad that they were there. Above all, we need a diversity of groups at the space. Meanwhile, others painted murals on the other side of the building. Finally, the space feels like an autonomous zone. There are different ideas of what people should be doing, nobody is dominating the space or disagreeing per se, and the diverse elements present become a source of strength rather than a source of confusion. This dynamic is what we refer to as the composition of the movement, and at this moment the zone is undefeatable.

Suddenly something changes. Unannounced, a group of about two hundred people dressed in all black and armed to the teeth shows up and marches through the Wendy's in a military-like formation. It's the all-Black militia NFAC. The gesture inspires awe in everyone present—now nobody would fuck with the space. But something strange happens. After posing for a picture in front of the building, the majority of them turn around and leave. These are specialists who, having never been to the space, quite literally qualified as outside agitators, even if they were Black. The mood changes. "A cloud swoops across the sky and blocks out the sun."

Four hours later, it's nighttime, and I've never been this happy with the occupation. The parking lot of a former fast-food restaurant opens up as a glimpse of paradise. We're eating food that someone cooked, waiting for fireworks to start going off, a little tired from blunts and the sun. I notice they start to block the streets off again, which they hadn't done since the cops stole their barricades three weeks earlier. It takes three dudes with long guns to block one lane of the road, since there's only a trash can as a barricade. I go home to change and get ready for the night, since there's a march in another part of the city later that evening. When I come back about an hour later, I'm ready to get active. I drank a Gatorade and was ready for anything. I notice the same problem as earlier—they need actual barricades to block the road.

When the bullets start flying, I lose all sense of orientation. I grab my best friend and pull her with me to the ground behind a car, hold her close, and when the shooting stops for a moment, we run low to the ground to the back of the parking lot. Someone opens up their car door for us, and we hop in and duck. We're not safe here. Blood-curdling screams ring out, I see shots fired and returned. Someone is screaming, "Whoever shot that black man is going to die!" *We're looking for our people, trying to figure out where they went, uncertain if we should leave or stay. The same voice rings out:* "If you do not have a rifle or a shotgun, leave now! If you do not have a rifle or a shotgun, leave now!" *OK, it's clear. We try to figure out an exit. I remember that someone got kicked out of the Wendy's for cutting a hole in the fence into the neighboring lot, and this is how we make our exit. I don't know if the kid who cut the hole in that fence knew that his mischief would one day save lives, but that's exactly what happens in that moment. We make our way out into the neighboring lot, hop some fences, run home. It's 9:00 p.m.; there's a march starting soon. We have less than an hour to decompress and take it all in before we hit the streets again. We're still dizzy from what just happened, but the adrenaline keeps us going for an all-night adventure. The next day, we hear that a little girl named Secoriea Turner had been shot in the crossfire of a dispute that had broken out at the blockades. I won't realize till weeks later how what happened that night scarred me.*

To Have Done with Gunslingers

America is that strange land where boomers are quicker to shrug off cops getting shot than broken windows: the former presents a legitimate form of self-defense, and the latter is an attack on property. It is wishful thinking to believe that demonstrations in America will be gun-free in the future, and for this reason it is important to deliberate on how best to engage with them. The problem is a difficult one. If fatalism points to a strategic problem of escalation without a clear horizon, then guns are the tactical counterpart to this strategy in the American context.

While guns were present from the very first night at the Wendy's, right after Rayshard was killed, they became a prominent feature of the occupation after the shooting on Juneteenth. This first shooting had two notable consequences: white people were temporarily banned from the space, and people started stockpiling weapons in the Wendy's parking lot. Regardless of whether or not this was the right thing to do, it must be said that the right wing's strategy depends on polarizing tensions around precisely these two axes: discord along ethnic lines and inciting armed conflict.

Since the traffic blockades eventually led to an armed confrontation, can we locate any specific strategic function they might have played? On the days following Juneteenth, road blockades made out of burned remnants of trash left over from the arson were set up in the streets and reinforced by young men with long guns. The blockade wasn't just at any random street in the neighborhood—it was at the first intersection after the freeway off ramp. To put it bluntly, it blocked the entrance to the entire neighborhood. Cars of Black people who showed solidarity or gave a fist were allowed to pass, while white people mostly turned around far before approaching the blockades. Had it been held for long enough, such a blockade is the kind of thing that could provoke white flight from the area, forcing people to abandon their plans to "clean up the neighborhood."

While it was the power of stone throwers and arsonists that claimed the territory, it was doubtless the presence of these guns that kept the police away for three weeks. Leftists are often appalled when police take a hands-off approach to armed right-wing demonstrators who attempt to blockade or occupy space, but the Wendy's showed that this could have more to do with the presence of guns than many leftists would like to believe. The visible display of guns made it so that the cops wouldn't dare to approach the place for fear of a shoot-out. Given the low morale of the Atlanta Police Department—many officers had walked off the job that week over the charges filed against the killer cop—it was clear that they were overstretched and didn't have the forces to engage in this kind of gun battle. Yet in an estimated total of seven shoot-outs that took place in three weeks, no fascists or cops were shot, and none of those killed were adversaries of the occupation.

What was the effect of guns at the occupation? Eventually, they became an ersatz for thinking about how to keep the space safe—and an ersatz for a strategy of collective power. As much as they contributed to keeping police away, they also became a substitute for other types of activity that could have strengthened the occupation: having more people there instead of less, building actual physical barricades in the street instead of leaving it up to gunmen to stop cars, etc. The increase in guns contributed to a regimented military vibe that dominated the camp. Thus, instead of sleeping at night, the security team was tasked with "patrolling" the space to look out for threats, a recipe for rapid burnout. There's no doubt in my mind that many people didn't come to the space because they were afraid of the guns, and not just white people. Black neighbors who fuck around with guns all the time also wouldn't come out, because they didn't see the guns as anything particularly impressive. For them, guns signaled something more like the specialized gang activity that is dangerous for their kids to be around, so they didn't have the same alluring effect that they did for many militants. In other words, the reliance on guns created a hostile environment that eventually ended up limiting the scope of the actors engaged in the camp, which made it even more vulnerable to violence and attack.

The problem was not the presence of guns per se, but the fact that carrying a gun turned into a specialized role. This specialization was most visible in the arrival of NFAC on the Fourth of July. Their alien presence, hardly more than a photo op, took no account of the situation whatsoever, militarized the mood, and definitely didn't make anyone safer. While the militia was called in to secure the space after fabricated threats of a KKK lynching on the Fourth of July, its presence was just plain dominating and created a situation that it was not actually there to take responsibility for. Even if it is a Black militia, it presents a pole of antagonism that escalates too quickly and falls into a trap of symmetrical warfare. The more armed actors become the leaders of the struggle, the less room to maneuver will be left to people throwing Molotov cocktails, breaking into buildings to hack electricity, or cutting fences to steal equipment.

The idea that the best way to respond to gun violence by the state is by more armed violence is a fallacy with a history. A similar debate played out in the 1960s between Eldridge Cleaver and Huey Newton: while the former advocated for an armed vanguard of lumpenproles to lead the struggle, Newton came to see the isolating effects brazen militancy had on the struggle and, thus, pursued survival programs instead. A more community-centered approach at the Wendy's might have created the space for real autonomous material power to grow, and broadening the scope of actors might have made the space less vulnerable to armed attack, reducing the number of guns necessary.

The guns at the Wendy's were not going to magically make a peace center appear. Aside from replacing any real strategy, guns did not help the Wendy's occupation leadership get any closer to their real goal, and in the end they were still reliant on negotiations with the state to get what they wanted. At the same time, it is clear that there would have been no way to launch a critique of the guns from an unarmed position. Any plea for nonviolence would have been laughed at and brushed aside. In hindsight, if we had wanted to make the space safer and more hospitable, we would have had to take over roles on the security team and neutralize the increasing militarization from within that role—a self-abolition of the armed partisan, if something like that is conceivable.

The question of violence will be a decisive one for the future of revolutionary movements in America. There's no doubt that said movements will need to arm themselves for self-defense. Yet, as also happened in the CHAZ in Seattle, the violence within the police-free zones often directly results in these spaces losing political support. When this is the case, the police do not even need to bother pursuing a strategy of direct repression. Instead they can just wait until their absence from the area allows for enough violence that eventually their presence seems justified. In contrast to this strategy, which is based upon minoritarian factions of armed shooters, the legacy of the nonviolent direct-action movement provides something that is able to maintain broad support. To point this out is not to make a case for moralistic nonviolence but, rather, to suggest that the strength of our movements will depend on broad social support more than on purely military victories.

Conclusion

The main problem at Wendy's was that the space was controlled by a hierarchical leadership who—by their own account—"privatized" the protest to the point of refusing any help from several dozens of people who were interested in contributing to the space in real ways. This factor increasingly isolated the space and made the leaders increasingly paranoid. As a result, the occupation relied on a dangerous strategy of armed escalation to strong-arm the state, which ended predictably with gun violence that made the space easily repressible and, quite frankly, difficult to defend, after an eight-year-old was murdered in the cross fire of the Fourth of July shoot-out. While the occupation galvanized an overwhelming display of militancy and courage, it ended with a dilemma similar to that experienced by many other rebellions across the country; it was unable to clarify what there was to build or affirm once the looting, burning, and destruction ended.

What does the Wendy's tell us about a strategy of escalation? What are we to think of the fact that guns both made the occupation possible and led to its demise? If it has been our task in past struggles to escalate things to their insurrectionary horizon, this must be differentiated from escalation as the mere increase of a capacity for violence. Kenosha is yet another situation in which violence quickly escalated past a point in which emancipatory actors were able to be effective. In these situations, the increased rate of escalation is unsustainable and, in the end, only accelerates the restoration of law and order. Revolutionary activity should be measured in terms of its capacity to be sustainably defended by as many people as possible. When revolutionary violence tends to isolate participants rather than defending them, it does more harm than good.

Beyond the issue of violence, the question emerges as to how to create a common perspective on what forms of action are possible in the absence of leadership structures or democratic proceduralism. As movements like the George Floyd Rebellion continue to appear, "organized

militants" might find themselves being outpaced and sidelined by proletarians who have little interest or regard for long-term revolutionary
or strategic objectives but, instead, are magnetized exclusively to looting and clashing with police. If we wish to avoid an easily foreseeable
outcome, it is important to clarify a measurable set of revolutionary
objectives beyond that of fighting increasingly militarized battles with
the state and fascists or becoming depressed or jaded when these dry up
or are no longer possible. Without any goals in mind, the escalation of
violence risks outpacing the capacity of movements to produce collective
affirmations beyond that of the enemies they hold in common. How do
we counter this escalation, while still advancing along a revolutionary
trajectory?

Insurrections and uprisings are one important piece of a protracted
revolutionary process, not necessarily their apocalyptic culmination. All
movements, being in their essence living organisms, are bound to die
out. However much we might wish to disavow this inevitable ending of
our movements, those frameworks that allow a sense of joy and celebration to accompany the end of movements are better positioned to foster
the growth of a sustainable long-term revolutionary force. It requires an
enormous amount of energy to weather the negative fallout of such big
ruptures and to avoid a sense of desperation that compels us to engage
in actions that merely mimic the feelings evoked during the movement
(the joy of destruction, now undertaken on an individual basis without
a mass of people) but do not have the potential to meaningfully open up
new paths of struggle. To avoid fatalistic actions, we must cultivate the
capacity to throw everything into these revolts, to give these battles our all,
while at the same time recognizing when their potential is exhausted or
when movements are "dead." This capacity to recognize when the terrain
is no longer one that we are determining is an essential part of what it
means to "be water."

As the recent debates around the desirability of civil war make clear,
there is no meaningful concept of revolution on offer today.[5] In the twentieth century, proletarian revolution was imagined as a process whereby
the working class would grow exponentially up to a critical threshold,
at which point it would become politically hegemonic, take power, and
produce a new world out of the shell of the old. Today, this is no longer
conceivable: we are collapsing under the shell of the old world rather than
finding meaningful ways to salvage it. Consequently, today's partisans

will have to be much more flexible in their expectations about what is desirable and possible in the coming years.

Beyond the internal strife our species is facing, we face the threat of extinction under a planetary catastrophe of unthinkable proportions. This calls on us to think, as Günther Anders phrased it, of an "apocalypse that consists of mere downfall, which doesn't represent the opening of a new, positive state of affairs"—an "apocalypse without kingdom." Fortunately, we're not the only ones faced with the difficulty of founding a new way of life. In the time to come, ruling elites will also find it increasingly challenging to establish and maintain law and order. As the horizon of governance recedes, more and more space will open up for us, allowing us to experiment with ever-larger regions of territory outside of their control. The Wendy's occupation gave us a very real glimpse of precisely this coming disarray. Our task now is to turn the challenges it faced into a touchstone to guide us through the coming abyss.

November 2020

Order Prevails in Louisville

Anonymous

The killing of Breonna Taylor in Louisville, Kentucky, was one of the most high-profile incidents of police violence in a year dominated by discussions of the subject, second perhaps only to the murder of George Floyd, captured on videotape, in Minneapolis. The call to "arrest the police who killed Breonna Taylor" has become, in addition to a major demand of the ongoing street protests, a cause celebrated by the likes of Beyoncé, LeBron James, and Joe Biden and something of a viral internet meme.

When, on Tuesday, September 22, 2020, the mayor of Louisville and the Louisville Metro Police Department (LMPD) announced a state of emergency "due to the potential for civil unrest," everyone knew that the state attorney general was preparing to make an announcement on the Breonna Taylor case. Everyone knew that they were not going to indict the officers involved. Everyone knew that this meant there would be a riot. A search for "Louisville" on Twitter that day would reveal an endless scroll of variations of "hope they burn Louisville to the ground #BreonnaTaylor," punctuated by the occasional plea from a verified Twitter account begging people to stay home. But Louisville did not burn down. This non-riot forces us to confront the limits and impasses present in this wave of struggle and to imagine how they may be overcome.

September 22

On Tuesday afternoon, a crowd began to gather in Jefferson Square Park to await news of the attorney general's announcement. The downtown park had been the site of daily protests since May 28, when thousands of people took to the streets in Louisville after Breonna Taylor's family leaked the audio of her boyfriend's 911 call. As afternoon turned to evening, those gathered began to grow impatient. When it became clear that no announcement would be made that evening, a hundred or so people began to march out of the park, chanting, "Breewayy or the Freeway." Breewayy was a family nickname for Breonna. Some also chanted, "Burn it down!"

Everyone there knew how the verdict would go. Many in the crowd were armed, and flak vests were abundant. Bottles of bourbon were passed around the march, and the smell of marijuana smoke was in the air.

The march wasn't huge, but it was rowdy and felt determined as it made its way through the empty, barricaded, boarded-up streets of downtown. As it approached the freeway, the I-64, commotion broke out. Emerging from a nearby parking lot, a lone white counterprotester flashed his gun at the march. The crowd fell back and in the midst of shouted debates began to march back to Jefferson Square Park. Along the way, arguments continued to break out throughout the crowd.

"Why bring all these guns, if you're going to act like cowards?"

"The women and children should head back to the park where it's safe, and the rest of us should keep going."

"The last time a white boy pulled a gun out on protesters, two people ended up dead."

"You're going to let a man pull a gun on you?" a group of women shouted from their car.

Tensions were high, and a sense of disappointment hung over the crowd. "Wait until tomorrow," people reminded each other. Tomorrow, it was assumed, the attorney general would finally make his announcement. Judging by the mood of the crowd, many anticipated there would be a riot.

Back at the park, some people got busy serving food or organizing donations. Someone played music from a small portable speaker, but most just milled about in small groups with their friends. A young Black man, particularly flustered by the night's events, made the rounds arguing for a more militant night march that would head to the nearest commercial strip. He made a short speech to everyone present, saying that we should not be so willing to back down, and that everyone who was serious should be ready to march again in twenty minutes. Before long, he made the rounds again with a rumor that the Three Percenters, a right-wing militia, was staging nearby. The march was called off.

September 23

A crowd began to gather in Jefferson Square Park again early the next day. At 1:30 p.m., an announcement was made. The state grand jury had recommended to charge one of the three officers with wanton endangerment but none of them with murder. Attorney General David Cameron, a young, charismatic Black Republican, followed this with a press conference at which he gave the speech of his life. As a television newscaster wondered aloud if this indictment would be enough to satisfy the protests, his station cut to live footage from Jefferson Square Park, where the crowd had already begun setting fires. Meanwhile, other protesters were seen starting to distribute shields out of the back of a U-Haul truck.

Soon, several hundred people were marching out of downtown, and then through the Highlands, the local equivalent of Brooklyn's Williamsburg neighborhood. At the front of the march were a row of banner-sized shields. Some windows were broken along the way, and fireworks were set off, which some, understandably, mistook for gunshots. The mood swung between tense and almost festive. Along Bardstown Road's strip of bars and shops, the march was intercepted by riot police. A scuffle broke out. Some in the crowd threw bottles, and the police responded with tear gas and pepper balls and made a number of arrests. The chaos broke up the crowd, but at least half of the protesters were able to regroup and keep marching.

"Frontliner gear," such as shields, helmets, goggles, masks, gas masks, and gloves, was everywhere, as were flak jackets. Lasers, though, seemed not to have caught on. The crowd was heavily armed. Some carried rifles, others had pistols with oversized clips sticking out of their pockets, and others still carried baseball bats or other makeshift weapons. While the armed demographic skewed male, there were plenty of women with firearms as well. A Black man on a mountain bike rode by with a rifle in one hand and no shirt on, followed moments later by a white woman on a Dutch-style bike with a bulletproof vest on and a pistol in a holster.

Militia-like organizations providing security for demonstrations has become an increasingly familiar sight in different parts of the country and has a particular history tracing back to the Civil Rights Movement. The scene in Louisville, though, was somewhat different. There was no armed body that distinguished itself from the crowd in any discernible way; rather, the demonstration itself was armed.

The march got bigger as it went. An ever-growing caravan of vehicles trailed behind: cars blasting music, with people hanging out of the windows or sitting on the roof; pickup trucks with their rear bed full of protesters, often carrying shields or rifles. The crowd was multiracial, but a significant majority was Black.

Arriving back downtown, protesters were confronted by the spectacle of militarization of their city. Concrete barriers blocked vehicular traffic from the city center. Almost every building was boarded up, and certain government buildings had fences built around them. Nearly every object that could be moved and, thus, turned into a barricade or projectile had been removed from the scene. Riot police and the National Guard seemed to be staging everywhere. Soldiers carrying rifles guarded the entrance to parking garages. Occasionally a garage door would open or close, giving a glimpse of rows of armored vehicles and armed guards. Helicopters and drones hovered overhead. By nightfall, these various state agencies were joined by their extralegal accomplices, as dozens of militiamen stationed themselves outside of a handful of gas stations and other businesses.

With some effort, a small group of protesters managed to push one of the concrete barriers out of the way, clearing the street for the caravan of cars trailing behind the march. Riot police quickly rushed to the scene. The rear of the march paused to confront them, with some throwing plastic bottles, and then glass ones. Most of the crowd was already rallying at Jefferson Square Park by this point. Dozens more riot police slowly arrived, making a big show of pushing the barrier back into place, as if to make clear that even the smallest act of defiance would not be tolerated in this totally controlled environment.

Stepping away from this standoff, around one hundred protesters began to march out of the barricaded-off zone. Before they had made it the length of a block, the march was cut off and surrounded by riot police and National Guard. Those who could escape did, and the rest were kettled.

News began to spread that the mayor had declared a 9:00 p.m. curfew.

•

The crowd at Jefferson Square Park continued to grow over the course of the evening. As the sun set, fires were started, first in trash cans, then in the street. Soon the front of the Justice Center was set on fire, as the crowd basked in its vindicating glow. Riot police who emerged from the building to try to extinguish the flames were met with a volley of bottles and firecrackers. They responded in kind with pepper balls and flashbangs, before making a hasty retreat back inside. A loudspeaker began to announce that this was an "unlawful assembly," ordering everyone to disperse.

At 8:30 p.m., a crowd of around 350 began to march out of the park. People used baseball bats to shatter the glass on bus stations and any windows that remained unboarded, while trash cans encountered along the way were set on fire. However, riot police managed to stay ahead of the crowd, blocking every exit out of the downtown corridor. Repelled onto Broadway, the march found itself facing a line of police charging down the avenue. A volley of projectiles emerged from the crowd. There was the sound of fireworks, then of flash-bangs, followed by gunfire.

The line of police scattered. For a moment, the world stood still. "He's firing a real gun!" a woman screamed. A man had emerged from the crowd and opened fire on the police while running. Suddenly, most of the crowd dispersed, taking off running into alleys or down the street or taking cover behind cars. The police, who had retreated to a neighboring parking lot, fired off a volley of pepper balls, and then reemerged with their guns drawn. The LMPD would abandon the pretense of less-than-lethal weapons for the rest of the night and would patrol the area with live ammunition ready.

Brief moments of chaos punctuated the night. One minute, dozens of kids could be seen running as fast as they could down Broadway, leaving a trail of broken glass in their wake. A minute later, a caravan of cars was speeding out of downtown toward the gentrified NULU neighborhood. Rumors abounded about where the crowd might be regrouping or what might be taking place in the rest of the city, but the crowd never regained the upper hand. Order prevailed in Louisville.

The small groups wandering downtown that night, trying to find the action, or at least find each other, often just found themselves arrested at gunpoint and forced to lie face down on the sidewalk while handcuffed. By midnight, a hundred protesters had managed to regroup at Jefferson Square Park, only to be dispersed, with many ending up in a mass arrest. At least 127 people had been arrested by the end of the night.

Meanwhile, diffuse looting began to spread throughout the rest of the city. Taking advantage of the concentration of police downtown, crews drove around the highways and neighborhoods that circle the city, breaking into strip malls. Stores were occasionally set on fire as well. Liquor stores and pawn shops were the common targets, as well as Family Dollar, Walgreens, and Home Depot. At least sixteen stores were looted, according to the LMPD. This pattern of looting and arson spreading throughout the county after the protests downtown wound down was repeated every night for the rest of the week.

September 24

Most of those arrested the night before were held in a jail neighboring Jefferson Square Park. The crowd, which once again gathered in and around the park and grew steadily as the afternoon went on, cheered for them as they were released over the course of the day. While the news focused on the two police officers who were shot, they were both quickly released from the hospital and faded from the public's view.

At 7:00 p.m., like clockwork, a march left from the park, this time heading to the nearby Hampton Inn, the downtown hotel that militias were rumored to be staying at. Protesters poured into the hotel parking lot, aggressively confronting the not-yet-geared-up militia members, who kept their composure and refrained from responding but as the confrontation dragged on slowly started unpacking guns from their trunk. The protesters fell back and tensely marched back to the park. Arguments broke out along the way. This was now the fourth march in three days that was repelled back before it was able to get out of the several-block radius around the park.

Back at Jefferson Square, tensions were high. An argument about the course of the march turned into a fistfight. A circle formed around the two men and watched them punch it out and then fight to a finish on the ground. Their friends stopped anyone from intervening. Later, an older man, told to keep his voice down while a venerated civil rights leader gave a speech, pulled out his gun.

There were other similar incidents throughout the course of the night. More than once, arguments within the crowd led to guns being pulled. Frantz Fanon would likely have something to say about how, unable to direct their capacity for violence at what oppresses them, the oppressed redirect it toward each other. Violence is also simply more present in the lives of Black proletarians than it is for many other Americans. Different levels of proximity and accustomedness to violence is something that multiracial struggle will have to come to terms with, one way or another.

The crowd was again heavily armed. A man in a bulletproof vest, with a pistol in a holster, rested his rifle nozzle-down on the sidewalk while he smoked a blunt with his friends. Another man walked around with a large branch that he'd wrapped the ends of in duct tape to serve as grips.

Someone else carried a sword. Crews of women wandered the park with bats. It would be hard to speculate how many in the crowd had concealed pistols.

At 8:00 p.m., an hour before curfew, several hundred people dressed mostly in black marched out of the park, moving quickly to try to clear the barricaded-in perimeter before police could get the jump on them. Once outside the perimeter, protesters began breaking windows and covering whatever surface was available in graffiti. The sound of shattering glass elicited cheers from the crowd. Although moving swiftly to evade the LMPD, the march was determined to leave a defiant trace.

The largely evacuated downtown left few options for the *potlatch of destruction*,[1] except to move elsewhere. But the LMPD was determined to contain the march within the area and managed to stay one step ahead. Any exit toward other neighborhoods or onto the freeway was blocked.

Those most determined to do something set their sights on whatever hadn't yet been boarded up and emptied out. Would-be rioters vandalized city buses, broke the windows of a hospital, and threw a flare through the window of a public library. Bonanno remarks somewhere that liberatory action is often excessive by nature. It is like the blow of a tiger's claws that rips but does not distinguish in its destruction.

After an hour of trying their best to stay ahead of the police and not get kettled, several hundred protesters ran into the First Unitarian Church, which had earlier offered itself as a sanctuary for protesters violating curfew. The LMPD and National Guard quickly formed a perimeter around the church. Debates broke out. The most militant faction felt like they had been led into a trap. The clergy warned everyone not to use profanities in a holy space. The smell of tear gas wafted in the air.

Small groups trying to leave the church were arrested. This included a state senator and a prominent organizer, both of whom were charged with multiple felonies, partially related to the "arson" attempt at the public library. The union representing the public library workers, AFSCME Local 3425, released a statement the next morning saying more or less that throwing a flare through the window of a library isn't that big of a deal. After several tense hours, the clergy negotiated safe passage for everyone who agreed to return to their cars. At least twenty-six arrests took place that night.

For the second night in a row, diffuse looting spread along the highways that encircle the city. The LMPD reported at least sixteen cases of break-ins. One Game Spot had an SUV drive through the front entrance. A Home Depot in a largely white suburb was set on fire. For a second time, rumors that the Jefferson Avenue Mall was being looted turned out not to be true.

September 25

The first public call for a demonstration was for Friday, a full two days after the grand jury announcement. The crowd that gathered in Jefferson Square Park wasn't substantially larger than previous days, but was significantly whiter. The demonstration marched through the gentrified NULU neighborhood, stopping to shame various local businesses that hadn't supported the movement, before being kettled and dispersed.

Protesters slowly regrouped in Jefferson Square Park. The crowd was significantly less armed than previous nights. At 8:00 p.m., an hour before curfew, protesters marched back to the First Unitarian Church, without making any pretense of being disruptive or of violating curfew. A Black teenager marching with a road flare was publicly shamed. LMPD and the National Guard again surrounded the church, but after a few hours clergy was able to negotiate safe passage for protesters back to their cars.

Diffuse looting throughout the county took place again, but with a little bit less energy than on previous nights. A Home Center in the city reported at least twenty televisions stolen.

The next day, a call for a "massive occupation" of Jefferson Square Park didn't exactly pan out. Protesters instead gathered at the square until an hour before curfew, and then held an orderly march to the church. After an hour of sanctuary, two dozen protesters marched across the street, breaking the windows of several buildings at a nearby college and using fireworks to set a security car on fire.

Twenty-two people were arrested that night for curfew violations. At least seven stores were looted, including a phone store, a pharmacy, and two GameStops.

•

"George Floyd got some kind of justice because Minneapolis burned, while Breonna Taylor got nothing because Louisville didn't" has become something of a truism this summer. Friends around the country with little previous exposure to radical politics find in that phrase justification for their sudden enthusiasm for riots. The phrase was repeated over and over again in the streets of Louisville this last week, in between variations of the chant "Burn it down!" Why, then, didn't Louisville burn?

Initiative

Anti-police riots tend to be spontaneous and, thus, require some event to prompt them. Police brutalize or murder someone, people from the neighborhood gather, and that gathering magnetizes people from across the city. Or an event of police violence is recorded, and that recording is later released and goes viral, causing outraged people to pour into the streets, even days or months after the initial event occurred. Such was the case with Breonna Taylor, as well as Daniel Prude in Rochester. Or the announcement of the non-indictment or acquittal of the officers involved sparks protests that spill over into riots. Of these circumstances, it is the latter the state is most able to predict and, thus, prepare for.

The most intense rioting in Ferguson, with reverberations across the country, followed the non-indictment of Darren Wilson, the officer who killed Michael Brown. Similarly, the 1992 LA riots took place following the acquittal of the officers who beat Rodney King. This specter has been haunting the city of Louisville and the State of Kentucky for months. Thus, they did everything they could to prepare.

A state of emergency was declared, along with a 9:00 p.m. curfew. The entire city police force was mobilized, as were the Kentucky National Guard and state police. The downtown area was boarded up, with barricades controlling traffic in and out of the zone where protests were expected. Every measure normally taken to suppress a riot already underway was in place well before anyone had taken to the streets.

The handling of the announcement itself was also carefully curated. Declaring a state of emergency gave everyone a sense of what to expect, but by pushing back the actual announcement they gave the city a chance to let go of some of the tension and blow off some steam. Simply by having the press conference early in the day, they gave the crowd an entire afternoon of marching and repression to exhaust itself. Indicting one of the officers involved and having that indictment announced by a young Black district attorney left just enough ambiguity for the public to hesitate.

After a long summer on the defensive, the state was finally able to recapture the initiative, choosing the time, terrain, and content of the battle. The movement obligingly agreed to meet it on its own terms. The obvious explanation for that is somewhat unsatisfying. Why did the movement choose to meet the state on its own ground? Why did a critical mass of the city never come into the streets? Why didn't the movement try to innovate tactically, taking advantage of the particular opportunities available in Louisville? Does this experience provide any lessons?

Territory

Jefferson Square Park, located in the heart of downtown and surrounded by City Hall, the Metro Police Department, the Sheriff's Department, the Department of Corrections, the Hall of Justice, and a number of court-houses, was the site of daily protests beginning in late May. Over the course of June, the park swelled into a sprawling encampment, complete with a library, a grill, a makeshift kitchen, several tables and tents for serving food and sharing donated supplies, and porta-potties. A statue in the middle of the park of Louis XVI, the king of France who was beheaded during the revolution and who is the city's namesake, was vandalized by protesters. It was eventually removed by the city. At the heart of the park is a memorial for Breonna Taylor, as well as for Tyler Charles Gerth and David McAtee, the local movement's martyrs. After a shooting in late June, the LMPD raided the park and cleared out all of the structures.

This follows a familiar pattern. Throughout the summer, protesters in cities across the country set up occupations or "autonomous zones" outside of symbolic government buildings as a way to keep momentum going, including Seattle's Capitol Hill Autonomous Zone and New York's City Hall Autonomous Zone. From Cairo's Tahrir Square to Manhattan's Zuccotti Park, from Gezi Park in Istanbul to Occupy Central in Hong Kong, occupations of public parks have been a recurring feature of this last decade's cycle of struggle. Compared to the 2014–2015 Black Lives Matter protests, which were unable to sustain themselves, due, in part, to participants not having a space to gather and get organized, this year's proliferation of autonomous zones feels like a significant step forward. Sharing a space gave the movement a shared rhythm and a spontaneous way to organize itself. It's entirely possible that the movement in some cities would not have been able to develop and sustain its momentum without them. In another sense, though, the intuitions at play seem to lag behind the struggle in Hong Kong, where the movement abandoned any ambition of holding space, instead aiming to "be water."

In this case, a sentimental attachment to a territory left the movement increasingly incapable of taking the initiative or acting strategically. In anticipation of suppressing the riot before it happened, the state sought to take advantage of the movement's attachments, amassing its forces for a symmetrical conflict on favorable ground, and the movement obliged.

Protesters would have had better odds trying their luck nearly anywhere except where they were accustomed to. Shifting the terrain, for instance, to the city's West End, where a majority of Black residents live, and where David McAtee was killed by police and National Guard in early June, may have provided, if not more numbers, at least a sympathetic environment with more room to maneuver. That part of town was also the site of Louisville's May 1968 riots. Instead, the movement was stuck in a loop of regrouping exactly where the enemy's forces were most concentrated, and then being either dispersed or corralled. All the state had to do was make this particular territory uninhabitable, and the movement had no way to regroup.

Composition

Throughout the year, in any number of cities, we've seen that if enough of the population takes to the streets, regardless of the strength of the police, they can make the city ungovernable. At no point following the announcement did a critical mass come into the streets of Louisville. There was never a large enough crowd to outnumber, let alone overpower, the police. It's possible that, judging from the show of force by the police, much of the city decided that nothing was possible and stayed home. It's also possible that the size of the crowd would have swelled the night of the indictment had the initial demonstration not been scattered, but the composition of those who came out seems to tell a different story.

An out-of-towner at the demonstrations that week would be forgiven for assuming that the population of Louisville was largely Black. Across the country, protests this summer, with the exception of perhaps the most intense moments of rioting, have fairly accurately reflected the racial composition of the cities they were held in. In Louisville, though, Black people make up only 22 percent of the metro area, and only 35 percent of the city itself (statistics are a bit hard to track, because the city and county boundaries recently merged), but tended to make up at least 80 percent of those in attendance at demonstrations. How do we explain this demographic inversion and the low turnout overall?

Louisville has been ranked one of the safest large cities in America, but the demonstrations there this summer have been particularly marked by violence. On May 28, the first day the city poured into the streets, seven demonstrators were shot from within the crowd. A few days later, on June 2, David McAtee was killed when LMPD and the National Guard opened fire on a social gathering in violation of curfew that was taking place several miles away from the protests. There were also at least three shooting incidents at Jefferson Square Park during protests. At a rally held by the Not Fucking Around Coalition, a semi-informal Black militia, a gun was accidentally fired after a demonstrator dropped it, wounding three other participants. Twice arguments among protesters at the park escalated into shootings. Tyler Charles Gerth, a white photographer documenting the movement, was left dead after being hit by a stray bullet during one such incident. At that point, all but the most committed began to ease away from the movement, and white Louisville, in particular, generally stopped going to Jefferson Square Park. Violence, it seems, raised the stakes of participation to the point where many who agreed with the movement's demands were intimidated away from actually participating.

Logistics

Violence aside, across the country, participation in the movement has waned over the summer. Cities that experienced a second flare-up around a local instance of police violence rarely had the same critical mass in the streets. Instead, they were able to make their power felt through some innovation in tactics. Following the shooting of Latrell Allen in Chicago, a "looter caravan" marauded through the city for a night. After the death of Rayshard Brooks in a Wendy's parking lot, demonstrators in Atlanta burned the restaurant down and began an occupation of the now-empty lot. No such tactical leap occurred in Louisville. When an individual fired on the police, it was, in a sense, a tactical novelty, but one that didn't generalize beyond the actions of a lone individual. If the struggle had been able to step away from its sentimental attachments and risk a tactical leap, it would probably have wanted to take advantage of the particular opportunities available.

"Breewayy or the Freeway" can be seen spray-painted on the few remaining structures at Jefferson Square Park and can be heard shouted enthusiastically at nearly every march. It functions as something of a watchword for the movement: if Breonna doesn't get justice, we shut down the freeways. (It also functions as a way to give literal direction to the marches. Breewayy has become the semiofficial name for the corridor around Jefferson Square Park.) Blocking the freeways may seem to some like a relic of the past. The most advanced tactic to generalize from the 2014 wave of struggle now feels quaint in comparison to the lootings and arson of this summer. But the slogan points to a particularly sensible reading of the possibilities available in that city. Louisville is, at its heart, a logistics city.

Located near the Ohio Falls, and nestled close to the center of the country, Louisville has a long history as a significant center of the country's shipping and cargo industries. Today the city is home to one of the country's largest inland ports and sits at the intersection of three major freeways. Most significantly, the Louisville International Airport is home to the UPS World Port, the largest automated package sorting facility in the world, processing roughly two million packages a day.[2] A strategy of disruption in Louisville could do much to bring the country's economy to a halt. Anyone who thinks protesters shutting down an airport is just a little too ambitious need only remember the country-wide airport blockades in January 2017, in response to Trump's Muslim ban.

Party

Anarchists, and their fellow travelers, certainly played a significant role behind the scenes, helping the movement develop infrastructure, but besides the stray anarchist slogan on a shield or the lone black bloc-er, there was no legible pro-revolutionary pole in the streets. The political ecology of the movement in Louisville is split between different factions of reformist organizations. Despite the armed demonstrations, even the political leadership at the camp is largely in the hands of career activists from well-funded national organizations.

One could argue, with some credulity, that the movement's avant-garde, the Black proletarians who tried over and over again that week to kick things off, is so deeply anti-political that it simply doesn't feel an obligation to express itself in terms legible to the left. It was certainly a pattern that those who acted the most spoke the least and had literally no interest in engaging in debate with those who weren't going to act with them. It is in precisely these moments, when movements come face to face with their impasses, that militants have the most to offer, by drawing on their own experience of struggle and their understanding of what is happening elsewhere to experiment with ways to move forward. As the barriers we collide with become trickier to traverse, the role of a revolutionary minority, those who help build the capacity and collective confidence of revolt, may become more important. In this sense, the absence of a pro-revolutionary pole was felt.

At times, during those nights of frantic cat and mouse games with the police, it felt as if everyone we met in the streets was from out of town. They all fit a similar profile: they were Black, working-class, probably in their twenties; they were invariably wearing some assortment of frontliner tactical gear, and often dressed in full black bloc attire. Everyone had a similar story: in late May, they had dived headfirst into the riots in whatever small city they lived in. They then tried to keep the momentum going where they were for as long as they could. Since then, they've been traveling the country to whichever city it kicks off in: Portland, Kenosha, Rochester, Louisville. Some had made a lifestyle out of it, installing a bed in the back of their pickup truck. Others had kids at home they had to get back to.

Perhaps lacking theoretically consistent perspectives, they are driven by an intuition that whatever hope there is in the world, in this strange plague year, can be found in pushing this struggle toward its limit. Whether this cycle of struggles is able to overcome the impasses it currently faces depends, to a certain degree, on whether these new militants are able to find each other and what sort of shared perspectives they develop. There is nothing guaranteeing that, like the generation of 2014, many of them do not end up mired in one of the numerous left or nonprofit swamps, becoming yet another barrier that future struggles will have to overcome. But if a collective material force is to emerge out of this sequence, we can get a glimpse of its possible contours in the lines traced by these circulating militants.

Future victories will spring from this defeat. Today, order prevails in Louisville, but that order is built on sand. Tomorrow, the revolution will rise up again, clashing its weapons, and proclaim with trumpets blazing: I was, I am, I shall be!

October 2020

The End of the Summer

Gilets Jawns

Nearly every week since the beginning of this long, hot summer, a different city has occupied the center stage of this particularly American drama. Through this passing of the torch, the sequence of riots has dragged on for far longer than anyone could have expected. Every time it seemed as if the wave had finally crashed, another city went up in flames. In the last days before the election, Philadelphia, the largest city in perhaps the most significant swing state, had its turn to carry the torch.

But, in the aftermath of the climactic violence in Kenosha, each new riot has been less able to mobilize wider layers of society or capture the public imaginary. It is too soon to tell whether this summer of unrest has finally run its course or if a faction of Black proletarians will continue to carry forward the struggle on their own. It may be that, for now, the spectacle of the election simply towers over the spectacle of insurrection. Nonetheless, the riots in Philadelphia leave us with questions about the composition and tactics of the movement and the role of revolutionaries within it.

•

Walter Wallace Jr., a father and aspiring rapper with a history of mental illness, was having a crisis and acting erratically. Someone from Wallace's family called 911, hoping to have him temporarily hospitalized. Soon, rather than the ambulance his family expected, the Philadelphia Police Department (PPD) arrived. Officers on the scene were told by his family that Wallace was having a mental health crisis. Nonetheless, within minutes Wallace had been shot at over a dozen times. Walter Wallace Jr. was pronounced dead soon after arriving at the hospital.

Shaky cellphone footage capturing the incident ends with Wallace's family and neighbors confronting and screaming at the police officers on the scene. Everybody knew it was about to explode.

That afternoon, the video began to circulate on social media, along with a flier calling for a demonstration that evening at Malcolm X Park in West Philadelphia, not far from the site of the shooting. Several hundred joined a rowdy march to the nearby 18th Precinct, through the neighborhood, and eventually back toward the precinct. A breakaway march left for University City, where a campus police station and substation and a police cruiser had their windows broken.

Clashes between demonstrators and riot police broke out near the 18th Precinct, and the crowd spilled over onto 52nd Street, the nearest commercial strip, where a police car was set on fire and another one had its windows broken. Dumpsters were dragged into the street and set on fire as well.

With the police retreating, a festive mood set in. The crowd set off fireworks and set about looting. Along that stretch of 52nd Street, most of the storefronts belong to small, Black-owned businesses: bookstores, beauty salons, restaurants. This initially constrained the spread of the looting. When riot police eventually charged the crowd, most people took off, ran down side streets, jumped into cars, and disappeared.

Looting soon broke out all over the city, as groups drove around breaking into pharmacies, liquor stores, and chain stores.

A crowd regrouped in West Philadelphia, where things began to take on the form of a classic community riot. Police were driven back with bricks and bottles, until they retreated. On the stretch of blocks now vacated by the police, much of the neighborhood was out in the street or on their porches. Young people broke up bricks on the sidewalk, in anticipation of another battle. Others drank, debated, enthusiastically greeted their neighbors, shared looted goods, and cheered on the youth as they fought with or ran from the police. Everyone present shared in the revelry of the moment, even if they didn't partake in, or even openly criticized, the *potlatch of destruction*.

People calmly walked in and out of bodegas and pharmacies, taking what they needed: "Is there any kid's cereal left? If you don't have kids, you might not know this, but that shit is expensive." A whole range of people from the neighborhood walked the streets, trash bags weighed down with looted products slung over their shoulders. Drunk men took on the role of town criers, walking from block to block enthusiastically shouting the news from elsewhere in the neighborhood: where looting was taking place, where groups were headed now.

When riot police inevitably tried to retake the street, just like earlier in the evening, most of the crowd either took off running to their cars or went back inside their homes. Someone yelled out an intersection in the neighborhood. People dispersed, regrouped there, and began looting, until enough police arrived that it was time to disperse and regroup elsewhere. This pattern was carried on for much of the night.

October 27

The next morning, it was announced that the National Guard had been mobilized and would arrive within the next forty-eight hours. The riot, thus, had a limited window of time.

A flier circulated for another demonstration at Malcolm X Park that evening. In an almost comically exaggerated act of what the movement has come to call "swooping," the Party for Socialism and Liberation (PSL) put out a separate call for a march at the exact same location an hour earlier. This confusion led to the crowd splitting, with some following the PSL toward Center City and others marching toward the 18th Precinct.

Over the course of the evening, the group gathered at the precinct, a noticeably larger and more diverse crowd than the previous night, growing to approximately four hundred people.

Meanwhile, a caravan of cars descended on the Wal-Mart in Port Richmond, on the northern end of the city. Helicopter news footage showed a parking lot densely packed with idling cars, while dozens of people ran out of the store with full shopping carts or flat-screen TVs and home appliances. One man even managed to get away with a washing machine. Police speculated that up to two hundred people were in the store at once.

The caravan marauded along Aramingo Avenue for the next several hours, storming a Foot Locker, a furniture store, a kid's clothing store, and other box stores along the way. PPD estimated that up to one thousand people participated in the caravan. Wal-Mart announced later that week that due to the threat of continued social unrest they would be taking guns and ammunition off of their shop floors.

The crowd at the precinct marched to 52nd Street, where some people began building barricades in the street. A line of riot police was forced to retreat under a volley of bottles and bricks and was chased nearly back to the precinct. Most of the crowd did its best to avoid the street fighting. The march carried on along 52nd Street, but was soon cut off by a line of riot police, with much of the crowd either being kettled or dispersing. Several smaller marches crisscrossed the neighborhood for the rest of the evening. One such march, avoiding the heavily policed area around 52nd Street, left a trail of burning barricades and a looted liquor store in its wake.

Around midnight, with the streets largely evacuated of activists, youth from the neighborhood began to gather. They dragged dumpsters into the street, setting them on fire, and threw bricks at the line of riot police on 52nd Street, until the police eventually charged at them. They led the police on a chase for much of the night, stopping occasionally to break up bricks and wait for their enemy to get within striking range or to drag improvised barricades into the street and set them on fire. Several vehicles were set on fire as well, including an Xfinity van. "That's for cutting off my wifi, bitch!" The whole proceeding had a festive air to it.

A solidarity demonstration that night in downtown Brooklyn threw bricks at the police and broke the windows of a police car, a court building, and numerous businesses.

October 28

The next morning, the FBI arrested four people in Philadelphia, including a prominent community organizer. They are being charged with arson for their alleged involvement in riots earlier this summer. Similar FBI raids took place in Atlanta that week as well.

A 9:00 p.m. curfew was declared. No protest was called for that evening.

As soon as the sun set, looting started to spread all over the city.

A small crowd, composed of more journalists than protesters, gathered outside of the 18th Precinct that evening. After being warned by community affairs officers that the gathering was illegal, most of the crowd went home. For the rest of the night, youth from West Philadelphia sporadically clashed with the police and set off fireworks.

Along City Avenue in Merion Park, a caravan of looters ransacked strip malls and big-box stores. Groups of cars swarmed the area, storming businesses, and then stopping at gas stations to regroup and discuss their next move. At times the swarm of looters was so dense that there were traffic jams along the highway.

Dispersed looting continued for the next several days, as did the occasional daytime protest, but neither found a way to relate to the other or to pick up momentum on its own. Several days of bad weather didn't help. This was, perhaps, the first time since May that a curfew had been declared and large crowds did not come out to challenge it. The National Guard finally arrived on Friday, too late to prevent the rioting.

By the time the unrest had died down, there had been an estimated 225 arrests, 60 injured police officers, 617 incidents of looting, 18 damaged vehicles, and over 50 ATM explosions, according to the city.

Innovation

To stay dynamic and overcome the impasses they face, movements need to constantly innovate the tactics they use. In many cities, including Philadelphia, as the large-scale riots and *social looting* of late May ran their course, the unrest was kept going through a turn to *diffuse looting*. Rather than struggling with police over a particular territory, groups spanned out by car throughout the entire city and surrounding suburbs. For a time, this happened on such a large scale that there was little that could be done to contain it. Diffuse looting has reemerged sporadically in recent months, during the unrest in Louisville and Philadelphia, as a way to disrupt the city in the absence of large-scale protests.

Philadelphia's unique tactical innovation has been the introduction of ATM bombings: groups detonate small explosive devices on an ATM and, ostensibly, walk away with the cash. During the heady days of May and early June, the sound of explosions became a part of the background ambiance of the city where American democracy was born. This tactic reemerged during late October's unrest. There were likely a dozen ATM bombings on each of the three major nights of unrest. This tactic has yet to spread elsewhere, likely due to the amount of technical knowledge required.

The major innovation of this summer has its origins in Chicago. After police shot Latrell Allen on Chicago's South Side, a caravan of looters poured into the downtown Magnificent Mile, Chicago's most famous shopping district, breaking windows and emptying out luxury stores. For the next few hours, this caravan marauded throughout the city, evading the police and looting luxury boutiques, pharmacies, and liquor stores.

This tactic was repeated on a smaller scale in Louisville in September and on a perhaps larger scale in Philadelphia.

These tactics indicate a much higher degree of coordination, organization, and boldness of initiative than is within reach of any activist, leftist, or revolutionary group at the moment. The fact that innovations like the caravan tend to leap from city to city indicates that proletarians are paying attention to how the struggle is unfolding elsewhere. It also shows that the choice of tactics isn't arbitrary but is grounded in an intelligent read of the situation proletarians find themselves struggling within.

Up to this point, these innovative tactics have allowed comparatively small groups to overwhelm police departments and disrupt the flows of the city, but there are clear limits to how much these high-risk actions might generalize. They, in fact, seem premised on the boldest layers of the proletariat acting alone. This perhaps indicates that Black proletarians no longer expect the large multiracial crowds that joined them in the outbreaks of rioting and proletarian shopping earlier this summer.

Composition

These recent nights in Philadelphia pose a challenge to the hypothesis that this has been a multiracial uprising. Or, rather, they seem to indicate that the "rigid lines of separation" that appeared to break down in May are quickly reemerging.[1] Throughout the country, the crowds that flooded the streets in May and June closely corresponded to the demographics of the cities they were in. White people, in fact, were often overrepresented compared to their share of the total population of the given city. It was only during some of the most intense moments of looting that the participants were mostly Black, but never exclusively so. The riots and demonstrations were also rarely confined to particular Black or working-class neighborhoods but, rather, tended to envelop the entire city.

Instead, during the recent riots in Philadelphia, Black proletarians stood largely alone. When multiracial crowds did come together, they were generally unable to overcome the separations that had been so easily dissolved earlier in the summer. If these activists had hoped to express their support for the rioting, they had the perhaps inverse effect of stifling it, as people from the neighborhood hesitated, waiting to see how these newcomers might act. For moments on Monday and Tuesday night, a multiracial crowd worked together to build barricades and attack the police, but more often than not, even when different elements of the crowd took part in the rioting, they did so separately. Each night, by midnight, almost no one was left on the streets who wasn't Black.

A certain amount of hesitation around whether or how to act in the streets likely results from anxiety around these "rigid lines of separation." Debates abounded in the streets, on Telegram channels, and within activists' circles about the proper way to relate to the Black struggle. It is worth remembering that this anxiety is often one-sided. People from outside of the neighborhood who showed up for the riots were at times treated with suspicion, until they made it clear that they were there for the same reasons as everyone else. Then they were widely embraced. Those taking initiative in the streets were glad that others had joined them, especially if they had something to contribute.

It is not simply that separations reasserted themselves within and between the crowds. The riot did not spread from neighborhood to neighborhood, and only a minority of any given neighborhood ever participated in a significant way. No wider layers of the class ever came into the streets, and the activist crowd that mobilized never exceeded a few hundred people. Solidarity demonstrations, with the exception of the one in Brooklyn, were small and attended only by committed activists.

What Are We to Do?
Those of us who want to see the leap from riot to insurrection, to see this long, hot season stretch into an endless summer, will need to find ways to contribute to this unfolding. Rather than being paralyzed by anxiety, revolutionaries should consider what practical knowledge and capacities they have to offer.

This is often quite simple. One way that revolutionaries can make themselves useful is by holding on to the memory of lessons learned in previous struggles and experiments. This can be as basic as reminding people to wear masks or showing them how to use Telegram to outsmart the police. There are certain gestures, such as circulating a call for a demonstration, that often only anarchists will do, that can be necessary to keep things moving forward.

The effects of these small steps are fairly clear in hindsight. Despite their awkwardness, the two evening demonstrations spilled over into riots, while the other nights only saw more diffuse actions. This is because they provided a space for those who wanted to take initiative to find each other. Likewise, for those who may not want to take initiative but support the riots, the demonstrations allow them to express that publicly in a way that provides cover for others. The evening demonstrations also provided cover for the looting happening elsewhere by occupying much of the city's police force along 52nd Street.

With the declaration of a curfew and the threat of the National Guard, providing some basic street presence to act within by calling for another evening demonstration could have created the conditions for the unrest to keep going for a few days longer. In this sense, a small intervention by pro-revolutionaries could have been significant.

Otherwise, pro-revolutionaries try to read the dynamics of a given struggle and how to contribute to its unfolding. This can look like trying to take initiative in a way that may resonate and be taken up by other members of the crowd. Even if we may stand out from the crowd, when the gestures we take prove themselves to be sensible, people tend to recognize them. Other times, simply having the foresight to bring tools, whether crowbars, fireworks, umbrellas, or a sound system, can go a long way toward contributing to the dynamic of an event.

This point may seem banal, but it's worth remembering. After the first days of the uprising in New York City, much bigger crowds began to come into the streets. In these moments, the "rigid lines of separation" between elements of the crowd could be felt reemerging. Many of the new participants were inspired by images of the uprising but, in person, were as afraid of the actuality of the riot as they were of the police. They desperately looked for people to appoint into leadership roles, who then tried their best to micromanage the demonstrations. Young Black proletarians in the crowd began to sense their isolation and, by the end of the first week, stopped coming out. If others in the crowd had also tried to take initiative, it's possible they could have contributed to a circumstance where the Black avant-garde didn't feel so constrained, perhaps extending the uprising even longer.[2]

In this sense, solidarity literally means attack. The more pro-revolutionaries have felt the confidence to act, the more they have been able to meaningfully contribute to the unfolding of this struggle set in motion by Black proletarians.

The leaps forward in proletarian self-organization and tactics this year present pro-revolutionaries with a particular dilemma. If our role has been to contribute to the intensification and generalization of struggles, to push toward their insurrectionary horizon, what is our role when proletarian self-activity takes on a form much more daring and riskier than many of us are ready for? When these tactics already entail such a degree of coordination and intensity, even if pro-revolutionaries are to participate, it is not clear what we have to contribute.

The election is now in the rearview mirror. While the dust has not yet settled, it may turn out to be the case that the left's fascination with the possibility of a coup or civil war only obscured from us the more difficult questions raised by this moment. The Black avant-garde may continue to blaze ahead on its own, struggling with an intensity that many cannot participate in. In the coming weeks or months, we may continue to see riots with the same intensity as Philadelphia but also with the same isolation. If we cannot find a way to meaningfully contribute to this dynamic, pro-revolutionaries might face a difficult choice of whether or not to join them on this path, taking increasing risks without a clear horizon. This riddle may solve itself as struggles once again generalize and new tactics proliferate, but that is not something we can take for granted.

November 2020

PART III
STRATEGIES AND TENSIONS

The Rise of Black Counterinsurgency

Shemon

From May 26 to June 1, 2020, a Black-led multiracial rebellion attacked police stations, destroyed cop cars, assaulted police, redistributed goods, and took revenge for the murder of countless Black and non-Black people by the police. By the first week of June, everything seemed to have changed, everyone seemed to have forgotten that any of this had happened, and, instead, we became good protesters, we became nonviolent, and we became reformists. Instead of attacking police, we endured countless marches with no point other than to continue marching. From revolutionary abolitionists, we became reformist abolitionists. What happened?

There are many easy answers, all of them incorrect. One potential answer would point to the police repression of the movement, which resulted in over fourteen thousand people being arrested. Another would point to the white people who joined the movement, and who brought with them all their liberal politics and strategies. Finally, the most ridiculous answer of all maintains that the militant phase of the rebellion was never a real movement of Black and non-Black proletarians to begin with but was, in fact, a product of outside agitators.

In reality, something much more dangerous and sinister took place, something organic to racial capitalism, with roots extending back to the African slave trade and the Haitian Revolution. A counterinsurgency campaign has fundamentally altered the course of the movement. While the retreat and defeat of the movement that it induced may turn out to be temporary, such campaigns present significant obstacles to further radicalization and, therefore, must be addressed. This counterinsurgency campaign on the ground was spearheaded by the Black middle class, Black politicians, Black radical academics, and Black NGOs. This may come as a shock to people whose impulse is to think of Black people as a monolithic political group. This conception is false.

This was not a local phenomenon in one or two cities but a dynamic that has taken place across the United States. A widespread rebellion demanded a widespread counterinsurgency. While there is no doubt that behind the Black-led counterinsurgency lie billion-dollar philanthropies, universities, the state, and the white middle class, the uncomfortable truth is that a Black-led rebellion could only be crushed by a Black-led counterinsurgency program. None of this could have taken place if there was not a significant layer of Black counterinsurgents across the United States.

The rise of the Black middle class is an organic development of class stratification under racial capitalism. It is the starting point for understanding the counterinsurgency that is presently strangling the George Floyd Rebellion. The latter has its social basis in the Black middle class, who seek at most a narrow reform of the system, namely, the transformation of racial capitalism into simple capitalism.

In the long run, the Black middle class is the enemy of the Black proletariat: the unemployed, wage workers, sex workers, etc. The true partners or accomplices of the Black proletariat are the Latinx and white proletarians, the Indigenous peoples of Turtle Island, and the international proletariat. So far, few in this country seem to have figured this out, let alone the political and strategic implications that follow from it. Although none of these problems are new, it is worth returning to them once again.

The Black Middle Class

There has always been a tension in the struggle for Black liberation over the question of the Black middle class: doctors, lawyers, professors, managers, and business owners. Not over its existence but over its political role and behavior in the struggle against white supremacy.

In many ways, the Black middle class is no different from other middle classes. At their core, all middle-class politics are electoral, legislative, and reformist. Their strategies are about respectability, the protection of private property, and, ultimately, following the law. Middle classes have always felt entitled to speak for and represent their respective proletariats. They advocate for multiracial unity among their class peers, at the same time as they use racial loyalty to advance their own positions under racial capitalism. All middle-class analysis sees the proletariat as a threat or a victim; none see the proletariat as a revolutionary class. Those few middle-class people who see the proletariat as revolutionary either work to repress the latter or else wind up joining them in struggle.

In 1931, W.E.B. Du Bois argued that so long as Jim Crow limited the Black middle class's opportunities, the Black proletariat and the Black middle class needed to fight together against white supremacy. By the 1960s, however, the Black Panther Party and the League of Revolutionary Black Workers were already convinced that the Black middle class and Black proletariat had parted company. With the defeat of Jim Crow in the 1960s, middle-class Black people found a path to success, resulting in vast differences between themselves and their dispossessed neighbors.

The movement to defeat Jim Crow did not destroy racial capitalism or anti-Blackness; rather, while it opened up new avenues for a small handful of Black people, their victory at the same time become a devastating defeat for the masses of Black proletarians, who remain stuck in their miserable conditions, with the sole difference that their workplaces and neighborhoods are now managed and policed by the "victorious" Black middle class. In this respect, the Black middle class is not entirely lying when it casts itself as the culmination of the Civil Rights Movement and Black Power. These contradictions existed prior to the movements of the 1960s, and they have never been clarified on a mass level since. The Black middle class has been, and remains to this day, the contradiction of the Black Liberation Movement.

The essential difference between the Black middle class and the white middle class is *strategic*: the Black middle class uses Black proletarian struggles to advance its own cause. Since it is not strong enough to advance its cause on its own, it leverages the fear of riots and street protests to push its own agenda. The Black middle class cannot completely dissociate itself from the militant phase of the rebellion, because it needs to wield riots and violence as a potential threat for the rest of society. At the same time, the Black middle class cannot identify itself with the riot, because to do so would contradict its own desire to be integrated into the capitalist state, whose laws and order secure the existence of private property.

The result is a confused and contradictory relationship marked by a triple dynamic: (i) the Black middle class strives to achieve the wealth and power of the white middle class, (ii) yet this requires it be willing to discipline the Black proletariat, (iii) with whom it nonetheless shares a sense of linked fate driven by the inability of the police and other white people to distinguish poor Black people from the hood from their suburban counterparts. This threefold dynamic finds expression in the general thrust of mainstream Black Lives Matter protests, whose middle-class activists advocate simultaneously (i) for police to stop confusing the Black middle class with Black people from the hood, (ii) for the state to spend more money on social reproduction in the hopes of catapulting more Black people into the Black middle class, and (iii) to create more positions for the Black middle class in universities, corporate boardrooms, etc.

All of Black middle-class society is poised to gain from the efforts of Black proletarians. In the coming months, the victories won from the rebellion will come in the form of the new and worthless diversity positions, pointless academic conferences and articles, and pitiful salary bumps. For now, the current protests must maintain their parasitic relationship with the initial George Floyd Rebellion. Following the militant phase of the rebellion, protests have gone into a zombie-like phase of endless marches, often through already empty streets and on empty highways. It is as if police stations were never besieged, smashed, and burned down. Protest after protest happens, without a meaningful reflection upon what took place that first week. Whereas 2014 introduced highway blockades to the tactical repertoire of anti-police struggle, we might have thought "burned precincts" would be remembered as Minneapolis's contribution. Instead, the advances made in Minneapolis are being buried under the street marches across the country, as Black leadership reinforces reactionary divisions between peaceful and good protesters, on the one hand, and violent and militant rioters, on the other.

Revolutionary versus Reformist Abolition

There are two kinds of abolition: revolutionary abolition and reformist abolition. Revolutionary abolition is the self-activity of the proletariat fighting against the entire carceral logic of the state and racial capitalism. This includes burning down police stations, destroying cop cars, attacking police officers, and redistributing goods from Target and Versace. Revolutionary abolitionism stands in alliance with revolutionary anti-capitalism, since it grasps that abolition is only possible when tied to anti-capitalism, anti-statism, anti-imperialism, anti-homophobia, and anti-patriarchy. Prisons have to be abolished, but so do schools, social workers, and the army of middle-class institutions and do-gooders. Therefore, the expansive dynamism that it names cannot stop with the police but must extend its attack to the wall separating the so-called United States and Mexico, to detention centers, to courts, and to the vast infrastructure of the carceral state and capitalism.

Revolutionary abolitionism quickly reached a boiling point during the first week of the rebellion, with a resurgence again this past week, on July 25. In the interim, revolutionary abolition was largely displaced by a reformist abolition, a current largely defined by the activity and politics of professional activists, NGOs, lawyers, and politicians and concerned primarily with "defunding," policy, and legislative shifts. This perspective continues to see politicians as the principal historical actors, in relation to whom it positions itself as a pressure group. In this way, reformist abolitionism removes proletarians from the terrain of struggle.

While it is correct to observe the gross injustice of police budgets by contrast with expenditures on health, infrastructure, schools, and other services, proposals to "defund" amount to little more than a monetary displacement from one section of the state to another. Moreover, even when reformist abolitionism begins to imagine abolishing the police, as is the case right now in Minneapolis, it cannot seem to grasp that the police cannot be abolished by legislation. What the reformist abolitionism fails to see is that it has always and only ever been actual or feared revolutionary wars that have abolished slavery. The shortest path to dismantling police and prisons is and has always been through revolt, as we saw last year when the uprising in Haiti led to entire prisons being emptied. Insurrection forms the centerpiece of revolutionary abolition.

In light of revolutionary abolition surfacing in the country, with attacks on DHS offices in Atlanta and the burning of courthouses, reformist abolition is a direct attack on these more militant means of abolition. Nowhere has this tension and relationship between reformist abolition and revolutionary abolition been more fraught than in Minneapolis. Reformists had been preparing for years in Minneapolis, and the rebellion provided them with the leverage to make their move. What began as an all-out assault on the forces of law and order in Minneapolis has since been transformed into a plethora of anodyne political projects. As the Black proletariat recedes, the Black professional activist comes to the forefront, until all is good and holy again.

NGOs and Academics

Black NGOs, including the groups in the Movement for Black Lives, have played a key role in this counterinsurgency campaign. Their social base is not the Black proletariat but the Black middle class and—most importantly—the white bourgeoisie, through the mediation of philanthropies. In order to co-opt the movement, the bourgeoisie is throwing money at problems generated by racial capitalism. In the NGOs, they have found a willing group of people who will happily accept their dollars. Money is falling from the sky: if you are Black, middle-class, and can say Black Lives Matter three times, money will magically appear in your lap. While these NGOs vary politically, they tend to have little or no background in struggle, no particular concern for movements, and, ultimately, no interest in overthrowing racial capitalism. They are merely a reflection of the various parasites sucking the blood from the historic struggle of Black proletarians. They solve nothing in the long run, and it is unlikely any of them will actually lead the movement, since they have no base. However, because the movement generated by the George Floyd Rebellion is new, many of its participants are still easily confused, and, thus, continue to display a servile willingness to follow any Black person who shows up with a megaphone. While it is inevitable that some NGO activists will once again split away from their groups and join the more radical elements in the movement, any strategic orientation that centers their potential energy is mistaken. Waiting around for the radicalization of the NGOs is like waiting around for unions to radicalize. Somehow, NGOs must eventually be kicked out of the movement.

What of the so-called "revolutionary Black intellectuals"? Since the word *revolutionary* is meaningless in nonrevolutionary times, and the restricted practice of being an "intellectual" is rendered inoperative during revolutionary times, we are dealing with a contradiction in terms. Whereas in nonrevolutionary times the activities of academic intellectuals reflect the standard capitalist division of labor between thinkers and manual workers, in insurrectional moments the division of labor tends to collapse and be rearranged, such that many proletarians suddenly find themselves engaged in forms of reading, writing, and theorizing that had previously been the exclusive task of intellectuals.

Let it be said clearly: the George Floyd Rebellion is the new criterion to which all theories and politics must be held to account. Not to tenure demands, not to academic journals, not to a community of so-called scholars but to the fire and heat of the proletarian struggle. They must answer to the demands of riots, strikes, occupations, blockades, insurrections, war, and revolution. In this regard, it must be admitted that the results so far have been a disaster. Black Marxism, Afro-pessimism, Black anarchism, and Black feminism have all been put to the test in this uprising, and all have failed. These theories have had little to no meaningful impact on the Black proletariat. In certain cases, their proponents have even enhanced their careers by lending their voice to counterinsurgent NGOs, which are only too happy to pay an honorarium.

What happened to Black revolutionary theory? For over fifty years, theories have been hiding in the academy. The university has completely commodified Black radical thought, which has divorced it from Black proletarians by determining who has access to it and who is able to make sense of its dense and obtuse language. The issues and questions that matter to the Black proletarian are never addressed on the terms, concepts, and traditions of the Black proletariat but, instead, are discussed in the much narrower and reformist terms of the academy. No idea in the academy is accountable to the Black proletariat, against whom a tenured job offers the radical academic the ultimate insulation. This lack of accountability protects outdated and useless ideas, allowing dusty old theories that were long ago defeated in the actual class struggle to continue to live on in the academy, becoming a dead weight on the movement's brain.

This stops now. The full force of a rebellion has cleared the debris in a manner that critique could never accomplish. Although the political consolidation of the rebellion has fallen to the Black counterinsurgents for now, the George Floyd Rebellion has allowed the next generation of Black revolutionaries from the proletariat, as well as some renegade middle-class people, to emerge and catch sight of themselves. In the upcoming months and years, we must do what we can to help them unburden themselves of the false divisions of intellectual activity and revolutionary activity that have long plagued our movements.

Conclusion

If capitalism is ever to be abolished, if a liberatory communist future will ever see the light of day, the proletariat must emancipate itself by force from its dependency on the bourgeois social order. But before the antagonism can reach this point, another battle must also take place, in which the Black proletariat politically and materially settles its accounts with the Black middle class. This is not a new reality but one with which every revolution involving Black people has had to wrestle. So far, the Black proletariat has lost every one of these struggles, resulting in a capitalism and state with a Black face.

If the Black middle class has been able to wage the counterinsurgency so effectively, this is in part due to the fact that it has captured key parts of the state. Lori Lightfoot in Chicago, Keisha Lance Bottoms in Atlanta, Chokwe Antar Lumumba in Jackson, and Bernard Young in Baltimore offer just a few examples of an aspirational managerial tier that is conscious of its class interests in a manner that the Black proletariat has yet to figure out. They attend the best schools in the country, allowing them to mobilize the kind of cynical arguments that are needed to articulate a reformist and counterinsurgent program.

The middle classes have their universities, elections, corporations, and other institutions to develop their version of the rainbow coalition. The proletariat is left outside of the process.

The Black proletariat can lead and spark the struggle but will win no decisive battles without accomplices in the white and Latinx proletariat and in Indigenous nations. As it cleaned out as many stores as it could, the Black proletariat fought together with other proletarians. For one week, an organic alliance was built, as different oppressed groups rained fire on police and redistributed goods across Turtle Island.

However, these organic alliances do not automatically lead to more permanent alliances. The gigantic eruptions of solidarity in riots and uprisings tend to quickly retreat back into antagonistic relations among proletarians soon after. After all, sharing a moment of combat is not the same as forging long-term trust and solidarity. What is more real, one week of shared unity or a lifetime of proletarian conflict with one another?

The Black proletariat competes with other proletarians for jobs, housing, and scarce resources. The respective middle classes promise to secure these goodies, as long as Black proletarians continue to vote for Black politicians, Latinx proletarians vote for Latinx politicians, and so on. Although this logic is a dead end for proletarian multiracial solidarity, it serves short-term aims that are often difficult to ignore for dispossessed folks. In this way, the fragile unity forged in moments of revolt are dissolved back into the separated social relationships of everyday life. Proletarians occasionally build solidarity with each other on a daily level, but on the whole they lack the mechanisms or institutions in racial capitalism to develop this unity. This is why attacks on the infrastructure of capitalism are so key and why new spaces of social reproduction are vital.

Nonetheless, our wager must be that the uprising has changed the proletariat. We have to believe in the possibility that everyday relations are also beginning to change. This is a guess and must be tested in battle.

Ultimately, some kind of larger process of crisis—war, economic upheaval, pandemics, ecological collapse—will be required to force a strategic unity between the different racialized groups of proletarians. Without fetishizing organizations, some organizational forms will be needed to crystalize and concentrate this alliance. The proletariat will have to develop its own class-race-gender interests against the Black and white middle class simultaneously through action, organization, and program.

Since the 2007–2008 economic crisis the entire world has entered a period of mass struggle. It has been uneven, with Greece one moment, the Arab Spring the next, Marikana or Haiti another, with respective counterrevolutions or counterinsurgency as part of the process. The George Floyd Rebellion is part of this ongoing process to deal with the massive inequality, police violence, and other forms of oppression. I have emphasized defeat-retreat in the current moment, because that is what we immediately face. But in the near future the movement will attack once again, because there will be no other choice. Defeat is temporary; struggle is permanent.

July 2020

References

While I did not cite any references, the following works informed my argument and analysis:

Allen, Robert L. *Black Awakening in Capitalist America*. New York: Doubleday, 1969.

Carter Jackson, Kellie. *Force and Freedom*. Philadelphia: University of Pennsylvania Press, 2019.

Du Bois, W.E.B. *Black Reconstruction*. New York: Free Press, 1998 [1935].

Du Bois, W.E.B. "The Negro and Communism." c. 1931.

Ferguson, Karen. *Top Down: The Ford Foundation, Black Power, and the Reinvention of Racial Liberalism*. Philadelphia: University of Pennsylvania Press, 2013.

INCITE. *The Revolution Will Not Be Funded: Beyond the Non-Profit Industrial Complex*. Durham, NC: Duke University Press, 2017 [2007].

James, C.L.R. *The Black Jacobins: Toussaint L'Ouverture and the San Domingo Revolution*. London: Penguin Books, 2001 [1938].

Robinson, Cedric. *Black Marxism: The Making of the Black Radical Tradition*. New York: Penguin Books, 2021 [1983].

Rodney, Walter. *How Europe Underdeveloped Africa*. London: Verso, 2018 [1972].

Williams, David. *Bitterly Divided*. New York: New Press, 2008.

The Return of John Brown: White Race Traitors in the 2020 Uprising

Shemon and Arturo

> "What is the prognosis? ... The prognosis is in the hands of those
> who are willing to get rid of the worm-eaten roots of the structure."
> —Frantz Fanon

The summer of 2020 was a summer of mass revolt. The revolt that started on May 26 in Minneapolis rapidly swept across the country, as crowds of people attacked police, set fire to cop cars, looted and redistributed goods, and engaged in all kinds of property destruction. This first week was Act I.

This initial uprising was repressed by the National Guard, police, and vigilantes, as well as by NGOs, nonviolent activists, and politicians. Whether by iron first or velvet glove, order was reimposed across the country. But this process of decomposition was uneven—the counterinsurgency was not able to fully stamp out the revolutionary upsurge, and in some places, we began to see a simultaneous process of recomposition. In Seattle, the Capital Hill Autonomous Zone attempted to prefigure a world where police did not exist. Another rebellion erupted on the streets of Atlanta following the police murder of Rayshard Brooks on June 12. In Portland, militants battled with federal agents throughout June and July. This was Act II.

Then there was Act III. On July 25, revolutionary abolition surfaced once again, taking the offensive in solidarity with the struggle in Portland. The construction site for a youth jail in Seattle was set on fire, as was a courthouse in Oakland. Courthouses were smashed in Los Angeles and Aurora, Colorado. In Atlanta, people smashed the windows of an ICE/DHS office. In the days that followed, solidarity marches across the country quickly turned into small street riots. Back in Portland, militants continued to clash with federal agents, laying siege to a federal courthouse. Then, on August 10, caravans of looters from all over Chicago ransacked high-end stores in the downtown section of the city.

Act IV began toward the end of August, when a new rebellion kicked off following the police shooting of Jacob Blake in Kenosha, Wisconsin. During the riots a Department of Corrections building was burned down, and then an armed militia member murdered two protesters on August 25. Less than a week later, in Portland, an antifascist—Michael Reinoehl—shot and killed a member of a far-right group Patriot Prayer during street battles between Trump supporters and Black Lives Matter protesters. A few days after this, on September 3, a team of US marshals located Michael Reinoehl (who was in hiding) and murdered him. Then, a few days after this, several days of rioting took place in Rochester, New York, after the police murdered yet another Black man, Daniel Prude.

The last act for now, Act V, began in mid-September, when a riot erupted in the small town of Lancaster, Pennsylvania, following the police murder of Ricardo Muñoz. A few weeks after this, at the end of September, a short wave of riots emerged following the grand jury decision that failed to convict the cops that murdered Breonna Taylor in Louisville, Kentucky. In response, a small rebellion popped off there, during which two police officers were shot in downtown Louisville, while solidarity protests throughout the country also turned into violent clashes with police, notably in Seattle.

This sequence of revolts has been unlike anything we've experienced before. Over the course of the summer and fall, crowds of people came together to attack the police and storm the commercial corridors of dozens of cities, causing more property damage than has ever been recorded in US history. In "Theses on the George Floyd Rebellion" (this volume, pages 25–29) and elsewhere, we argue that the self-activity of the Black proletariat is the driving force of this revolutionary trajectory. In this essay, we explore the role of the white proletariat.

Hearing the battle cry of Black Lives Matter, a considerable minority of white people participated in the uprising. This is what we saw with our own eyes, over and over again throughout the summer and fall. White people even died and killed other white people in the uprising. All of this reveals a deep split within white society, something that has only happened a few other times in US history—in the 1960s and, most notably, during the Civil War and the Reconstruction era.

Anyone with a basic understanding of the history of the US recognizes the significance of this event and all the potentials, contradictions, and dangers that it raises. There is nothing more dangerous to the US bourgeoisie than a multiracial insurgency. At the same time, there is nothing more dangerous to the class struggle in the US than the treachery of the white proletariat, which, over the course of its history, has forged an alliance with capital and the state and betrayed the proletariat of color. While the material basis of the cross-class alliance among whites is deteriorating and fissures are emerging, it continues to be the glue that holds US society together.

The road ahead is filled with possibilities but also with mortal dangers. Friends can quickly become enemies, and long-standing enemies can become dedicated comrades. Although history can serve as a guide, if a successful revolution is to take place, we will have to charge into the unknown. To become stuck in the patterns of history is to create another prison for ourselves. The George Floyd uprising and the rebellions that have followed give us the tools to finally break down not only the prison of racial capitalism but the prison of history.

Reactions

Our focus on the white proletariat will anger and shock many on the left. We will be accused of paying too much attention to whites. There will be reactions from many different angles, but the reactions that really concern us come from within the "BIPOC" (Black, Indigenous, people of color) left.

The first kind of reaction comes from BIPOC who cannot, on principle, stand any discussion of white people as agents of revolt. Because of their experiences in a white-dominated world, they see whites as eternally lost to racism, settler colonialism, and empire. This is understandable, and there is no point in trying to convince people otherwise. It is only through the concrete experience of fighting alongside whites that BIPOC will come to see the strategic error of lumping all of them together in a counterrevolutionary bloc.

The second reaction comes from BIPOC who are worried that the spirit of the uprising will be diluted and betrayed, especially in majority white cities like Kenosha, Seattle, Portland, and Minneapolis. These people might have white comrades and might have a perspective that includes them in a revolutionary process, but they are nonetheless skeptical of focusing on the white proletariat, because they don't want to lose sight of the proletariat of color. This is also understandable. We can only ask that comrades with these concerns read this text in its entirety and judge it for what it says. A serious discussion of the white proletariat does not have to take anything away from the proletariat of color.

While recognizing these concerns, we nonetheless believe that a revolutionary strategy must take white people into account. The most obvious reason for this is that they constitute a gigantic part of the US population. According to the US Census, this country is 60.1 percent white European. Let that sink in. The next largest group is Latino at 18.5 percent, followed by Black or African American at 13.4 percent. Next is Asians at 5.9 percent, and Indigenous people at 1.3 percent. In other words, there are still more white people in the US than all non-white people combined. It is unclear how a revolution could succeed unless it develops a strategy that splits the whites.

A Blurred Understanding

The conceptual tools that encourage us to view white workers as fundamentally reactionary—white privilege, settler-colonialism, anti-Blackness, the labor aristocracy—are powerful, because they are rooted in historical reality. But what happens when whites act in a revolutionary manner? Are we able to recognize when these analytic tools no longer function and, instead, block our ability to see what is happening? While we should not discard these concepts, we believe that the Black radical tradition provides other means for making sense of this situation.

The Black radical tradition positions itself in relation to whites in a strategic manner. In The Black Jacobins,[1] for example, C.L.R. James showed how, during the Haitian Revolution, Black insurgents played different colonial powers against one another, while also forging an alliance with anti-slavery whites in the French Revolution. Similarly, in Black Reconstruction,[2] W.E.B. Du Bois showed how, during the American Civil War, former slaves joined the Union army and took advantage of its occupation of the South, as well as the fact that white soldiers were deserting the Confederate army. In A Dying Colonialism,[3] in a chapter entitled "Algeria's European Minority," Frantz Fanon showed how, during the Algerian Revolution, the National Liberation Front welcomed white Algerians into its ranks in the fight against French colonialism. The list goes on and on.

Today, it's once again necessary to develop a strategy concerning whites, to exploit similar opportunities. However, given the current theoretical environment in the US, it's not at all clear how this would happen. Most of the American left sees white workers as privileged, anti-Black, colonizers, and bloodsuckers of the global proletariat. When this analysis goes so far as to become quasi-ontological, it is unclear how whites could ever fit into a revolutionary strategy.

The Ethical Commitment of the Black Radical Tradition

While a central virtue of the Black radical tradition is the love and liberation of Black people, we believe that this tradition also encourages love and liberation of all people. Chapter 7 of Cedric Robinson's *Black Marxism* offers some striking examples of this basic respect for human dignity.[4] Here Robinson notes that "Blacks have seldom employed the level of violence that they [Westerners] have understood the situation required." He then goes on to ask some very powerful questions: "Why did Nat Turner, admittedly a violent man, spare poor whites? Why did Toussaint escort his absent 'master's' family to safety before joining the slave revolution? Why was 'no white person killed in a slave rebellion in colonial Virginia'?" Robinson reminds the reader that these are not mere anecdotes but a pattern repeated throughout the centuries: "The people with Chilembwe in 1915 forcibly marched European women and children to the safety of colonist settlements." We've seen a similar dynamic in more recent times during violent clashes between fascists and antifascists, where, after physically overpowering them in the streets, Black antifascist militants have saved white fascists from being beaten to death. This happened recently in London during clashes between BLM protesters and fascists. It has happened before in the US. Our point here isn't to argue for nonviolence but, rather, to highlight the sort of deep ethical commitment within the Black radical tradition, which, in opposition to the pathology of race, orients itself toward the transformation of humanity.

In her essay "1492: A New World View,"[5] as well as in other essays, Sylvia Wynter examines how modern divisions of race, gender, and nation—divisions formed through the colonization of the Americas, the rise of the Atlantic slave trade, and the globalization of capitalism—are normalized and reified as fixed subjectivities. As she sees it, however, the goal is neither to celebrate these subjectivities nor to deny them but, rather, to break down the field of power that reproduces them. For her, "the general upheaval of the 1960s made possible a new opening" that challenged the historical and social basis of these "symbolic representational systems." We would imagine that, for Wynter, the present revolts also constitute such an opening.

From Slavery to the George Floyd Uprising

The division of race has been particularly powerful in the US. While there is a history of multiracial class struggle, it is a highly fraught and contradictory one. Before the establishment of the US nation-state and the widespread development of the racial order that haunts us today, European servants, alongside African and Indigenous slaves, fled colonial farms and joined maroon communities. In "The Dragon and the Hydra," political prisoner Russell "Maroon" Shoats describes how "indentured European workers, who had escaped that status … allied themselves with both Amerindians and Africans who had also escaped from slavery and servitude, all of whom combined into maroon communities in areas that are now part of the United States."[6] From these early class solidarities, racial divisions developed following Bacon's Rebellion in 1676. This was a class war in which white indentured servants and Black slaves joined together to fight against the colonial elite in Virginia, but this struggle was also premised on settler colonialism against Indigenous people. In response to this rebellion, the colonial elite implemented laws that deepened racial divisions. Interracial marriage was criminalized, and subsequent laws abolished Black people's right to vote, hold office, and bear arms. Harsh new slave codes cut off previous legal avenues to freedom for Black slaves. The Atlantic slave trade continued to grow, and as the price of a slave diminished, more Africans were enslaved than ever before. By the time of the American Revolution, Black chattel slavery had become a widespread institution, while the previously predominant system of white indentured servitude, by contrast, was on the decline. The victory of the Americans in the war against England further cemented the slave system in the newly formed United States.

It was not until the rise of militant abolitionism and the Civil War that whites would once again join Black people in a common struggle. Thousands of whites would give their lives in a conflict that ultimately resulted in the overthrow of Black chattel slavery. Of course, as before, this was a contradictory process. Letters from white soldiers show that most of them were racist. Nonetheless, through their determination and resistance, Black Americans transformed the war for the Union into a war

to abolish slavery, and in the process pulled some of the white proletariat closer to the Black struggle. While the white working class as a whole was not interested in abolishing slavery, white workers nonetheless played an important role in slavery's downfall throughout the course of the war. Following the war, this contradiction arose again in the Populist Movement, a left-wing agrarian movement that included a layer of Black farmers. Here too, most of the whites involved were racist. Nonetheless, Black farmers and sharecroppers carved out a space for themselves within this movement, most notably in the form of the Colored Farmers National Alliance and Cooperative Union.

This tension within the white worker, between whiteness and humanity, would continue into the twentieth century. In the 1900s, the Industrial Workers of the World (IWW) attempted to forge a relationship with Black people in the South but was eventually crushed there. In Philadelphia in the 1910s, the IWW managed to organize a powerful labor union among Black and Irish dockworkers, the Local 8, which was led by Ben Fletcher. Later on, in the 1930s, the Communist Party made inroads with Black proletarians but quickly lost their respect on account of its popular front politics, which shut down anti-racist struggles in an effort to support the Allies during World War II. With the explosion of mass struggles in the 1930s, Black and white workers temporarily came together in the Congress of Industrial Organizations (CIO). With the exception of the IWW in the 1900s and 1910s, various kinds of racism coursed through all of these struggles. In many ways, class struggle among white workers assumed a form of anti-Blackness, which led some Black workers to refer to the United Auto Workers union (UAW) as "You Ain't White."

When the Civil Rights Movement and Black Power exploded onto the scene in the 1960s, white workers were largely absent from the urban rebellions that took place. There were certainly white people involved in the Civil Rights Movement, highlighted in the early days of CORE and SNCC. Still, by most accounts, whites did not fight alongside Black people in the rebellions in cities like Birmingham, Harlem, Philadelphia, Detroit, etc. If they did, this was highly marginal or was largely confined to college campuses. Although Fred Hampton's Rainbow Coalition formed alliances with some white proletarians in Chicago, overall, this effort did not generalize. The Black proletariat, unable to find an accomplice in the white proletariat, was forced to look outward in the 1960s to national liberation struggles in the Third World.

What can this history tell us about the present moment? One of the dynamics that it reveals is that the destinies of Black and white workers are tied together in the US. Of course, the popular assumption is that BIPOC communities have the deepest history of solidarity in the US. While it is true that non-Black people of color were not involved in the enslavement and mass murder of Black people to the same extent as white people, this alone does not ensure that solidarity is a de facto reality between people of color. The uncomfortable truth is that there is no automatic unity between any of the racial formations in the US. However, there is an even more uncomfortable truth: even with all their racism, white people have fought and died alongside Black people more than any other group of people in this country. Given the numerical majority of white people here, this really shouldn't be surprising. This is also why Black Americans have repeatedly made alliances with white people, as in the cases of the maroon communities and the US Civil War or via the original IWW or CIO. No doubt, these alliances did not automatically defeat racism and anti-Blackness among whites, who have repeatedly betrayed and excluded their fellow workers to defend racial capitalism and crush any threat to it. This counterrevolutionary tendency is precisely why we need to develop a revolutionary strategy to split the white proletariat.

Every time that the class structure is thrown into a revolutionary crisis, whiteness reorganizes itself. After the Civil War and the defeat of Reconstruction, Jim Crow re-cemented whiteness, and after the defeat of the Civil Rights and Black Power Movements, a certain kind of neoliberalism based on austerity and mass incarceration took hold and reconsolidated whiteness. The reconsolidation of whiteness is playing itself out now in its own way, with the return of nonviolent protests, the commercialization of the BLM movement, and the Biden presidential campaign. History shows us that one of the best ways to prevent this reconsolidation is by keeping the whites divided and deepening the split among them.

The Return of the White Proletariat

Following the lead of the Black proletariat in the George Floyd uprising, the white proletariat reentered the stage of history. Whereas the white proletariat largely did not participate in the Black rebellions of the 1960s, today there is a new generation of white millennials and Gen Z proles fighting and dying alongside militants of color. What do we make of this? How do we relate to white proletarians in these struggles? Can the forms of oppression they face be given a voice? Or does this inevitably lead to white supremacy?

Taking a cue from C.L.R. James, Noel Ignatiev warned against the dangers of trying to win over white workers at the expense of setting aside the demands of Black liberation. The critique of whiteness that Noel outlines in his 1972 essay, "Black Worker, White Worker,"[7] seems to be playing itself out today in the broader BLM movement. Without endorsing every aspect of BLM's program, anyone can see that it is more radical than that of Bernie Sanders or the Democratic Socialists of America (DSA). In terms of mass politics, BLM is the most radical anyone has gone in this country in generations. It would be a catastrophic mistake to water down BLM to win over more whites. At the same time, we can also acknowledge that much of BLM's politics, like most people's politics, remain trapped in the past.

The proletariat that Ignatiev was working with is different from the one that exists today. We have seen a hardening of the class divide between the proletariat and the bourgeoisie, including between the Black proletariat and the Black bourgeoisie. The white proletariat has also experienced this process of class immiseration. In the 1960s, it was riding the post–World War II economic boom, but the current white proletariat has suffered decades of deindustrialization and austerity, the opioid crisis, the 2007–2008 crisis, and now the pandemic. These crises have destabilized the glue of whiteness, which, as demonstrated by the 2020 uprising, cannot always be counted on to hold all whites together. The riots revealed a layer of whites who we can describe as *race traitors*—white militants who riot and fight against the institutions that uphold whiteness. This layer of whites is often referred to as "antifa," but most are not actually part of any leftist scenes or groups.

The phenomenon of white race traitors has yet to be fully integrated into a revolutionary strategy for Black liberation. Whereas Ignatiev regarded an orientation toward white workers as a basis for deradicalization and reformism within the Black struggle, the current moment might show a different dynamic, wherein the involvement of white race traitors makes the movement more radical and more revolutionary. For the most part, however, the white proletariat and the Black proletariat remain deeply divided. The fact that a considerable number of white people are fighting under the banner of Black Lives Matter is an important development, but many obstacles still stand in the way of a lasting revolutionary alliance. As long as the Black proletariat is convinced that the white proletariat isn't willing to fight racism to the finish, the horizon and possibilities of struggle will remain limited. The white proletariat has a lot of work to do on this front.

If Black and white proletarians fail to form a lasting revolutionary alliance, sooner or later the Black proletariat will have to stop fighting or, just as tragically, make alliances with other classes: the Black middle class, the white middle class, or even the white bourgeoisie. This is already happening within the NGOs and the Democratic Party. The white proletariat will continue to uphold its own alliances with bourgeois society, further blocking the development of a revolutionary class struggle.

The White Racists

The return of the white proletariat has also included the return of white racists. This should come as no surprise. Just as a Black-led uprising was countered by a Black-led counterinsurgency, the rise of white race traitors was countered by white racists. As rebellions continue to flare up, more and more white vigilantes are stepping forward to violently defend whiteness and the property relations it entails, leading to a rising death toll for the partisans of the riot. In this context, armed self-defense appears increasingly necessary for those in revolt. However, the larger question remains: What is our strategy?

Among the middle-class left, much of what passes for anti-racism amounts to an almost religious belief that whites can never change. As noted before, there are legitimate reasons for this belief, but it also generates major ethical and political problems regarding any strategy for revolution. Obviously, considerable sections of the white proletariat are racist, and we must be ready to engage them in battle. But if racism is not something innate, natural, and permanent, as the fascists maintain, then it means that these very same racists are capable of change.

While it might sound like we are advocating nonviolence, downplaying racism, or arguing for some essential class unity, nothing could be further from the truth. Violence with racists is inevitable, but there are enough of them, and they have enough guns and support from the state that we cannot defeat them on a military basis alone. Confronting them on the streets is important, but in the long term we need to convince some of them that their commitment to whiteness only subordinates them to the bourgeoisie. This will be a slow, difficult, even dangerous process, but it can be done. Daryle Lamont Jenkins, who runs the One People's Project, for example, convinced several white nationalists to abandon their racist affiliations, and has facilitated their development into anti-racist militants. Many will justifiably not want to do this work—it isn't for everyone—but it is important work nonetheless. This work will not happen through some woke NGO workshop or Marxist journal but through shared experiences in mass struggles and tough conversations with other proletarians.

The White Ultraleft

While a minority of the white ultraleft has correctly oriented itself toward the riots and is in sync with the Black proletariat in high points of struggle, it returns to a segregated way of life during times of quiet. The paradox remains: the high points of struggle reveal the real relationship between revolutionary forces, but during most of our everyday lives racial capitalism continues to shape our relationships and common understanding of said forces. This is to be expected, but it poses a serious challenge to the development of a revolutionary movement.

Because of its separation from Black revolutionaries, the white ultraleft is struggling to overcome the political counterinsurgency that is raging throughout the country. When it's time to riot, it does what needs to be done, but afterward the political gains all fall to the counterinsurgent middle-class activists, who instrumentalize the riots as leverage for the reorganization of capitalism and the state. Meanwhile, white race traitors cannot intervene politically without being accused by these middle-class activists of being privileged, putting people in danger, speaking out of turn, etc., a dynamic that sidelines militancy and has the effect of transforming revolutionaries into foot soldiers for liberals, NGOs, and the Democratic Party. Unless Black revolutionaries step in to challenge the Black-led counterinsurgency and the Black middle classes more broadly, it's hard to imagine how white revolutionaries can avoid these pitfalls.

The Return of the Outside Agitators

The middle classes and bourgeoisie who believed they had firm control over the proletariat cannot fathom what is taking place. They cannot imagine why masses of people would violently revolt against society. Instead, they assert that white outside agitators are behind the riots. Of course, those of us on the ground know the truth: Black proletarians tend to initiate the most insurrectionary tactics. But the myth of the white outside agitator persists, and it is a powerful myth, designed to obscure the revolutionary nature of the uprising. Because of the hegemony of this myth, it is necessary to dissect it further.

The narrative of the white outside agitator first began to take shape during the era of Black chattel slavery. The old racist story goes that slaves were happy until white abolitionists from the North excited them to revolt. Then, after the defeat of chattel slavery, the story went that white Northern communists disturbed the peace, once again putting wild ideas of equality into the hearts and minds of Black people. Today, the white outside agitator returns in Minneapolis, Detroit, Richmond, and elsewhere. In this narrative, it is white people who are burning courthouses, fighting cops, and looting businesses. Taking the lead from the Black middle class, the middle classes, NGOs, and Democrats of all stripes resurrect the same argument dear to the slave owners and the segregationists of yesteryear, finding solace in their delusion that it is white agitators who are the active and driving force of history.

There is one current of outside agitators, however, that must be taken seriously. This is the racist white outside agitator. The middle classes have jumped on this, arguing that it is white racists who are burning down buildings, destroying Black-owned businesses, and pushing the country closer to another civil war. It is possible that a tiny layer of racist whites has used the riots to practice urban warfare. However, this alone cannot explain what is happening. It is not mobs of white racists who are attacking the police and capitalist property. It is a multiracial proletariat led by the Black proletariat.

Minneapolis, Seattle, Portland, Kenosha

In a *Washington Post* op-ed, E.D. Mondainé of the Portland branch of the NAACP mobilized the white outside agitator narrative to explain what is happening in Portland. He has called the Portland rebellion a "white spectacle." His critique hits on Naked Athena, the Wall of Moms, and the siege of the Federal Building. Mondainé argues that instead of rioting we should take the cause of Black Lives Matter into boardrooms, schools, city councils, the halls of "justice," and into the "smoky back rooms of a duplicitous government."[8] This is clearly a counterinsurgency strategy that could only ever lead to the end of the movement.

The question that has haunted the prospect of revolution in the US has been that of the white proletariat. Will it join the revolutionary struggle or will it defend class society? In Portland, white militants are fighting under the banner of Black Lives Matter. Black proletarians are taking notice, watching, seeing if these whites are serious. The historic question for revolution in the US has always been: Will white proletarians fight alongside Black proletarians and other proletarians of color? Portland, Seattle, Minneapolis, and Kenosha are answering that question in the affirmative.

Majority-white cities like Minneapolis, Seattle, Portland, and Kenosha have seen some of the largest and most militant rebellions of this cycle so far. How do we explain this? The answer is that these cities have the weakest Black middle classes, the weakest Black NGOs, and the weakest Black Democratic Party institutions relative to other cities like Atlanta, Detroit, Philadelphia, Baltimore, etc. In the majority white cities mentioned above, the Black counterinsurgency was sufficiently weak that these cities produced the high points of the revolt.

The Monster

The insurrectionary alliance that emerges through riots is frightening, scandalous, and monstrous. It upends all the contemporary notions of solidarity, politics, and organization. It displaces the leadership and control of the bourgeoisie and the middle classes of all colors. The left does not understand it and quite clearly sees it as a threat. The left has become so divorced from proletarian life, from proletarian forms of knowledge, and from proletarian culture that when the proletariat finally takes the lead in this country, it can appear only as an abomination to be contained and disciplined.

We have seen this happen many times throughout history. The Bolsheviks who crushed the Kronstadt rebellion and the Makhnovshchyna offer only the most classic examples. Frantz Fanon and C.L.R. James noted the same counterrevolutionary tendency among the national bourgeoisie of the Third World. Whether in the Haitian Revolution, the US Civil War, the Mexican Revolution, the Chinese Revolution, or elsewhere—every appearance of the proletarian monster was grotesque and terrifying, because it undermined the boundaries of society.

The Revolutionary Crucible of the White Proletariat

Even with the current revolts, the reality is that race traitors represent a small minority of white workers, who, for the most part, remain unconvinced by what they have seen. The white workers must be dragged into learning the truth. This is not an endorsement but a recognition of a historical reality.

White workers will not learn their true interests from the public education system or the media, and certainly not through activist organizations, Marxist or anarchist magazines, newspapers, conferences, study groups, mutual aid, etc. The reality is that it is only through the bitter experience of crisis and struggle that white workers can become revolutionary.

Noel Ignatiev was correct that whiteness must be abolished, and that it will take millions of white race traitors to accomplish this, but the only way this will occur is through the lessons of crisis. John Brown's entire strategy was to provoke a national crisis and to drive the country into a civil war against slavery. If this were the 1850s, how many of us would support the strategy of escalation that Brown engaged in during Bloody Kansas? How many of us would support the raid that he and Harriet Tubman planned on Harpers Ferry?

Historically, the white proletariat has only figured things out when objective circumstances dragged it through mud and blood. The US Civil War forced it to fight against slavery, the Great Depression forced it to join Black workers in the CIO, World War II forced it to shoot fascists in Europe, and the Vietnam War taught it the cruel lessons of US imperialism. The pattern is the same. Crisis educates the white proletariat. There is no denying that a large section of white workers might reach the most counterrevolutionary and racist of conclusions from such a crisis, but there is no other way. Crisis, struggle, and polarization are inevitable. Revolutionaries need to reckon with this reality and act accordingly.

Theses on the White Proletariat

1. White people, like all people, are divided by politics and class. These divisions were revealed through the recent uprisings, which showed us that there are whites who are willing to go the distance, and there are whites who are willing to violently defend capitalism and the state. Our task is to deepen this split.
2. At the same time, this split is not permanent. At this very moment, whiteness is reforming and re-cementing itself. This is why it's important to develop a strategy for race treason.
3. Race treason is not an identity, nor is it a state of mind. Race treason is when white people fight against the institutions that make them white. This doesn't mean that people stop being racialized as white. It means that the racial order is getting attacked by a section of people who are expected to be loyal to it.

4. We need a revolutionary strategy for white workers not in spite of but precisely because of their racism and counterrevolutionary potential. Enrolling the white proletariat into a racial alliance has been a crucial tactic of American capitalism, for the simple reason that white workers have always been the largest demographic in this nation. A successful proletarian revolution requires breaking up this alliance.

5. The white proletariat has revolutionary potential, but this potential is simultaneously inflected with racism and anti-Blackness. This contradiction takes the form of a civil war within the white proletariat. This civil war is defined, on the one hand, by solidarity with the rest of the proletariat, and, on the other hand, by investment in the system of whiteness.

6. The so-called "white outside agitator" is the name for a living creature who breaks the spell of a united white bloc of civility, protocol, and allegiance to capitalism and the state. It reveals that there are white people who are not invested in whiteness.

7. As more white race traitors emerge, they too will be hunted down and murdered. In this sense, law and order is not only about disciplining militants of color but also white race traitors.

8. The white proletariat is not frozen. It can change, evolve, and break from its history of settler colonialism, racism, and imperialism. We do not need romantic illusions to see this. Actual people make revolutions, not saints and angels.

9. The historical moment that sheds the most light on the current white proletariat is the era of the Civil War. This history powerfully informs the trajectory of what will come. The Civil War and Reconstruction are the unfinished business of this land.

10. Only crisis, civil war, and revolution can smash the alliance between the white proletariat and capitalism.

Conclusion

"And the maps of spring always have to be redrawn again, in undared forms."
—Sylvia Wynter

The Black proletariat is the most revolutionary faction of the US proletariat, but it can't defeat capitalism on its own. In this essay, we have explored how the white proletariat is a piece of the puzzle. Another piece, which we have not yet examined, is the Latinx proletariat. Another piece is the Indigenous proletariat. Another is the international proletariat. There are many pieces in the puzzle of revolutionary strategy; how they come together was revealed in the experience of the 2020 uprising.

Capitalism has been chipping away at the wages of whiteness for decades now. As a result, more whites are joining the struggle against racial capitalism, but there is no guarantee of what will happen with the white proletariat. While there are revolutionary currents within it, its history is defined by racism. It has a lot of work to do to convince other proletarians that it is committed to revolution. This will require dedication of the likes we have never seen. It must be made clear, however, that the point of such an orientation isn't to assuage a guilty conscience. There is a lot of abstract and shallow accounting of how whiteness is to be overcome through guilt, self-sacrifice, charity, and interpersonal behaviors, but the clearest road ahead is when whites fight the police, burn cop cars, burn police stations, burn courthouses, and commit their bodies to the uprising.

The uprising forced everyone to take sides, raising the specter of civil war. How do we turn this civil war into a revolutionary war that abolishes whiteness, empire, capitalism, and patriarchy? For this to happen, a revolutionary alliance must develop between all sections of the proletariat, in opposition to the middle classes and bourgeoisie of all identities. The formation of this proletarian alliance will be on terms so different from what most people understand solidarity to mean that it will look like a monster. It will require strategy, organization, tactics, and politics that most of the US left is unprepared for. This does not mean that it has to stay this way.

Some will look at these rebellions and continue to think exactly as they thought before. They have nothing to learn from this experience. Riots, looting, and arson have accomplished more in one summer than what activists have been able to accomplish in decades. This summer has transformed an entire generation. It is not the NGOs or the left, not even the revolutionary left, that has done this. It is thousands of brave young people acting on their own initiative, their own perception of what makes sense, what feels not only logical and powerful but what a *dignified* response to state slaughter looks like. They are the ones we pay homage to—and to our fallen comrades.

If a revolutionary praxis is to emerge, it will emerge from the fires of these rebellions. Now, with a new recession, masses of people out of work, tens of thousands on the verge of eviction, and a pandemic that is getting worse, the crisis of America is only becoming more entrenched. Despite the push toward reformism and the spectacle of the election, the struggle continues.

We welcome the proletarian monster.

September 2020

Weapons and Ethics

Adrian Wohlleben

The ethical question is not about weapons but about which ones.

There is no such thing as a peaceful insurrection. This is America; there is no imaginable scenario in which social conflicts will continue and people will not be armed, on all sides. Whether weapons are necessary is an open question, but, in any case, they are inevitable. However, as friends noted some time ago, there is an important distinction to be made between "being armed and the use of arms." If guns are an inevitable feature of any American insurrection, it is a question of doing everything possible to make their use unnecessary.

For participants and observers of this summer's uprisings, the clashes in Kenosha following Jacob Blake's shooting have dragged the question of armed violence to the forefront of debates. Does the presence of guns on "our side" offer any sense of relief from danger? Do they make anything possible that isn't otherwise? Can we imagine them being used in a way that would open the situation up and make people feel more powerful?

In his "Critique of Violence,"[1] penned in the immediate aftermath of a defeated communist insurrection in Germany, Walter Benjamin attempts to bypass sterile oppositions between violence and "nonviolence," legitimate and illegitimate force, instead directing our attention to the more decisive difference between modes and manners of violence. By suspending the question of the "aims" or goals of violence—which, in Benjamin's view, quickly devolves into myth and metaphysics—and instead differentiating between its *means* and *uses*, we shift the problem from an instrumental or technical register to an ethical one. Instead of asking, "For the sake of what end does this act occur?" we should ask: *What is this act like from the inside? What does it do to us and those around us? How does it activate or deactivate our capacity to fully participate in existence?* In this way, Benjamin is able to reframe the problem of revolutionary violence: its difference from state violence resides not in the "tasks" or agenda it claims to serve but, first and foremost, in the relation to the world, to oneself, and to others that it engenders.

The same insight must today be applied to the presence of violence and weapons within rebellious movements. Violence is neither "good" nor "bad," nor is it helpfully framed in terms of the "ends" or purposes it serves. (Tradition offers us little in the way of a program, model, or vocation anyway.) Better would be to ask about the types of arms and the mode of their use: *How does our use of weapons work behind our backs to define the meaning and limits of our power? How does this choice affect and configure who feels able to join us, and even what we think of as "winning"? How can we make this choice explicit to ourselves?* To be clear, this question cannot be limited to the subject of firearms (my focus here) but embraces the entire domain of tactics—marches, blockades, occupations, rioting, looting, mutual aid, and so on. In the long run, it's our whole way of looking at things, at the meaning of revolution itself as an immanent and lived process, that is at issue here. All methods used by insurgents must be subjected to ethical concerns of this sort. We are in need of an earnest debate around tactics today: *Which practices have succeeded in deepening and widening social ruptures, thereby opening a real possibility for communism? Which have ended up confining insurgencies within a closed field of specialized problems, the better to govern and manage them?*

There is an ethics wrapped up in the selection of firearms and the visibility this entails. For instance, when we think about the presence of guns on the side of protesters, we need to distinguish guns openly carried versus those concealed. The leftist militia-style folks openly carrying long rifles often say they are there to "protect" the demonstration or the crowd outside the courthouse. For this reason, we think of them as being formally or ideologically aligned with the protesters, or "on our side." In reality, however, the crowd in Kenosha was already armed, only with pistols under their belts. Between these two groups, there are qualitative distinctions to be made around the mode and method of arms and how each brings their bearer to relate to the crowd around them.

Unlike the folks carrying long rifles and wearing bulletproof vests, those who had pistols concealed in their belts were able to continue to engage in more "social" forms of rebellion. By this, I mean those nonspecialized forms of action accessible to anyone who simply shows up, such as graffitiing, breaking windows at the courthouse, throwing rocks at police, setting dump trucks on fire, rioting and looting, etc. For the most part, while those conceal-carrying in the crowd often make no secret of the fact that they are armed, to the point of openly telling people next to them that they intend to shoot back if the crowd is attacked, they do not make their possession of guns into an exclusive vocation. Having a gun is not treated like an identity or a "social function" that distinguishes them from everyone else. In most cases, those moving alongside them in the crowd would not even see their guns until they were used, for instance to shoot open an ATM or when Kyle Rittenhouse opened fire, at which point at least a dozen pistols that had not been seen before came out of belts.

By contrast—and this is the sense in which the choice of a tool like the long rifle becomes ethical and not simply technical—the use of arms by Black or Black-adjacent militia folks tended to specialize itself, resulting in a form of social closure. With certain rare exceptions—as during the standoff with a BearCat that drove up on the crowd outside the Kenosha courthouse on the first night—the open-carry leftist militia folks keep to the edge of the demonstration and generally refuse to participate in any other way. On the one hand, one could, of course, read this decision as performing an equal "social" function, at least if you believe that the crowd needed "protecting" or guarding. Yet this feels like a misconception, since the protest was already armed and did not hesitate to draw when fired upon. In the meantime, however, those conceal-carrying pistols continue to combine and move together with other roles, practices, and forms of participation. They can engage in the same gestures of attack, defense, and care as everyone else, smashing up concrete benches and pulling up bricks, lasering police, throwing paint bombs at BearCat windows to immobilize them, escorting protesters wounded or blinded by police to safety, throwing fireworks, and so on.

The choice of weapons is not merely technical; it is at the same time ethical. Given the climate of mounting social hostility, the need for collective self-defense is an undeniable fact of current social ruptures. How we try to solve this problem will impact the possibilities of social composition on the ground. The more that armed violence detaches itself from other forms of struggle, the more it becomes something we treat as a specialized technical problem requiring esoteric knowledge, the more it will tend to become divorced from the intelligence and confidence of the crowd. This ultimately will result in a de-escalation, since it will ensure that people unversed in its methods continue to feel unwelcome or unprepared to engage.

By contrast, while I might be aware that there are pistols in the belt of the person throwing rocks next to me, this fact need not cancel other forms of engagement, participation, and collaboration. It is decisive that we maintain a common *plane of consistency* of practices that cut across armed and nonarmed people. By contrast, the militia-style practice of open carrying long arms risks producing a kind of tactical solipsism. The more people believe their only function in the demo is to be a "living gun," the less inclined they will be to participate in the collective intelligence of the crowd, which is often able to find solutions other than gunfire to problems that confront it. This accounts for the strange feeling one has marching alongside such folks or engaging in battles with the police in their presence; rather than remaining in fluid contact with the crowd or feeling like they are a part of what's going on, their disconnection gives the impression of them being a third or even a fourth type of force on the ground. They appear, in addition to police, protesters, and right-wing militias, like one more problem to deal with, one more unpredictable element with its own internal logic, inaccessible to those around it.

Do the guns on "our side" offer us any sense of relief from danger? Do they make anything possible that isn't otherwise?

Any sense of "relief" we might feel at the presence of either the pistols or the long rifles pertains solely to a scenario that is itself already basically terrifying—either police or right-wing forces opening fire on us—which, in any case, would result in a chaotic mess that would be destructive of the collective power of the crowd. To what extent does the knowledge that our side is armed help us relate to this possibility? In such a scenario, it *might* be good that the fascists are not the only force shooting—provided that return fire doesn't result in further casualties on our side. To be honest, the intensity of such situations so thoroughly exceeds what most of us are accustomed to that the kinds of gestures and tactics we know and understand cannot easily find their bearings in it. As a result, it makes little sense to associate them with anything positive or to say that the presence of guns generated a kind of opening within the situation outside of this eventuality.

In the final analysis, the only thing that the guns contribute to our side is the possibility of *slowing down a massacre*, since they introduce the potential for return fire. However, bloodshed is just bloodshed, and there is nothing to celebrate in it ethically or socially on its own terms.

September 2020

Letter to Michael Reinoehl

Idris Robinson

Dear Michael Reinoehl,

I must begin by apologizing for not writing to you sooner. That is, I need to say sorry for not getting this letter to you before it was all over—or, better, before they took it upon themselves to end it and had subsequently finished you off in the process. However, if there is any consolation that we can hold onto in all of this, then it is, as you and I both know very well, that it is never *really* over. As the old slogan goes, "Nothing stops; everything continues…"

Believe me, I will totally understand if there is simply no forgiveness left in that big heart of yours, since we all let you down when you needed us most. The sad fact of the matter is that everyone on our side claims to be waiting for the next John Brown, but when he finally appears before us, we line up to unanimously reject him. Later on, I think, most will come to acknowledge the tragedy in allowing history to repeat itself, yet very few will have the honesty to admit that you and your children were sacrificed so that we could continue to live our farcical lives of fear and shame.

What I mean is that there will be those who will continue to bear false witness, even though it is impossible to deny that it was none other than Ol' Brown who manifested himself through you. It is obvious to anyone who was courageous enough not to turn away that the piercing stare that the two of you share in common is, in fact, one and the same. Indeed, it showed itself to us as you sat in that wooded grove, where the unmistakable fire in your eyes made the same silent pledge that was also proclaimed in the black and white image of the great nineteenth-century abolitionist, with his palm raised. It is the look of a person, man or woman, who has declared an eternal war against slavery.

It all happened so fast… And almost immediately, in the very next instant, so many of those who once stood beside you found a convenient way to forsake those bonds by expressing worries, instead of using their words to strengthen the collective commitments of solidarity. Above all, what indicated the implicit hypocrisy in the whole matter was how quickly they arrived at certain conclusions, before they had even had a chance to learn the details of the situation.

The fact that it somehow did not manage to cross their minds that what happened was more than likely a legitimate case of self-defense is rather telling in and of itself. Since the uprising began, the list of those martyred by white supremacists, with or without a badge, continues grow almost daily: Calvin Horton, Sean Monterossa, Sarah Grossman, Italia Kelly, Marquis Tousant, Malik Graves, Victor Cazares, Robert Forbes, Oluwatoyin Salau, Victoria Simms, Erik Salgado… In that same week, when you set your course with a bold decision to act, we lost two other momentous figures of your stature in Kenosha: Anthony Huber and Joseph Rosenbaum. Since it is the martyr's blood and not abstract humanitarian life that must be deemed the most precious, I have to accept all of the fault for inevitably leaving out names that demand to be repeated, again and again. Thus, as we witness with each day, each week, and each month, another human being destroyed by firearms or automobiles, the question then poses itself more forcefully: Why did their initial assumptions stray from the predictable instance of self-defense, which you would later confirm in that final interview?

On the other side of things, there is no Black person—unless they are a complete and total Uncle Tom—who would've even had a second thought about giving you the benefit of the doubt here. This is because the course of our lives has shown us that anyone who plays with guns as recklessly as the fascists do will, eventually and unsurprisingly, get themselves shot. To put it bluntly, if we were talking about an inner-city gang affiliate, instead of a member of the far right, then there would certainly be no discussion about any of this.

What the double standard with regards to your situation reveals is how violence in America will always necessarily have a profoundly racial dimension. And it is precisely this—the terrifying core of racialized violence—that they are trying to repress when they lie to both themselves and others that their issue with what you did is a question of strategy or tactics. I mean, give me a break: in a country that is literally saturated in violence, from blind mass shooters to murderous police, no one can honestly claim that the few shots that you let off could in some way be construed as an escalation. There is simply no way to avoid the spiral of violence that began at the very moment the first wooden ships reached the shores of the Atlantic.

In truth, when considering that a veritable industry has been constructed to promote victimhood—where everyone except the most wretched is capable of cashing-in—what they are afraid of is not so much ending up on the smoky side of the barrel of a gun. Instead, what they are really afraid of is having another person's blood on their hands. Put better: it is what is implied by spilling another's blood that constitutes their deepest fears. It would mean that they would finally have to believe in something—that is, believe in something beyond themselves. Such a choice would necessarily involve a conscious transgression: crossing over a dangerous boundary, at the edge, at the limits, where whiteness ends; and once it has been breached, they could never find their way back.

What I am trying my best to get at, albeit poorly, is what Walter Benjamin once struggled to explain about the ethical stakes of the commandment "Thou shalt not kill":

> Those who base a condemnation of all violent killing of one person by another on the commandment are therefore mistaken. It exists not as a criterion of judgment, but as a guideline for the actions of persons and communities who have to wrestle with it in solitude and, in exceptional cases, to take upon themselves the responsibility of ignoring it.... But those thinkers who take the opposite view refer to a ... doctrine of the sanctity of life [and] profess that higher than the happiness and justice of existence stands existence alone. As certainly as this last proposition is false, indeed ignoble, it shows the necessity of seeking the reason for the commandment no longer in what the deed does to the victim, but in what it does to God and the doer. The proposition that existence stands higher than a just existence is false and ignominious, if existence is to mean nothing other than mere life.[1]

As holy as they come, John Brown fought with the utmost religious sincerity exactly this internal battle. By contravening the prohibition against murder, at Pottawatomie and at Harpers Ferry, he drew a line that elevated truth and justice above life itself. It demonstrated that all life will remain senseless and barren, so long as there are those reduced to abject servitude. And, yes, Michael, you did the same, when, in protecting both yourself and your friend, you brought to reality the chant, otherwise carelessly echoed, that "No Lives Matter until Black Lives Matter."

Such a conversion of words into deeds inherently involves a fundamental transformation of the self. This is what Benjamin meant when he said that it is more about what is done to the doer than to the victim. Once again, in our context, this has an irrevocably racial significance. To some extent, it boils down to the plain fact that I know so many white people who have never been in a fistfight, but, conversely, when you grow up Black, your grandma won't let you back in the house unless you stand up for yourself and throw hands. It is for this reason that I can so readily dismiss purported strategic concerns as irrelevant, because we are taught to fight even if we are sure to lose to a stronger opponent. In the larger struggle against America, it is clear that, in the same way, we have both nothing to lose and nothing to gain, except for that something "higher" that could only be abandoned by giving in. It's like James Baldwin once said, those who are forced to snatch their humanity out of the fire of cruelty, whether they survive or not, still come to know something that no school or church could ever teach. For others to accept this wager is to perpetrate the ultimate betrayal of their own whiteness. It is to become an abolitionist.

Conducting his raid, John Brown assumed precisely this peculiar blend of hope and despair in order to affirmatively take up his position on death-ground. Accordingly, his willingness to act was wholly reflected in his character. In this regard, there was always something about an account offered by the historian Margaret Washington that has stayed with me:

It's important to understand what an anomaly John Brown was during his time as far as his attitude toward people of African descent was concerned, because John Brown considered himself a complete egalitarian. It was very important for him to practice egalitarianism on all levels.... And even the [other] abolitionists, as antislavery as they were, the majority of them did not see African Americans as equals.... Well, John Brown was not like that. For him, practicing egalitarianism was a first step toward ending slavery. And African Americans who came in contact with him knew this immediately. He made it very clear that he saw no difference, and he did not make this clear by saying it, he made it clear by what he did.[2]

For lack of a better formulation, it could be said that *common sense* is very white, whereas *good sense* is totally anti-white.

What this entails is that much of academic debate about race, which has now become everyday parlance, is actually beside the point. It is neither biological nor social: whiteness is to be measured by the degree to which a person clings to the last vestiges of this dying and doomed country. It is to maintain a faith in the same constitutional protections that your summary execution again proved empty. It is to nurse feelings for that one racist family member who still manages to elicit affection and love. It is to believe that a job is actually deserved at a firm where the darker employees can only do cleanup. In short, it is the extent to which a person embodies life, liberty, and the pursuit of happiness. It is worthwhile to note that, according to this standard of evaluation, it follows that many of the people who are called "Black" must instead be judged as white.

To fend off its own dissolution, white supremacist society tells us that there is nothing more insane than the desire to be born with Black skin. This is how they present Rachel Dolezal to us. John Brown was forced to wear this label for more than a century, and it will, unfortunately, be attached to you, Michael, for some time to come. However, this is nothing but a projection of a far more widespread cluster of pathologies pervading white America: a situation in which opiates and self-inflicted wounds have become the only means to temper the pain of rapidly disintegrating personal relationships.

Likewise, the dire emotional state of the individual citizen is being mirrored in the way the country as a whole is crumbling before our eyes. To be more precise, I'd say that the American government is doing its best to overthrow itself. Yet, so accustomed to disappointment, I should have expected some of the loudest voices within the movement to express skepticism, a defeatist attitude, and acquire a defensive posture through their reluctance. It brings to mind the old "Chapter Report on the S.D.S. Regional Council" distributed by Up Against the Wall Motherfucker:

A "WHITE RADICAL"
IS THREE PARTS BULLSHIT
AND ONE PART HESITATION,
IT IS NOT REVOLUTIONARY
AND SHOULD NOT BE
STOCKPILED
AT THIS MOMENT.[3]

Despite certain grandiose delusions of white mastery and control, it is becoming increasingly evident that civil war is inescapable. It is not up to anyone. Rather, it is a play of forces that does not need to make any excuses for itself—once the tiger has been let out of the cage, it doesn't go back in without trying to turn its former captors into prey. In other words, it doesn't look like Black people are going to sit down anytime soon, unless Mister Charlie figures out a way to strap us back down into his chair. Therefore, the strategic question is, then, not so much how to stop it but how to win a civil war.

So the misgivings about what you did tend to tread on thin air. What's more, they all turn a blind eye to the concrete lessons taught to us by history. That is, the criticism and apprehensions, which I'm sure you have also heard, tend to ignore the extensive tradition of militant self-defense, which has consistently been the red thread capable of uniting the most advanced and revolutionary sectors of the Black freedom struggle. Only by neglecting this legacy can one mistakenly suppose that racist terror will somehow disappear on its own or be checked by the authorities.

Alas, I have written too much. With that said, if all this is too overwhelming, don't feel compelled to hurry in writing back—even when I don't hear from you, I know that you're still around. To close, I should mention that, in these difficult times, with their disorientating ups and downs, I find myself telling my friends, more often and in earnest, that I love them.

Love and solidarity,
Idris Robinson

October 2020

Memes without End

Adrian Wohlleben

"What counts is no longer the statement of wind, but the wind."
—Georges Bataille

The revolt against police power in the wake of George Floyd's murder forms the unsurpassable horizon of our moment. The limits it hit upon mark the boundary of our political and vital possibilities today. The reflections offered here attempt to trace just a few of these thresholds. They began as notes jotted down on the fly, conversations between friends amid the fire and smoke of a long, hot summer. The basic argument can be summarized in four propositions:

1. Insurrection today depends less upon the consolidation of leading identities than on the circulation of leading practices or gestures.
2. Last summer's rebellion began not as an abolitionist politics centered on policy changes but as a viral contagion of demolitionist desire directed at police stations, vehicles, and courthouses. However, when it burned the Third Precinct, the movement advanced a leading practice that it was unable to repeat.
3. Counterinsurgency does not take place solely through external maneuvers "against" the movement but also by channeling untamed and decivilizing forms of race treason, rebellion, and communication back into recognizable frameworks of what a "social movement" is supposed to look like, the better to manage and pacify it.
4. The real movement's offensive capacity last summer was divided into two modes, political riots and storefront riots, whose externality to

one another placed a ceiling on the insurgency's power. Breaking this apparatus would require disentangling the placemaking impulse from its one-sided inscription in the political riot and the logistical intelligence from its restriction to the storefront riot. However, this task implies a qualitative and not simply quantitative leap for which there is no linear strategic path.

Leading Subjects/Leading Gestures

A few years ago, after witnessing firsthand the explosive insurgency of the Yellow Vests in France, Paul Torino and I began asking whether it wasn't far more likely that an insurrection capable of suspending the ruling order would be assembled through a *memetic* rather than a conventional social movement logic. In an article we wrote at the time, we set out an opposition between classical social movements and what we called *memes with force*, by which we mean real-life conflicts organized memetically through contagious gestures.

> The social movement paradigm refers to a process by which groups get organized around their distinct experience of social institutions (or around their distinct experience of oppression, as in the case of the New Left), work to advance the interests of their respective constituencies, and link up with other institutional segments along the way. From the Worker-Student Action Committees of May 1968, to the failed alliance between French rail workers and university occupations exactly 50 years later, this Trotskyist model of organization continues to exert a lasting influence on how an escalation of conflict comes to be imagined.[1]

By basing themselves on a "dialogue" with power, social movements are forced to accept and move *within* the given terrain of truth, making it easy for the ruling elites to de-escalate, derail, and defang them (more on this below). By contrast, the Yellow Vests showed us that conflicts originating in memetic activities are far more difficult to contain, since they have the power to open the vortex that invites ever wider circles of people to jump in and innovate within them. What if mass memetic experiments could—with a lot of tact and a bit of luck—escalate into genuine crises for the ruling-class order, opening the window for mass experiments in noneconomic sharing and self-organization? Might the meme be how insurrections get started in the twenty-first century?

When we speak of "memes with force," we are not referring to digital memes used as propaganda for promoting radical social ideologies but to movements that spread *as* memes. In a nutshell, our argument is that the apparent strength of social movements actually constitutes a limitation from the point of view of an insurrection. Social movements are indexed to *institutional subjects*, meaning that they are assumed to originate in shared experiences of suffering that you or I have at the hands of an institution. These could originate inside an institution, like the university in the case of students or the factory for workers, or else by being placed outside one, as when undocumented folks are denied papers, youth experience racialized policing, etc. Since they're designed like dialogues between inferiors and superiors, or service recipients and providers, social movements make a lot of sense if you're trying to rectify or improve an institution. But what if you want to overthrow capitalist society? According to the mythology of the left, the revolutionary potential of social movements depends upon a so-called "convergence of struggles," a much-touted but rarely achieved moment in which various separate struggles suddenly staple themselves together into a common fighting force through "solidarity." Although the American left excused itself from articulating any practical strategy for producing revolutionary ruptures decades ago, the social convergence logic still implicitly underwrites today's "intersectional" left. Unfortunately, such convergences never work: the myriad social separations, narrowly circumscribed "interests," and disavowed hierarchies baked into social movements from the jump are more than adequate to ensure that everyone stays in their separate lanes, and that no one hopes for anything more than defensive wins. While its depressive boom-bust cycle sponges up fresh radical energy year in and year out, its ultimate significance is to reproduce a demoralizing cynicism as to the prospects of revolution in our time.

The appeal of the meme lies in the possibility of leaping over or sidestepping this whole problem. The intrinsically viral character of the meme can facilitate the absorption and coordination of rage and anger from all different sorts of people without becoming canalized by institutions.

Let us be clear from the outset: there is no question of denying or avoiding social contradictions. Anyone can see that class domination and racial abjection constitute the structuring logic of suffering in this land. But how is an uprising against exploitation and abjection *composed*?

Mainstream political rationality has trained us to believe that the fate of uprisings depends upon the identity of the actors involved (students, Black people, women, factory workers, migrants, etc.), since it is this that determines the radicality of "demands" the movement can imagine making, as well as the concessions sufficient to pacify it. Consequently (this thinking goes), only if the struggle is led by those whose demands are too radical for the system to accommodate can it ever hope to overcome the system itself. The problem of composition, therefore, appears, from this perspective, as reducible to the social content of the struggles. Who led? Who took control? Whose demands were centered? Did the middle-class activists co-opt the movement? Did those whose social position *ought* to have compelled them to join end up staying away, and, if so, how do we explain that? Much analysis of last summer focuses on the class and race identity of the participants, while comparatively less attention was paid to the grammar of action that drove it.

What if we were to shift our focus for a moment away from the identity and "intentions" of the actors to the practices of the movement? What if the precondition for a revolution today lies not in the political consolidation and social command of a "leading identity" (the working class, the subaltern, the lumpen, the Native, the Black, etc.) but, rather, in the contagion and ramification of *leading gestures*?[2]

Gestures don't "lead" in the same way social groups were once thought to, i.e., by asserting historical or moral claims that would grant them the legitimacy to direct struggles. A gesture leads by (i) being copied and imitated, accumulating instances of repetition; (ii) by forcibly rearranging the field of intelligibility into which it is inserted, by *changing the problem,* such that neighboring practices must be rethought and reorganized in response to it, even if only temporarily; and (iii) by facilitating other interventions around it, by "leaving, escaping, but while causing more escapes."[3] The mark of a leading gesture is that it becomes a vessel into which a broad swath of singular antagonists feel invited to pour their outrage, aggression, and ferocious joy. Coherence, resonance, and contagion measure the success of a decisive act.

Truckers angry about surveillance regulations get organized autonomously through Facebook groups and begin doing mass slow-rolls on freeways,[4] *blocking interstates and city centers. The gesture quickly spreads not only to other truckers but also to locals who start showing up in their civilian vehicles for their own reasons, driving alongside the truckers, until they outstrip the truckers entirely, leading to swarms of vehicles caravanning through city centers.*

Police are filmed getting soaked by crowds of shrieking teens after attempting to disperse a water pistol fight.[5] Within days, cops are being stalked and soaked by massive mobs of youth two states over.

Teenagers responding to fare hikes on public transit organize a subversive game they call "Mass Evasion,"[6] which they promote on social media. The game adapts an everyday form of individual subversion—not paying for the train—transforming it into a collective gesture that people can do in groups. State repression of the game only spreads it further and wider, catalyzing an insurrectionary sequence that is still unfinished to this day.

Just as it is meaningless to speak of "revolutionaries" outside of the revolutions they take part in, gestures are never liberatory per se but only as a function of the situation they intervene in. What matters is the space of play each opens up, their power to *invite* autonomous responses from onlookers ("yes, and…"), and the experiments that fill the space they open up as more people throw themselves in.[7] The mark of a "meme with force" is that, before anyone realizes what's happened, thousands of people suddenly feel authorized to take initiative and begin attacking the source of their suffering, starting from where they stand.

Both the Occupy movement of 2011 and the 2016 Labor Law movement in France (with its *cortège de tête*) consisted of a mix of memetic gestures and recognizably leftist and social movement grammar.[8] However, the first mass uprising to explode entirely through a memetic platform was the Yellow Vests struggle in France. Here, it was the *gesture* of "putting on the vest" that placed one on a common plane with all others who have done the same.

If memes can circulate beyond and across institutional and even national boundaries, this is not because they are somehow "universal." On the contrary, memes are always seized upon for *local* reasons, even if these resonate with broader forms of social violence (austerity, atomization, abjection, etc.). Unlike political organizations, which generate consistency by translating singular experiences of violence into shared ideologies, one can put on a yellow vest and show up at a traffic circle and remain a singularity. Whereas one "belongs" to a political organization by joining it, we join ourselves to gestures only by repeating them and by introducing variations into them. However, the difference concerns not only who and how one "belongs" but also *how* one fights. Whereas the tendency of the social movement is to articulate conflicts in terms of demands made of this or that institution—tuition, work benefits, papers, etc.—a "meme with force" does not come with a ready-made set of demands, nor must we belong to any certain social group to gain entry into it. Since there are few preliminaries, prerequisites, or preconditions, memes allow individuals to move alongside one another, while preserving their own respective reasons for fighting, thereby inviting each of us to trust in our own singular evaluation of the situation. This has the great advantage of allowing memetic movements to harness and leverage the *ante-political* forms of life in which each of us already participate:[9] think of the hooligans and ultras who fought in Turkey's Gezi Park uprising, the mutual aid networks and autonomous hubs that fed into frontliner formations, or the motorcycle clubs and sideshow drivers whose revving engines became a permanent sensory feature of the George Floyd uprising. When conflicts kick off, these ante-political lifeforms suddenly become potentiated in new ways: they bend, crisscross, and weave together like so many shards of light through the kaleidoscope of the event, adding fuel to the fire. When a fighting force is assembled in this way, it can grow and multiply along paths that are responsive to the really existing terrain of the situation, rather than relying on obsolete rituals handed down by the institutional left. Since there is no distinct subject whose "interests" can be appeased or bought off to quell the escalation, no expiration of hostilities is programmed into the movement in advance.[10] Although it always meets its limits in reality, at a formal level memetic antagonisms are limitless, since they have no reconciliatory horizon.

This tight link between memes and ante-political forms ensures that politics remains connected to our intimate everyday life, which it also weaponizes. At the same time, it belongs to the nature of all memes to be wrenched out of their context and away from their creators, since anyone can pick them up and pull them in another direction.[11] Memetics lodges itself within this *tensor* between intimacy and anonymity, between banality and contagion: its locus lies in the switching point where life becomes combat, where nonpolitical practices and cultures, such as singing "Baby Shark" to an anxious toddler, jumping subway turnstiles, or carrying an umbrella in Hong Kong, suddenly become magnetic and find themselves incorporated like machine parts into combative formations. The real secret, the one that Western ideology has always worked to conceal, is that *there is no separation between "politics," on the one hand, and "life," on the other.* There is only a single flat surface—experience, everyday life—articulated into various grammars of suffering and populated by countless ante-political forms that here and there reach a threshold of intensity that polarizes them, often (but not always) under the sway of larger events.[12] What matters is identifying, in this or that situation, how unowned, inappropriable, anonymous practices originating in everyday life become magnetized by conflicts and what potential reach each might still pack within it.

While it is difficult to imagine an insurrection in the USA today taking the form of a disciplined consolidation of marginal social groups—e.g., a crystallization of crowds into "classes" through solidarity or by forming new racially separatist militant cadres[13]—it is considerably easier to imagine a viral contagion of actions that respond intelligently to their moment escalating into mass experiments in communist sharing on a variety of scales. Whether these approach the horizon of becoming an insurrection will depend on whether such experiments are sufficiently empowering in material and ethical ways to render the return of normal life and bourgeois economics undesirable for millions of people.

While there is nothing wrong with paying attention to, and even participating in, social movements organized around institutional or identitarian demands, we should not see them as terrains of victory in their own right but as laboratories for new "memes with force." From this angle, the aim of insurgents within social movements is to propagate memes across them, like anonymous viruses on a hostile platform. The black bloc was one such virus. The car caravan was another. The plaza occupation—a tactic now approaching its exhaustion, at least in North America—was a third. What forms of action constitute the cutting edge of what's thinkable today? What minor gestures have already emerged but missed their chance to spread?

Open the vortex and extend the meme to the point of ungovernability.[14] Repeat, expand, innovate. Do what you can to ensure that the movement stays inviting and open to new and wider groups of people. Try to prevent any group from ideologically hegemonizing it—not only the far right but *also* the far left.[15] Only in this way can we generate the conditions in which mass experiments in living outside of the rule of money, measure, and racial abjection might take root.

The party is not its ends but its gestures. It is only as it does. And—like substance for Spinoza—it always goes as far as it can.

Demolition/Abolition

The first phase of the George Floyd Rebellion was qualitatively different from the policy-friendly social movement that later strove to supplant it. The spontaneous practical intuition of the crowd signaled an entirely logical response to the forces that murdered George Floyd: push the police out, sabotage their bases, sink their battleships. Destroy the places from which their violence is organized—precincts, substations, courthouses—as well as the cars and vans that circulate it. By contrast with the abolitionist campaigns to "defund" police departments or (in its weaker versions) to supplement them with "civilian review boards"—discursive, dialogical, and demand-based frameworks that leave the initiative in the hands of the state—*demolitionism* aims to materially flatten the organs of state power, to make it logistically and socially impossible for the police and courts to assert their claim to rule: in short, to render the situation ungovernable and to make this fact *flagrant* for all to see. It was demolitionist practice and not abolitionist policy that burned the Third Precinct. And what of the pillage of several hundred businesses that accompanied this historic feat? It is important to recall that looting is not simply an attack on the commodity form or a renegade form of consumerism. It is also the most direct way possible for a crowd to concretize, exhibit, and feel the power it has wrenched away from the state and its police, to make this power real, to *fulfill* it. No activity more directly confirms the absence of police control over a territory, the suspension and inoperativity of the law, than looting.[16]

That the burning of the police precinct was a meme was evident to anyone paying attention during the first few days of the revolt. No sooner was the Third Precinct burned than the crowds in Minneapolis spontaneously attempted to torch another one. Similar efforts took place in other cities, including Brooklyn, Reno, and Portland.[17] On May 29, 2020, in Minneapolis, a fierce battle took place over the Fifth Precinct. As happened with the Third, police took to the roof, using flash-bangs and rubber bullets to hold the crowd at bay. That the crowd intended to repeat its successes from days prior was evinced not only by the chain of businesses and government buildings set ablaze across the street and all down the block but more immediately by the Molotov cocktails hurled against the outer walls of the precinct itself. While it is difficult to know for certain, it's quite possible that the Fifth Precinct *was, in fact, evacuated* during the conflict, as police formed a line in the street and pushed the crowd back into a nearby strip mall under a barrage of chemical munitions and flash-bang grenades. Although the crowd made a valiant final push back toward the precinct, it was ultimately unable to disperse the police line before the National Guard stepped in. The battle for a second precinct was fought and lost. The logical task of the movement could not be continued.

The next major opportunity to continue the meme was in Seattle. Although there were elements in the crowd who pushed for burning the precinct after the police withdrew, a combination of paranoid fantasies and arbitrary forced choices (destruction *or* occupation, etc.) ultimately succeeded in deterring them. As a result, what occurred instead was a reversion to the familiar leftist tactic of outdoor occupations popularized during Occupy and more recent anti-ICE protests.[18] From the moment Seattle failed to reproduce the meme of burning precincts, this first phase of the rebellion ended. Other towns would come close: courthouses were briefly set ablaze in Oakland, Portland, Nashville, and Seattle; construction buildings at the site of a new youth detention center were torched in Seattle—yet all fell short of the bar set by Minneapolis.[19] It was not until the eruptions in Colombia and Nigeria that the Minnesotan attack on police infrastructure would be successfully memetically reproduced and the bar raised once again.[20]

As was noted elsewhere, the calibration between *sense* and *gesture* is dynamic and fluid.[21] In some struggles the slogans, ideas, and thought falls short of the tactics and gestures that we're engaging in, and we find ourselves demanding things we already possess or framing things in terms or oppositions that the movement has already surpassed at a practical level. Other times, thought runs ahead of the tactical repertoire, such that every effort to elaborate a practice appropriate to the affective declension of hostilities and the ideas in people's heads seems to fall short. When the George Floyd Rebellion failed to develop its central meme, the ensuing absence of a horizon opened the way for a *social movement apparatus* to insert itself into the confusion and redraw the stakes of the conflict.[22]

Race Treason and the Real Movement

Considered from the outside, the George Floyd Rebellion appears as a historically aberrant "coalition" between socially contraposed identities. While this language makes sense from a certain sociological perspective, the limitation of this point of view is that if one was white-skinned and went hard in the George Floyd Rebellion, one can only articulate this experience negatively, as the position of the "race traitor," and not positively. Since it interprets actions exclusively through their subjective positions within the structure or "diagram" of the racial caste system, the rhetoric of race treason grasps the situation correctly yet externally, from the side of governance. Meanwhile, the phenomenology of race treason—i.e., the description of this subversion from within—remains unwritten.

Nothing is more intimately real than moving in an anonymous mob alongside one another, pulled like moths toward the flame. To describe the experience of last summer's rioting as "treason" is to read it only through the "ban" that structures the anti-Black civil society it left behind, while passing over in silence the penchant that it *abandons itself to.* When we consider things internally, what could appear from the outside only as a betrayal of hegemonic norms often feels like quite the opposite. From the inside, it felt like the *recovery* of a type of qualitative experience that racialized bourgeois society has starved us of: a luminous and confident presence to a shared situation, rich with practical stakes, shared risks, and mutual dependencies. An opportunity to express our nonbelonging to the dominant historical order. Before we can betray our ascriptive identities, we must first put an end to that *treason to ourselves,* that ceaseless betrayal and mutilation of our senses demanded of us by the "sensory religion" of Empire.[23] Whereas "race treason" looks upon this moment from the outside, from an internal or modal perspective—a perspective focused on the grammar of action and experience of presence—we will speak instead of the *real movement.*

Any integral understanding of political events like looting and fighting the police must also account for the restoration of experience that first makes such attacks possible, a restoration of an *ethical* nature. By "real movement" I refer not only to a specific repertoire of methods and gestures but also to the restoration of confidence these presuppose, a certain presence to the world within us to which they attest. *Every uprising is first of all an explosion of vital confidence in our own perceptions, a sudden willingness to take our own lives seriously as the site and source of "legitimate" truth.* The riots last summer would never have happened without a singularization of this sort, in which we refuse to decouple ourselves from our own perception, from our contact with the world. Before it can set out to demolish the present state of things, the real movement first coincides with the messianic assumption of our singular entry into the world: the suppression of mediations, the end of waiting, the moment we stop asking for permission or dialoguing and start doing what makes sense to us for our own reasons. "As one wise vandal sprayed-painted on a wall in Minneapolis: *Welcome back to the world.*"[24]

This internal ethical movement is reflected in the grammar of action of the riot. During the first week of conflict last summer (but also in the explosion in Kenosha, the resurgence of looting in August in Chicago, in Philadelphia after Walter Wallace was murdered, etc.) there was a radical absence of classical discursive political practices. Hardly anyone bothered identifying or subjectivizing themselves, there was virtually no formal or informal dialogue with the state, nor were decisions vetted through assemblies, town hall meetings, or other quasi-democratic forms. By contrast with the amputated speech that characterizes Western classical politics, wherein citizens come together to debate ideas in a space formally separate from the domain of everyday life, when people wanted to "say something" they wrote it with spray paint on the windows and walls of businesses and state property. This linkage of *thought* and *gesture* typifies the real movement. We might even say that the real movement begins the moment people stop looking for some external source to legitimize their actions and instead begin trusting in and acting upon their own sensibilities, their own perception of what makes sense versus what is intolerable. From this moment forward, the whole apparatus of official politics begins to collapse, allowing everyone to see it as the managerial hell it is.

To the extent that the real movement signals an exit from the apparatus of classical politics, we might be tempted to speak here of an "anti-movement" or a movement of "anti-politics." However, the negativity of such formulations would be misleading.[25] What is in question is a positive liberation of conflictual action from established rules and customs, a departure from the constituent logocentric "game" in which politics discovers its consistency in discourse, opinions, and ideological programs and the replacement of this game by another.[26] As Maurice Blanchot knew in his day, any "rupture with the powers that be ... with all the places power predominates" must also be a rupture with "a speech that teaches, that leads, and perhaps [with] all speech." However, as he was quick to insist, this "is not merely a negative moment" but must be understood as a "refusal that affirms, releasing or maintaining an affirmation that does not come to any arrangement but that undoes arrangements, even its own, since it is related to dis-arrangement or disarray, or even the nonstructurable."[27] Hannah Black put it nicely: "communism is a movement away from the state and toward each other. Everything that happens in the street is a lesson because it is a point of contact."[28]

However, what there is of "community" in the real movement is not easily named or identified in a positive sense from without. To speak of a fidelity to one's penchants or of an end to self-treason is not yet to speak positively of community with others. To conjure up a new political subject or "species" (the George Floyd rebel) as some friends have done only avoids the issue without solving it.[29] It is not an accident or an oversight that America has no language by which it could describe race treason internally. Perhaps the problem should actually be reversed: whereas racialization has its origins in a triangular diagram that articulates the humanity of full and partial subjects through the abjection of a third nonsubject position (more on this below), race treason in the Americas belongs within a long lineage of desertion and opacity that affirmatively refuses to appear on the map of dominant history. From the lost colony of Croatan to the Lowry Wars, from Bacon's Rebellion to the Free State of Jones, a powerful yet subterranean history of racial defection and anonymous secession has punctuated American politics since it began.[30] As Kiersten Solt is right to insist, "contrary to every spectacular perspective, the relation between revolutionary elements and their would-be representatives is that of a persistent and asymmetrical conflict."[31] Whether the offer on the table from civil society looked like membership in a failing English plantation economy or entrepreneurial inclusion in the beautiful hell of a racialized late capitalist spectacle, the primary, raw fact of the real communist movement in this country has always responded to a single formula: *recovery of experience = decomposition of the social; the commune in/as the desertion of the social experience we are offered.* The communication experienced during last summer's riots belongs within this lineage: it was "a movement of contestation that, coming from the subject, devastates it, but has as a deeper origin the relationship with the other which is community itself."[32] As Keno Evol observes, to assemble a fighting force is always also to assemble "relations of sustained regard" that, we must add, always remain illegible to the spectacular order.[33]

The Social Movement Apparatus

How was the George Floyd Rebellion defeated? Sixty years ago, an expert in the theory of counterinsurgency warfare distilled the basic strategy into a lapidary formula: the task of counterinsurgency is "[to] build (or rebuild) a political machine from the population upward."[34] When taken to heart, this formula offers a fresh perspective on the repression of the George Floyd movement last summer.

The pacification of the revolt did not occur solely or even primarily through flash-bangs and tear gas but by waging a war over the meaning of the war itself. In response to their messianic self-authorization, the forces of order not only attempt to frontally "crush" the most intense and threatening forms of rupture and rebellion from outside but also to deploy "soft" modes of capture and displacement designed to ratchet down the stakes of conflict by *translating* the conflict into a social movement. This apparatus of translation-pacification of the real movement may be referred to as the *social movement apparatus*.

As Laurent Jeanpierre reminds us, even when they oppose the official institutions of society, social movements "are institutions themselves, since they depend upon legal rules and customs, rules for the game of contestation."[35] In 2014, state media, the left, and the police crushed the Ferguson revolt not only by gassing, beating, and arresting insurgents in the street but also by canalizing the rebellion itself into the framework of leftist politics (Black Lives Matter™). Today, the campaign around "defund" plays a similar role.[36] The operation is always the same: jam the rebellion into a watered-down and sanctioned form of dialogue between recognized constituents and marginalize and criminalize any grammar of action or form of communication that doesn't fit within it. That the apparatus leverages both existing institutional influence and moderately disruptive protests should not mislead us as to its essential meaning, which consists in neutralizing and pacifying the joyful collective confidence that the rebellion instilled in thousands of angry people. By displacing the terms of confrontation from a demolitionist wave to abolitionist demands the social movement apparatus alters the terms of conflict, redirecting the wild, unmediated forms of cooperation, rebellion, and action that initiated the rebellion back into recognizable dialogical grammar of politics, the better to manage and pacify them.

Moreover, while it is customary to associate the term *social movement* with a contestation of state or economic power (whether from the left or the right), dominant institutions also spontaneously adopt its forms when their legitimacy is challenged. We see this both at a superficial level, when police and private property mobilize victimhood structures to shore up their own discredit, and also at a deeper level that penetrates to the very core of the racial matrix in this land.

Locals may recall a farcical moment in 2017, when, after losing control of downtown St. Louis to riotous demonstrators for over an hour, the cops who retook control felt the need to chant in unison, "*Whose streets? Our streets!*" The next night, the police union headquarters had its windows smashed, its walls graffitied, and its police service vehicles vandalized. The union responded by posting a sign on their door declaring, "*We are open. We won't be defeated.*" A union spokesperson told the press that day that the vandals were "trying to intimidate us," that they had "declared war on us"—in fact, police in this country have unceasingly complained of suffering "hate" at the hands of the public ever since. How many times last summer did cops "take a knee" like Colin Kaepernick? It's not just the police either. When businesses write "minority-owned" on their windows in the hopes that they'll escape being looted and torched, we see a similar logic at play: the petty bourgeoisie, seeing that the regime of property is being called into question, translates its claim to ownership into the identity politics of the anti-oppression social movement. In both cases, it's as if a wounded social-institutional structure, noticing that its legitimacy is in the gutter, suddenly begins speaking no longer in the majoritarian voice of juridical society but rather as one organized clique or faction among others. By taking over protest chants and poster slogans, the forms of social domination spontaneously adopt the social movement form to reassert their credibility.

At a deeper level, however, if the racial order on this continent cannot be overthrown by means of a social movement, this is because it was originally produced by one. The structuring racial *diagram* of the Americas does not begin in Port Comfort, Virginia, in 1619;[37] it was forged exactly one hundred years earlier, as a plea to address the suffering of the (part civilized, part savage) "Indian," to which the enslavement of Africans offered a *solution*. The proposal to import slaves en masse from Portugal to the Americas was among the first fruits of a nascent decolonial rationality, when, in his 1520 audience with the crown, the great "Protector of the Indians" Bartolomé de Las Casas proposed replacing the recalcitrant and rapidly dwindling labor supply of Native populations with Africans,[38] a group he believed to be "better suited" to a lifetime of back-breaking toil and social death.[39] It was through Las Casas's civilizing gesture that anti-Blackness entered America, by distinguishing rightful claimants to the mantle of civilization (its junior partners) from those who never can or will find a place in it, because they do not appear on its "anthropological map."[40] The civilizational analogy between the settler and the Native that Las Casas mobilized in his struggle to guarantee recognition for the "Indians" within the universal community of humanity was founded both economically and ontologically on the fungibility of the African slave. In other words, when anti-Blackness first sailed to the Americas, it did so under the indemnifying flag of respectability politics.

The racial order of the "New World" was a binary machine (civilized/savage) only for approximately thirty years; from the 1520s onward, it became a ternary structure (major/minor/nonsubject). Its signature was forged by a decolonial anti-racism that understood that for the "Indians" to become junior partners to Western civilization, the unchallenged enslavement of Africans was necessary. Of course, the half century Las Casas spent pleading his case to the empire did little to halt the genocide of Native Americans. It did, however, serve to install a triangular social apparatus that remains with us today. It is only an apparent irony that Las Casas, "the man often pilloried for advocating, hypocritically, the initiation of the African slave trade," would later be regarded as "one of the philosophical and spiritual progenitors of the abolitionist movement that sprang to life a century and a half after he died."[41] After living through last summer, the irony dissipates. In his moralism, in his pseudo-universalism, in the naiveté of his faith in Christian values and in the conscience of the ruling class, Las Casas remains the disavowed father of Western leftism avant la lettre. The fact that the institution of anti-Black slavery crossed the Atlantic passage cosigned by a salvific humanitarian gesture offers a pertinent reminder that the West is a civilization that can save with its *left* hand only by relegating others to the whip with its right.

This insight also offers a clue about how (and how not) to fight. The ultimate function of the ternary racial diagram was not merely to legitimize the rapine and enslavement of non-European life, it was also a desperate effort to patch the dangerous cracks in its own ruling fiction: the fiction of unitary civilization per se. To defend the universality of Christendom's claim to absolute truth against the major anthropological crisis that menaced it from *without*—"the possibility of multiple true worlds"[42]—but also already from *within*—in the form of an unruly peasantry—a liminal figure was needed. As Ronald Judy has shown, if the Indians were deemed not "irrational" but *unrational* in the manner of children, this was because assigning them the status of "*potentially* civilized" allowed European ideology to internalize and defang the threat they signaled to its order, relegating it to a harmless alterity. By straddling the gap between inside and outside, reason and unreason, the racialized junior partner allows civilizational epistemology to position itself both inside and outside of its own order and, thereby, to master its edges. It is by becoming the principle of both itself and its *other*, by making *its* actuality the destiny of all potentiality, by learning to anticipate forces of subversion and grant them a (subordinate) place in its world that humanism becomes the governing paradigm of the social. "The moment in Western history when the recognition of alternative worlds becomes possible—in the Spanish encounter with the Aztecs—is also the moment when humanism achieves hegemony."[43]

The result, as Frank B. Wilderson has shown, is an ethical ambivalence that becomes foundational for modernity: Do we imagine emancipation in terms of the analogy between "savage" and "settler" and organize ourselves through claims to sovereignty, humanity, inclusion, and recognition (the social movement),[44] or—and this sets up the legacy of race treason in the USA—does one pursue a paradigmatic alliance with Blackness and desert the project of Western humanism? It is a decision that must be made not only by Native Americans and Jews, whose grammar of suffering leaves them suspended between genocidal dislocation and junior sovereignty, but by everyone else too. Those who are not Native must also decide whether to "adjust their logic" to fit that of genocidal ontology or to make their peace with anti-Blackness.[45] However, whereas Wilderson reads this possibility exclusively through worldlessness and ontological death, Judy's insistence on racialization as a response to the "possibility of multiple true worlds" opens up another path: whereas the social movement inherits the civilizational project of *internalizing* all exteriority and alterity through partial inclusions, while Blackening that which it cannot digest, *race treason seeks not inclusion but to explode the fiction of a unified society itself*, by allowing the multiplicity of worlds and forms of life it crushed under its weight to burst forth.

The recent rehabilitation of "vitalist" thought in North America could perhaps be understood from a similar perspective: less an import of European communist thought than a continuation of the American legacy of secessionist race treason. Once wrenched away from the jaws of the spiritualist far right,[46] an affective idea of life can help draw attention to the vital multiplicity that rumbles pitilessly beneath the surface of civilization's unitary façade, undermining the latter's claim to include all subjects actual *and potential*. For instance, applying this insight to the George Floyd Rebellion, H. Bolin and Sonali Gupta describe the virality of its combatant crowds as "a mode of contagion that destabilizes the way constituted groups interface with one another, confusing their position within the established order, which prepares the ground on which destituent powers can emerge."[47]

Neo-abolitionist approaches to decarceration and "non-reformist reforms," beginning in the 1980s, were intended to serve as a combative intervention against the carceral leftism of their day, by helping to "imagine the possibility of shrinking the prison-industrial complex and ending reliance on imprisonment."[48] However, with the return of the real movement, abolitionists now face a stark choice: hold onto the strategy of "non-reformist reformist" policy or accept the strategy of demolition-as-abolition developed in response to George Floyd's murder. If abolitionism's line of flight has now been captured, for it to produce new escapes—into the real movement—it is necessary to *break the frame*.

Just as the real movement can be captured and canalized into the social movement, social movement formations can undergo becomings that place them in contact with the real movement, allowing them to outstrip their managerial frameworks. This is what happened to the Loi Travail movement the moment the *cortège de tête* flipped it into a meme. This is what happened for two months to the established BLM organizations in Chicago last summer, once they allowed themselves to be swept into a physical confrontation with the police and a taboo embrace of imprisoned looters.[49] It is what happened in Portland's "frontliner culture" as new and varied groups of people began showing up at the Justice Center in gas masks and hockey gear spoiling for a fight. As often happens, many of these becomings eventually became blocked, routed, or trapped within a resurgent activist consciousness. But these defections and recompositions were real desubjectifications and desertions in their moment.

We must neither abandon nor embrace social movements; rather, we must explode their frame, cause them to break away, force them to *encounter* their outside and keep them in contact with it. In short, we must place them into *flight*. What we want is both more and less than a social movement: more antagonistic than an institutional framework will ever be able to express—more contagious, more viral, more complex and capable of absorbing becomings, mutations, self-destructions, and rebirths of subjects, and not simply "recognition" of their existing demands—but also less than a social movement, since we don't always want to have to "appear" to one another or to power as a social entity. We don't want to play the games of language, dialogue, critique, and negotiation. We're tired of games whose playing field is stacked against us from the start.

The anthropologist Pierres Clastres defined primitive or "classless" societies by the techniques they develop internally to hold the state function in abeyance. In a similar spirit, today we should seek to identify those features and dimensions of struggles that succeed in warding off capture not simply by the state but also by the social movement apparatus. This is, once again, why some of us have begun to theorize revolt and communist potentialities through the framework of partisan memetics. Memes invite us to take our own singular perception seriously, since they call us to answer them, to *repeat* them, according to the contours of our own life, our own situation, to respond in ways that reverberate with our bodies, while undermining the rigid separations through which the racial order governs our separation. Yet, in and of itself, this is not enough to put us on a long-term revolutionary timeline. Memes alone cannot offer us a *living form* in terms of which we can exist together with others in a long-term way, a shared world to inhabit. What they can do is place the social movement apparatus in flight, break its frame, refuse its discursive and representational interpellation, its episodic temporality, and suppress its tendency to adopt governmental subject-forms as its practical language, but they are not enough to escape the cycles of recuperation, capture, and burnout, nor do they provide a soil in which to plant ourselves in the long term. The meme is a moving train. In the long run, we need to plant roots on something slightly more stable.

Unlike during the Yellow Vests, whose implantation on the roundabouts shifted the *site* of the political to bases situated in an extreme proximity to everyday life, which they filtered through the collective blockades and cabins they constructed, efforts to territorialize the George Floyd Rebellion met with mixed and often disappointing results. From the Capitol Hill Autonomous Zone (CHAZ) in Seattle to the armed paranoia of the Wendy's no-cop zone in Atlanta, the experiments in placemaking—although too locally heterogeneous to be subsumed under any consistent patterns—generally failed to establish lasting consistencies that point beyond the suspended time of the battle. The horizon of the George Floyd

Rebellion remained, for better or for worse, the horizon of the riot, and once its offensive capacities were throttled the real movement had no other possibility but to recede.

Political Riot and Storefront Riot

The movement's offensive capacities, as well as its imagination of its own power, were distributed across two distinct dynamisms. On the one hand, *political riots* target the symbols and halls of state power (city halls, courthouses, police precincts, monuments and statues but also the media); on the other hand, *storefront riots* target merchandise, from big-box stores and banks all the way down to 7-11, cell phone shops, GameStops, etc. Whereas the political riot generally consists in a stationary geography in which crowds attempt to *beat back* police lines and, if possible, sink the enemy's battleship, the merchandise riot is defined by a mobile crowd *in flight* from the police. While the two riots might occur on the same day, or even within the same approximate space (as in Minneapolis), they are distinguished not only by their selection of targets but by the affective dynamism that organizes the crowd: Are we moving forward or backward, toward or away? Is the aim to attack and disperse the police or evade them as long as possible, while consummating our momentary independence? Whereas the siege mentality of a political riot depends upon the sustained conflict with personnel outside highly symbolic sites of state power (e.g., the Justice Center in Portland), in the merchandise riot, the experience of collective power is felt through the maelstrom of vandalism, looting, and arson along its flight path.[50]

Generally, the pattern is for political riots to mutate *into* storefront riots when crowds are driven away from state targets.[51] Sometimes, the mobile crowd may encounter state property along the way, as happened when the Bureau of Corrections building was torched in Kenosha on the second night, but this does not fundamentally challenge the dynamic difference at play in the two riots. This difference is the kernel of truth of that cynical lie by the state when it attempts, as part of its divide and conquer strategy, to drive a wedge between "good" and "bad rioters." In point of fact, the two crowds were already divided, even if neither can be reduced to "pure crime," as the state sought to do.[52]

The combination of these two vectors resulted in a wave of material devastation surpassing any North American rebellion in the twentieth century. Between May 26 and June 8 alone, an estimated $1 to $2 billion dollars in damages were recorded, with mobilizations taking place in some 1,700 cities and towns.[53]

As the liberal-democratic peace was shattered, the ruling classes leveraged all its forces to contain the assault waged upon it. Well-accustomed to siege battles, the police had little trouble sustaining conflicts that were content to remain stationary. Even where they dragged out for quite a while, as in Portland, it is unlikely that the forces of order ever really feared the loss of life or their bases at the hands of the crowd. By contrast, the speed and agility of car looting created unforeseen problems: police would win back one block only to lose another one, and as soon as they pulled out of the first spot, looters would return.[54] Unable to fight *mano a mano* at the scale of the entire city, police were compelled to find another method of projecting their power across the terrain of the city. As a result, the forces of order initiated an unprecedented sequence of infrastructural counterinsurgency. The City of Chicago was truly exemplary in this respect. In response to the second wave of caravan looting on August 10–12, the cybernetic city was replaced by a medieval fortress architecture designed to selectively sever its circulatory flows: bridges were raised; city buses were repurposed as mobile barricades and shuttles for riot police; sanitation, trash, and salt trucks were deployed to block roads and highways; concrete barriers lined the shopping districts; etc. The aim was obvious to everyone: to functionally isolate the Black population from the rich neighborhoods, to raise the drawbridge between the castle and the wilderness beyond.

Infrastructural counterinsurgency carries risks for ruling powers. As the means of urban reproduction are drafted into the theater of war, the veil of social unity projected by the city during peacetime is torn asunder. In this way, by pushing the police order to react infrastructurally, the car looting completed the unprecedented destitution of the fictions of social peace begun by the initial street battles at the end of May.[55] Any pretense of neutrality is withdrawn: police and ruling-class politicians close ranks and defend their turf like the *gang* that they are, public transit is perfunctorily suspended, and capital's cities are exposed as little more than a cluster of apparatuses designed to funnel wealth into white neighborhoods, while containing the racialized proletariat on which it depends at its margins, "included *as excluded*." This visionary destitution of power marked the outer limit that the 2020 revolt was capable of reaching, nakedly exhibiting both the social cruelty and material fragility on which economic and police power rests. It proved that with enough determination, control of America's major cities can be wrenched away from police for days on end, and the avenues where the wealthy live can be devastated.

But the ruling class's counteroffensive was swift and effective. Once its *symbolic* centers were stolen away and its posh storefronts locked off or placed under twenty-four-hour-a-day police surveillance, insurgents were generally unable to develop effective alternate strategies for continuing the offensive. *It has been easy to embarrass power but hard to defeat it.*

It is with this in mind that, stepping back a bit, the twin jets of the political riot and the storefront riot now begin to appear in a different light, almost as if this division (*polis* and *oikos*) were two ends of a single apparatus in which the power of the insurgency had allowed itself to become trapped. What would it look like to overcome this apparatus?

According to a certain line of ultraleft thought, what is needed is for the merchandise riot to ascend the supply chain in reverse, for the storefront riot to mutate into an *infrastructure riot* capable of responding to police logistics by disrupting the circulatory flows on which the economy depends. On this view, short-circuiting the arterial web of capitalist circulation by targeting ports, warehouses, and factories presents a far greater threat to power than emptying retail outlets in shopping districts.[56] Whence the bated breath around the Breonna Taylor verdict,[57] as materialists fantasized about the riots leaping over themselves and disrupting the UPS WorldPort, a key artery for the regional circulation of commodities.[58]

Rather than starting from the map of capital and working backward, we should ask how the impulses that the movement itself engendered might be extended in new directions. On the one hand, it is undeniable that looting by car—to say nothing of the looting of freight trains[59]—already includes within it a certain degree of partisan logistics (encrypted communication, mobile coordination, mastery of the terrain, ingress/egress, etc.), yet one that remains subordinated to the dynamism of the merchandise riot.[60] On the other hand, the occupations of the CHAZ/CHOP in Seattle, the federal courthouse plaza in Portland, and city hall in New York City all attest to a powerful impulse toward placemaking, yet one whose preferred locations were subordinated to the dynamic of the political riot.[61]

For the movement to break the apparatus in which its power was captured would mean disentangling the placemaking impulse of the movement from its one-sided inscription in the political riot and, second, extending the logistical intelligence of car looting beyond the form of the storefront riot.

It is possible—if not entirely easy—to imagine frontliner culture, which has been generally constricted to street battles with police, mutating into an antagonism in a more explicitly infrastructural context. During the insurgency against the authoritarian Chinese state in Hong Kong, the dialectic of repression and retaliation escalated to the point where rebel youth declared open season on the city's public transit system writ large. Four years prior, after the murder of Remi Fraise in France, ZADists teamed up with survivors of police violence to organize a weekend of actions outside a police munitions factory, resulting in fiery demonstrations so dangerous that they shut the factory down for days.[62] While the strength of both approaches lay in aiming their sights *past* the social enemy toward the infrastructural grids on which its power depends, their weakness lay in the exhausting willpower such attacks require to sustain themselves and—in the case of the Nobelsport factory—the remoteness of the terrain from the space of combatants' everyday life.

In this regard, when it comes to combining logistical initiative with situated placemaking, the unsurpassed model remains the roundabout occupations of the Yellow Vests.[63] By embedding themselves in close proximity to the space and time of everyday life, by blocking circulation not at the point of greatest importance *to capital* but at the point where capital enters the space of everyday life (freeway offramps into towns and cities), they politicized the membrane between life and money on terms amenable to them. The true strategic horizon of hinterland blockades is not to suspend the flows of the economy tout court but to produce inhabited territorial bases that *restore* it to the map of everyday life at a level at which it can be *seized upon* and *decided*. As the highway barricades erected by Oaxacan teachers in 2016 clearly demonstrated, successful blockades are *selective*. The model is not the trench but the filter: enemy corporations are turned back or plundered, while the community is waved on with a smile.[64]

However, in the US context, such a leap would imply a qualitative mutation for which there is no linear path. A new memetic repertoire would be necessary, one that speaks not only to decaying suburbs but also to the further out hinterlands: occupations of gas stations and toll booths, slow-rolls, the takeover of vacant strip malls, coordinated looting of Amazon warehouses and freight trains, etc. None of this can happen without the movement posing a radically new *problem*.

Any choice of terrain is a way of posing a question to ourselves about the nature of the war we are fighting. The problem of logistics, as well as that of place, must be understood from this point of view. There is no inherent connection between the riot, the strike, or the blockade of infrastructure, nor is there a natural or quantitative escalation envisionable that would organically lead from one to the other. Herein, we confront some of the ultimate challenges any insurrectional movement must face: how to shift from one frame of war to another and from one image of victory to another, how to change the nature of the conflict *while fighting it*, and how not only to engage in a conflict but to wage a "conflict over conflict" from within its midst, thereby posing a new problem.[65]

Could another rebellion against the police murder of Black lives open up the vortex sufficiently wide that capitalist command comes under fire? Is it possible from within the demolitionist moment to imagine a second, third, or fourth "rhythmic marker" introducing another dynamic into such revolts, as happened in Chile when the memetic rebellion initiated by students mutated to absorb the rage of feminists, Indigenous communities, anarchists, and other groups, becoming a *general antagonism* in which the very notion of constituent power itself is up for grabs?[66]

Without End

No one needs to be told that this world stands on a precipice. The evidence is everywhere. Yet nothing about the catastrophe through which we are living makes a revolution inevitable. What is decisive is not to denounce or critique but to study the seams that allow situations to split open, that let antagonisms spread and generalize, restoring motion and confidence to our lives *here* and *now*. Contemporary struggles don't expand around ideas or ideologies but around gestures that make sense of their moment, around situated truths worth defending. A million correct ideas about the present are swept away by a single act that alters that reality.

When the intolerable explodes again into a public scandal, everything must be done to push for its irreversibility. How do we pivot from demolitionism to collective experiments in nonmonetized sharing? How do we suppress and deactivate the organs of representation that seek to incorporate and disarm us? How do we *exit* the terrain of the social, while creating spaces of communion, desertion, and contact along the way?

While the movement has died back for the time being, the fictions on which social peace rests remain as fragile as ever. Nothing is over. With a lot of tact and a little luck, next time will hit even harder.

May 2021

Publication Information

All articles have been lightly edited for this volume.

Anonymous, "The Siege of the Third Precinct in Minneapolis: An Account and an Analysis," first published in CrimethInc., June 10, 2020.

Shemon and Arturo, "Theses on the George Floyd Rebellion," first published in Ill Will, June 24, 2020.

Inhabit, "A Gift for Humanity: The George Floyd Rebellion," first published as "Dignity: On the George Floyd Rebellion," in Inhabit: Territories, June 29, 2020.

Jarrod Shanahan and Zhandarka Kurti, "Prelude to a Hot American Summer," first published in *Brooklyn Rail*, July–August 2020.

Idris Robinson, "How It Might Should Be Done," first published in Ill Will, August 15, 2020.

New York Post-Left, "Welcome to the Party," first published in It's Going Down, June 24, 2020.

Anonymous, "Frontliners to the Front," Parts I and II, first published in It's Going Down, July 8, 2020.

Nevada, "Imaginary Enemies: Myth and Abolition in the Minneapolis Rebellion," first published in Ill Will, November 21, 2020.

Fran, JF, and Lane, "In the Eye of the Storm: A Report from Kenosha," first published in Hard Crackers, September 7, 2020.

Anonymous, "Rhythm and Ritual: Composing Movement in Portland's 2020," first published in Ill Will, October 14, 2020.

Anonymous, "At the Wendy's: Armed Struggle at the End of the World," first published in Ill Will, November 9, 2020.

Anonymous, "Order Prevails in Louisville," first published as "Breewayy or the Freeway: The Rise of America's Frontliners and Why Louisville Didn't Burn," in It's Going Down, October 15, 2020.

Gilets Jawns, "The End of the Summer," originally published as "About to Explode: Notes on the Walter Wallace Jr. Rebellion in Philadelphia," first published in It's Going Down, November 12, 2020.

Shemon, "The Rise of Black Counterinsurgency," first published in Ill Will, July 30, 2020.

Shemon and Arturo, "The Return of John Brown: White Race Traitors in the 2020 Uprising," first published in Ill Will, September 4, 2020.

Adrian Wohlleben, "Weapons and Ethics," first published in Ill Will, September 18, 2020.

Idris Robinson, "Letter to Michael Reinoehl," first published in Ill Will, October 23, 2020.

Adrian Wohlleben, "Memes without End," first published in Ill Will, May 16, 2021.

Notes

Introduction: Welcome Back to the World

1   On the role of smaller cities in the George Floyd uprising, see Shemon, Arturo, and Atticus, "Fire on Mainstreet: Small Cities in the George Floyd Uprising," It's Going Down, January 4, 2021. For a reconstruction of the entire revolt according to its various sequences or "acts" (to borrow a phrase from the Yellow Vests), see K.N. and Paul Torino, "Life, War, Politics," Ill Will, November 15, 2020. A similar breakdown is found in Shemon and Arturo, "The Return of John Brown: White Race Traitors in the 2020 Uprising," this volume, pages 196–212.

2   See Anonymous, "At the Wendy's: Armed Struggle at the End of the World," this volume, pages 145–61.

3   See "Lessons from Grant Park," Black Lives Matter Chicago, August 2020; also see Anonymous, "Accounts from the Battle of Grant Park," CrimethInc., July 21, 2020.

4   See Anonymous, "Rhythm and Ritual: Constructing Movement in Portland's 2020," this volume, pages 122–44.

5   On "the production of revolutionaries," see "Onward Barbarians," Endnotes, September 2020.

6   See Shemon and Arturo, "Cars, Riots and Black Liberation," Mute Magazine, November 17, 2020; "Spontaneity, Mediation, Rupture," Endnotes, September 2013.

7   W.E.B. Du Bois, *Black Reconstruction* (New York: Free Press, 1992 [1935]); C.L.R. James, "The Historical Development of the Negro in the United States," in Scott McLemee, ed., *C.L.R. James on the "Negro Question"* (Jackson: University Press of Mississippi, 1996).

8   Rosa Luxemburg, "Order Prevails in Berlin," *Die Rote Fahne*, January 14, 1919.

The Siege of the Third Precinct in Minneapolis: An Account and Analysis

1   Editor's note: the partially constructed 189-unit housing complex referenced here ("Midtown Corner") was not, in fact, condominiums. Midtown Corner was a mixed-use development, with retail space on the first floor and a full 189 units of affordable rental housing comprising the upper five floors. Some public confusion may have arisen due to the fact that only 38 of the 189 units were designated "deeply affordable," meaning the rent would be pegged to 60 percent or less of Area Median Income. However, the remaining approximately 150 units were not priced at luxury or market rate; they were designated "affordable," with rent pegged to 80 percent or less of AMI. The development did not contain a single residential unit not slated for affordable rent pricing.

A Gift for Humanity: The George Floyd Rebellion

1   See Matthew Impelli, "54 Percent of Americans Think Burning Down Minneapolis Police Precinct Was Justified After George Floyd's Death," *Newsweek*, June 3 2020.

2   The modern conception of race is deeply tied to the ways in which it was codified in law, incorporated into juridical frameworks, and regulated by courts in the seventeenth century. These legal frameworks laid the groundwork for the deadly ramifications we see today, not just in the popular understanding of race but in institutional/structural inequalities and police violence.

3   We're thinking, for instance, of online commenters desperate to find out the identity of which (white) people committed which acts of destruction. This reactionary quest was exemplified nowhere more than the campaign that resulted in the arrest of Rayshard Brooks's girlfriend for allegedly setting fire to the Wendy's where he was killed by police.

4   The relatively unknown history of the Great Dismal Swamp is an inspiring lesson in what we called that other history of race/resistance. For one of the better accounts of this multiracial exodus, see the indispensable chronicle of the American history of insurrection Saralee Stafford, *Dixie Be Damned: 300 Years of Insurrection in the American South* (Oakland: AK Press, 2015).

5   This point, and the title of this essay, draws considerably on the work of Fred Moten. For Moten, Blackness is always less than and more than. It's a "horrible gift" that he wants to share, because it upends Western ontologies about the subject. Blackness, which is positioned as the object of race, is shaped by struggle against slavery and captivity. In escaping these, Blackness also shapes itself as a new form of life in fugitivity. This gift exposes us all to the fact that we were never subjects to begin with, and, most importantly, that the racial nightmare is undone through inhabiting what he calls the undercommons—the community founded in escape.

Prelude to a Hot American Summer

1   James Baldwin, *The Fire Next Time* (New York: Vintage, 1993), 76.

2   Keeanga-Yamahtta Taylor, "The Black Plague," *New Yorker*, April 16, 2020.

3   Loïc Wacquant, *Prisons of Poverty* (Minneapolis: University of Minnesota Press, 2009); Loïc Wacquant, *Punishing the Poor* (Durham, NC: Duke University Press, 2009); Cedric Johnson, "The Panthers Can't Save Us Now," *Catalyst*, Spring 2017; Mark Jay, "Cages and Crisis: A Marxist Analysis of Mass Incarceration," *Historical Materialism* 27, no. 1 (2019): 1–42.

4   David Campbell, "Stick-Up at Rikers Island," Hard Crackers: Chronicles of Everyday Life, May 1, 2020.

5   C.L.R. James, *The Black Jacobins: Toussaint L'Ouverture and the San Domingo Revolution* (New York: Vintage Books, 1963 [1938]), 138.

6   Unicorn Riot livestream, May 28, 2020.

7   "The Siege of the Third Precinct in Minneapolis: An Account and Analysis," CrimethInc., June 6, 2010.

8   See JF, "The Old Mole Breaks Concrete," Unity and Struggle, December 11, 2014.

9   Unicorn Riot livestream.

10 Sergei Klebnikov, "Floyd Protests Go Global—from Mexico, London, Germany and France—and Sometimes Violent," *Forbes*, June 6, 2020.

11 Rob Picheta, "Protesters Tear Down Statue of Slave Trader as Anti-Racism Demonstrations Take Place Worldwide," CNN, June 8, 2020; Eric Williams, *Capitalism and Slavery* (Chapel Hill: University of North Carolina Press, 1994).

12   Azi Paybarah and Nikita Stewart, "Symbol of N.Y.C. Unrest: The Burning Police Car," *New York Times*, May 31, 2020.

13   Emily Witt, "Protesting Past Curfew in New York City," *New Yorker*, June 4, 2020.

14   Back the Blue (@ChicagoPD19), "Great job protestors. The Chicago Police Department has one hundred less cars to serve and protect the citizens of Chicago. Tax payers will pay for new cars!" Twitter, June 4, 2020, accessed March 28, 2022, https://twitter.com/ChicagoPD19/status/1268685906250215425.

15   Fernando Alphonso III, "CNN Center in Atlanta Damaged during Protests," CNN, May 29, 2020.

16   James Stephens and JJ McAffee, "In the Streets of Philadelphia," Hard Crackers: Chronicles of Everyday Life, June 14, 2020.

17   John Bowden, "25-Year-Old Arrested for Allegedly Setting Fire to Nashville's Historic Courthouse," Hill, May 31, 2020.

18   Allison Pries, "These Are All the Cities Where Protests and Riots Have Erupted Over George Floyd's Death," NJ.COM, June 2, 2020; Saja Hindi and Sam Tabachnik, "Denver Businesses Assess Vandalism, Looting Costs After George Floyd Protests," *Denver Post*, May 30, 2020; Matt Galka, "Unrest in Downtown Phoenix amid Protest over Deaths of George Floyd, Dion Johnson; Two Arrested," Fox News 10 Phoenix, May 30, 2020.

19   Jesse Paul, "Police Arrest 83 for Curfew Violations, Denver Mayor Calls After-Dark Mayhem 'Reckless, Inexcusable and Unacceptable,'" *Colorado Sun*, May 31, 2020.

20   Aaron Mesh, "Video: Portland Protesters Smash Windows and Set Fires inside Multnomah County Justice Center," *Willamette Week*, May 30, 2020.

21   "The Siege of the Third Precinct in Minneapolis."

22   Hallie Golden, "Seattle Protesters Take Over City Blocks to Create Police-Free 'Autonomous Zone,'" *Guardian*, June 11, 2020.

23   "The Siege of the Third Precinct in Minneapolis."

24   Tim Balk, "These 13 Protestors Have Died Since George Floyd Protests Started Last Week," *Daily News*, June 3, 2020.

25   Brakkton Booker, "Louisville Hosts Public Viewing for David McAtee as Details of His Shooting Emerge," NPR, June 12, 2020.

26   Jennifer Wadsworth, "SJPD Mains Activist Who Helped Train Officers About Implicit Bias," *San Jose Inside*, June 6, 2020.

27   Brandon Conradis, "Clashes, Fires Near White House as Protests Escalate," Hill, May 31, 2020.

28   Molly Olmstead, "White House Goes Completely Dark as Protests Rage Outside," Slate, June 1, 2020.

29   Ryan Browne, Alicia Lee, and Renee Rigdon, "There Are as Many National Guard Members Activated in the US as There Are Active Duty Troops in Iraq, Syria and Afghanistan," CNN, June 1, 2020.

30   "Minneapolis Protest," All Gas No Brakes, June 8, 2020.

31   Matthew Impelli, "54 Percent of Americans Think Burning Down Minneapolis Police Precinct Was Justified After George Floyd's Death," *Newsweek*, June 3, 2020.

32   Kuwasi Balagoon, "Brinks Trial: Closing Statement," *A Soldier's Story: Writings by a Revolutionary New Afrikan Anarchist* (Montréal: Kersplebedeb Publishing, 2003 [2001]).

33   Unicorn Riot livestream.

34   George Ciccariello-Maher, "Blaming 'Outside Agitators' Is a Centuries-Old Ploy," *Wall Street Journal*, June 7, 2020; "This is a Public Service Announcement (Without Guitars)," Hard Crackers: Chronicles of Everyday Life, June 2, 2020.

35   Sanya Mansoor, "Local Officials and Trump Were Quick to Blame Out-of-State Agitators for Minneapolis' Violent Protests. Arrest Records Suggest Otherwise," *Time*, May 31, 2020; Eric Flack and Jordan Fisher, "Nearly 90% of People Arrested for Riot Crimes and Vandalism Are from DMV, Police Say," WUSA9 News, June 8, 2020; Ted Oberg and Sarah Rafique, "13 Investigates: Most of Houston's Protest Arrests Were Locals," ABC 13 Eyewitness News, June 2, 2020; David Krowman and Lilly Fowler, "'Outside Agitator' Narrative Not Supported by Data," Crosscut, June 3, 2020; Michael McGough and Dale Kasler, "Sacramento Leaders Blamed Recent Havoc on Outsiders. Nearly All Arrests Were Locals," *Sacramento Bee*, June 3, 2020; Monique Madan, Joey Flechas, and David Smiley, "Miami Chief, Mayor Deride Arrested Protesters as 'Outsiders': But 30 of 57 are from County," *Miami Herald*, May 31, 2020.

36   Oliver O'Connell, "Questions Raised Over Masked White Man with Umbrella Seen Calmly Smashing Windows Before Minneapolis Riots," *Independent*, May 29, 2020.

37   Katie Kim and Lisa Capitanini, "Extremist Groups May Be Infiltrating Protests," NBC Chicago, June 5, 2020; EJ Dickson, "People Claim Authorities Are Intentionally Planting Bricks to Bait Protesters," *Rolling Stone*, June 3, 2020.

38   Neil MacFarquhar, Alan Feuer, and Adam Goldman, "Federal Arrests Show No Sign That Antifa Plotted Protest," *New York Times*, June 11, 2020.

39   This is discussed at length in Cedric Johnson, *Revolutionaries to Race Leaders: Black Power and the Making of African American Politics* (Minneapolis: University of Minnesota Press, 2007); Keeanga Yahmatta-Taylor, *From #BlackLivesMatter to Black Liberation* (Chicago: Haymarket Books, 2016), chapter 7.

40   For a historical account of the role of criminal justice nonprofits in the wider counterinsurgency strategies of the New York City ruling class in the late 1960s, see Jarrod Shanahan and Zhandarka Kurti, "Managing Disorder in the 1960s: The New York City Model," Gotham Center for New York City History (blog), January 7, 2020.

41   Miller Jonathan Reuben, "Devolving the Carceral State: Race, Prisoner Reentry, and the Micro-Politics of Urban Poverty Management," *Punishment & Society* 16, no. 3 (July 2014): 305–35; Reuben Jonathan Miller and Amanda Alexander, "The Price of Carceral Citizenship: Punishment, Surveillance and Social Welfare Policy in the Age of Carceral Expansion," *Michigan Journal of Race and Law* 21, no. 2 (January 2016): 291–314; Ruth Wilson Gilmore, "In the Shadow of the Shadow State," in *Navigating Neoliberalism, Academy, Nonprofits, and Beyond* 13, no. 2 (Spring 2016); Zhandarka Kurti and Jarrod Shanahan, "Rebranding Mass Incarceration: The Lippman Commission and 'Carceral Devolution' in New York City," *Social Justice: A Journal of Crime, Conflict and World Order* 45, nos. 2–3 (2018): 23–50; Brendan McQuade, *Pacifying the Homeland: Intelligence Fusion and Mass Supervision* (Berkeley: University of California Press, 2019).

42   Mike O'Meara, Press Conference, June 9, 2020.

43   Grante Schulte, "George Floyd Protests Spread to Smaller, Mostly White Towns," ABC News, June 7, 2020.

44   Loïc Wacquant, *Punishing the Poor* (Durham, NC: Duke University Press, 2009); David Garland, *The Culture of Control: Crime and Social Order in Contemporary Society* (Oxford: Oxford University Press, 2001); Ruth Wilson Gilmore, *Golden Gulag: Prisons, Surplus, Crisis and Opposition in Globalizing California* (Berkeley: University of California Press, 2007); Mark Jay, "Cages and Crisis: A Marxist Analysis of Mass Incarceration," *Historical Materialism* 27, no. 1 (2019): 182–223;

Jack Norton, "Cut the Carceral System Now," *New York Review of Books*, June 6, 2020; for a global context, see Stuart Hall, *Policing the Crisis: Mugging, the State and Law and Order* (London: Palgrave, 1978).

45 Michelle Alexander, *The New Jim Crow: Mass Incarceration in an Age of Color Blindness* (New York: New Press, 2010); Adaner Usmani, "Did Liberals Give Us Mass Incarceration" *Catalyst* 1, no. 3 (Fall 2017); Alex Vitale, *End of Policing* (London: Verso, 2017).

46 "Freedom to Thrive: Reimagining Safety & Security in Our Communities," Center for Popular Democracy, June 4, 2017.

47 Jordan Camp, *Incarcerating the Crisis: Freedom Struggles and the Rise of the Neoliberal State* (Berkeley: University of California Press, 2016); Timothy L. Lombardo, *Blue-Collar Conservatism: Frank Rizzo's Philadelphia and Populist Politics* (Philadelphia: University of Pennsylvania Press, 2018).

48 Across the country a large section of the working class is homeless; see "Working While Homeless: A Tough Job for Thousands of Californians," NPR, September 30, 2018; D.W. Gibson, "Eight New Yorkers Explain Why It's So Hard to Stop Being Homeless," *New York Magazine*, March 2017.

49 Unicorn Riot livestream.

50 "Investigative Update on Critical Incident Concerning Minneapolis Police," Press Release Desk Minneapolis Police Department, May 26, 2020; Joe Prince, "Teen Who Filmed George Floyd Video Says She's Traumatized by Online Abuse," Complex, May 28, 2020.

51 MPR News Staff, "Timeline: The Jamar Clark Shooting, Aftermath," MPR News, November 30, 2015.

52 Maki Becker, "57 Members of Buffalo Police Riot Response Team Resign After Shoving Incident," *Buffalo News*, June 6, 2020.

53 Rebecca Hill, "'The Common Enemy Is the Boss and the Inmate': Police and Prison Guard Unions in New York in the 1970s–1980s," *Labor: Studies in Working Class History of the Americas* 8, no. 3 (Fall 2011): 65–96; Jarrod Shanahan, "Solidarity Behind Bars: NYC Correction Officers Benevolent Association," *Brooklyn Rail*, September 2017; Jarrod Shanahan, "'White Tigers Eat Black Panthers,' New York City's Law Enforcement Group," Gotham Center for New York City History (blog), March 21, 2019.

54 Chris McGreal, "Anger as Local Police Union Chief Calls George Floyd a 'Violent Criminal,'" *Guardian*, June 1, 2020.

55 O.H. Groth, "Don't Fall for the Copaganda: They'll Take a Knee, Then Tear Gas Thousands," *Left Voice*, June 3, 2020.

56 Carol Boyce Davies, *Left of Karl Marx: The Political Life of Black Communist Claudia Jones* (Durham, NC: Duke University Press, 2008).

57 Alexander, *The New Jim Crow*; Khalil Gibran Muhammad, *The Condemnation of Blackness: Race, Crime and the Making of Modern Urban America* (Cambridge, MA: Harvard University Press, 2011).

58 Kayleigh Skinner, Kelsey Davis Betz, and Aallyah Wright, "'Fed the F— Up': Why Young Activists Are Organizing Protests across Mississippi," *Mississippi Today*, June 5, 2020.

59 For further discussion of this theme, see "Accomplices Not Allies," Indigenous Action, May 4, 2014; "The East Flatbush Rebellion, Not 'Outside Agitators,'" Fire Next Time, March 14, 2013.

60 Anna Quinn, "Uptown Calls for Unity After Protest Confrontation Goes Viral," Patch, June 3, 2020.

61 Jacqueline Serrato, "Abandoned Communities Arrange Black and Brown Truce," *South Side Weekly*, June 9, 2020.
62 Théorie Communiste, "The Glass Floor," in Théo Cosme, *Les Émeute en Grèce* (Geneva: Senonevero, 2009).
63 Cited in TZ, "Burn Down the Prison," Unity and Struggle, December 11, 2014.
64 Randy Furst, "Minneapolis' Janeé Harteau Breaking the Mold as Chief of Police," *Star Tribune*, November 28, 2012.
65 Peter Callaghan, "The Professors and the Police: How a Minneapolis Project May Change the Way Cops Everywhere Relate to the Public," MinnPost, August 27, 2015.
66 Libor Jany, "Justice Department Releases Report on MPD 'Early Intervention System,'" *Star Tribune*, January 28, 2015.
67 Jamiles Lartey and Simone Weichselbaum, "Before George Floyd's Death, Minneapolis Police Failed to Adopt Reforms, Remove Bad Officers," Marshall Project, May 28, 2020.
68 "Use of Force Policy," Minneapolis Police Department, June 28, 2016.
69 "Progressive Police Initiatives," Inside MN PD, October 2016.
70 Libor Jany, Andy Mannix, and Eric Roper, "Minneapolis Police Chief Janeé Harteau Resigns; Protesters Shout Down Mayor Betsy Hodges," *Star Tribune*, July 22, 2017.
71 "Minneapolis Police Department 2018: Focusing on Procedural Justice Internally and Externally," Inside MPD, June 2017.
72 Jeff Hargarten, Jennifer Bjorhus, Mary Jo Webster, and Kelly Smith, "Every Police-Involved Death in Minnesota Since 2000," *Star Tribune*, May 31, 2020.
73 Zachary Siegel, "'Starve the Beast': A Q&A with Alex S. Vitale on Defunding the Police," *Nation*, June 4, 2020.
74 Campaign Zero, "#8CantWait."
75 #8toAbolition, "Abolition Can't Wait."
76 Critical Resistance, "Abolish Police"; Angela Davis, *Are Prisons Obsolete?* (New York: Seven Stories Press, 2003); Incite!, *The Revolution Will Not Be Funded: Beyond the Non-Profit Industrial Complex* (Boston: South End Press, 2007); Ruth Wilson Gilmore, *Golden Gulag: Prisons, Surplus, Crisis, and Opposition in Globalising California* (Berkeley: University of California Press, 2007); Dan Berger, Mariame Kaba, and Dave Stein, "What Abolitionists Do," *Jacobin*, August 24, 2017; Tyler Wall and David Correia, *Police: A Field Guide* (London: Verso, 2018); Michelle Brown, "Transformative Justice and New Abolition in the United States," in Pat Carlen and Leandro Ayres França, eds., *Justice Alternatives* (New York, Routledge, 2020); Mariame Kaba, "Yes We Mean Literally Abolish the Police," *New York Times*, June 12, 2020; Brendan McQuade, "The Camden Police Is Not a Model for Policing in the Post-George Floyd Era," Appeal, June 12, 2020.
77 Barr has been waiting for this moment since 1968, when as a freshman at Columbia University he joined the "Majority Coalition" to combat New Left protesters; see Paul Cronin, "The Time That Bill Barr Faced Down Protesters—Personally," Politico, June 7, 2020.
78 Mark Neocleous, *Fabrication of Order: A Critical Theory of Police Power* (London: Pluto Press, 2000).
79 Hannah Jones, "Black Visions Collective: Meet Some of the Protestors that Shut Down Pride," *City Pages*, July 2, 2018.
80 No New Jails NYC, "Close Rikers Now: We Keep Us Safe."
81 "Cutting Funding for Police Could Lead to a Better and Safer Chicago," *Chicago Sun Times*, June 8, 2020.

82   Nicole Sperling, "'Cops,' Long-Running Reality Show That Glorified Police, Is Cancelled," *New York Times*, June 9, 2020.
83   "Minneapolis Protest."
84   Julia Lurie, "They Built a Utopian Sanctuary in a Minneapolis Hotel. Then They Got Evicted," *Mother Jones*, June 12, 2019.
85   For the counterinsurgent history of the Ford Foundation, see Robert Allen, *Black Awakening in Capitalist America*, excerpted in INCITE!, *The Revolution Will Not Be Funded* (Boston: South End Press, 2009); Karen Ferguson, *Top Down: The Ford Foundation, Black Power and the Reinvention of Racial Liberalism* (Philadelphia: University of Pennsylvania Press, 2013); Shanahan and Kurti, "Managing Urban Discontent."
86   Eric Levitz, "Defunding the Police Is Not Nearly Enough," *New York Magazine*, June 12, 2020; Michelle Alexander, "America This Is Your Chance," *New York Times*, June 8, 2020.
87   New York City's homeless crisis costs over $3 billion a year and is managed largely through collaboration between the state and third-party sector; Melanie Grayce West, "New York City's Spending on Homeless Hits $3.2 Billion This Year," *Wall Street Journal*, May 22, 2019.
88   Kristian Williams, *Our Enemies in Blue: Police and Power in America* (Oakland: AK Press, 2004).
89   On this imperative, see Kali Akuno, "From Rebellion to Revolution," *Viewpoint*, June 11, 2020.
90   Karl Marx, *The Civil War in France* (Peking: Foreign Language Press, 1970), 73.

How It Might Should Be Done

1   Nikolay Gavrilovich Chernyshevsky, *A Vital Question; or, What Is to Be Done?* (New York: Thomas Y. Crowell, 1886).
2   Vladimir Ilyich Lenin, *What Is to Be Done?* (Moscow: Foreign Languages Publishing House, 1961 [1902]).
3   Tiqqun, "How Is It to Be Done?" Void Network, June 15, 2020.
4   "Interactive Map: Protests in Wake of George Floyd Killing Touch All 50 States," Ipsos, accessed July 10, 2020.
5   Jeffery Martin, "What Is Operation Legend? Trump May Use Federal Forces in U.S. Cities," *Newsweek*, July 20, 2020.
6   Peggy McIntosh, "White Privilege: Unpacking the Invisible Knapsack," National Seed Project, July 10, 2020.
7   John Clegg and Idris Robinson, "Racial Capitalism and Disposable Populations in the Time of Covid," Red May TV, May 15, 2020.
8   Toni Cade Bambara, ed., *The Black Woman: An Anthology* (New York: Washington Square Press, 2005 [1970]).
9   James Baldwin, "Going to Meet the Man," in *Going to Meet the Man* (New York: Vintage Books, 1993 [1965]).
10   Black Liberation Army member Sundiata Acoli was arrested and imprisoned in 1973. He received parole in 2022, at the age of eighty-five.
11   John Clegg, "How Slavery Shaped American Capitalism," *Jacobin*, August 28, 2019; L. Robin Einhorn, "Slavery," *Enterprise & Society* 9, no. 3 (September 2008): 491–506.
12   Marten Bjork, "Phase Two—The Reproduction of This Life," Tillfällighetsskrivande, June 23, 2020.
13   The Invisible Committee, *To Our Friends* (Los Angeles: Semiotexte, 2014).
14   "Zombie Preparedness," Center for Disease Control and Prevention.

15   Kenneth Rexroth, *An Autobiographical Novel* (New York: New Direction, 1991).
16   W.E.B. Du Bois, *Black Reconstruction* (New York: Free Press, 1992 [1935]).
17   Pier Paolo Pasolini, *In Danger: A Pasolini Anthology* (San Francisco: City Lights, 2010).
18   Walter Benjamin, "Theses on the Philosophy of History," in Hannah Arendt, ed., *Illuminations* (New York: Schocken Books, 1969).

Welcome to the Party
1   Corey Kilgannon and Juliana Kim, "New Woe for a Jittery N.Y.C.: Illegal Fireworks Going Off All Night," *New York Times*, June 19, 2020.

Frontliners to the Front, Part II: Between Politics and Rebellion in Atlanta
1   See Larry Buchanan, Quoctrung Bui, and Jugal K. Patel, "Black Lives Matter May Be the Largest Movement in U.S. History," *New York Times*, July 3, 2020.

Imaginary Enemies: Myth and Abolition in the Minneapolis Rebellion
1   The present article is based on a talk first delivered across the street from the burned remains of the Third Precinct in Minneapolis, Minnesota, on October 29, 2020.
2   In Minnesota, the state's attention to Boogaloo Bois continued months after the attack on the Third Precinct. On October 24, the FBI charged a Boogaloo Boi for shooting his gun at the Third Precinct after it was surrendered by the police on May 28. This relatively minor act was magnified by news media outlets to falsely portray the destruction of the police building as the work of white supremacist agitators.
3   This insight comes from the essay "Memes with Force." The authors argue that in the logic of the Yellow Vests movement there lies a way out of the traditional political narratives to which I refer here. Before going on to show how looting and vandalism marginalized the influence of the far right, they urge us to see "radical actions," not "radical actors": "Contemporary politics sees in action nothing but a *conversation* between constituencies and populations in society. It is for this reason that, when radical activity emerges in a way that is relatively anonymous, that lacks a consistent author, and persistently refuses to answer to our compositional ('who are you?') and projectual questions ('why are you doing this?'), it tends to be unrecognizable to political analysts and activists alike. It is precisely this received wisdom that the Yellow Vests have been laying to waste, week after week. What is emerging today in France is a radical form of collective action that does not rely on a coherent ideology, motivation, participant, or regional location. Above all, it is not proceeding by means of a dialogue with its enemy"; Paul Torino and Adrian Wohlleben, "Memes with Force: Lessons from the Yellow Vests," Mute Magazine, February 26, 2019.
4   For further analysis of the "outside agitator" as a strategy of delegitimation, with historical comparisons to the George Floyd Rebellion, see "The Anti-Black and Anti-Semitic History of 'Outside Agitators': An Interview with Spencer Sunshine," It's Going Down, June 2, 2020.
5   Marquis Bey, *Anarcho-Blackness: Notes toward a Black Anarchism* (Oakland: AK Press, 2020) cites Fred Moten and Stefano Harney, *The Undercommons*, which also meditates on this refusal of ideological exclusion: "Upon a re-reading of *The Undercommons*, I was drawn, obsessively, to one phrase, one that struck me

NOTES TO PAGES 106-109

at first as dangerously wrongheaded. But, then, the revolutionary will always be dangerous. The revolutionary call that Moten and Harney require and that I've been obsessed with is this: they insist that our radical politics, our anarchic world-building must be 'unconditional—the door swings open for refuge even though it may let in police agents and destruction.' As my grandmother might quip, what kind of foolishness is this? But it is not foolishness precisely because the only ethical call that could bring about the radical revolutionary overturning we seek is one that does not discriminate or develop criteria for inclusion and, consequently, exclusion." In an interview from 2013, Moten discusses Fred Hampton's statement, "White power to white people. Black power to black people." Moten follows: "What I think he meant is, look: the problematic of coalition is that coalition isn't something that emerges so that you can come help me, a maneuver that always gets traced back to your own interests. The coalition emerges out of your recognition that it's fucked up for you, in the same way that we've already recognized that it's fucked up for us. I don't need your help. I just need you to recognize that this shit is killing you, too, however much more softly, you stupid motherfucker, you know?"; see Stefano Harney and Fred Moten, *The Undercommons: Fugitive Planning and Black Study*, edited by Erik Empson (New York: Minor Compositions, 2013), 140–141. On this connection, see Shemon and Arturo's text on the participation of white people in the revolt and its significance; Shemon and Arturo, "The Return of John Brown: White Race Traitors in the 2020 Uprising," this volume, pages 196–212.

6   I am building off of what philosopher Giorgio Agamben has proposed to call a "destituent power," which has influenced the writings of other revolutionaries on the uprising, such as a piece that appeared in CrimethInc. earlier this summer: "Unlike protests, which employ a means (e.g., a march or a blockade) to reach an end (e.g., sending a message or making demands), the events of the uprising ... blur this distinction. They create a kind of means-as-end, or means-without-end, in which the purpose is inextricable from the lived experience of the event itself. To fuse means and ends in this way, we have to move beyond the predetermined choreography of protest to a more transformative paradigm of action. 'I'll never forget that night' reads the latest graffiti written on the barricades surrounding the precinct, referring to the night of May 28 on which unrelenting crowds forced police to retreat from their station and established a brief yet real police-free zone—*abolition in real time*."; "July 4 in Minneapolis: The Logic of Autonomous Organizing," CrimethInc., July 6, 2020.

7   Idris Robinson has argued that the attack on this inner connection between race and property was at the heart of the George Floyd Rebellion. He says: "Whitey loves property. Property enjoys a special prestige in American life, it has a special kind of sanctity.... There is a very important reason that property has this particular kind of sanctity in America, as many historians are starting to confirm and argue. For most of its history, the most important property in America was human property, shackled and chained. We need to weaponize this argument, and say that whenever property is protected, it is protected for white supremacist ends. If property is truly the pursuit of happiness, in that trifecta of life, liberty, and the pursuit of happiness, the existence of that happiness and property is premised upon the negation of Black life and the negation of Black liberty. So the protection of property is something that we need to attack explicitly"; Idris Robinson, "How It Might Should Be Done," this volume, pages 61–76. In her recent book, *In Defense of Looting*, Vicky Osterweil traces the inextricable history of race, settler-colonialism,

and property, building off thinkers like Cedric Robinson, who coined the term *racial capitalism*. The thrust of what I have written here can be summed up by the following passage from her book: "Not only is capitalist development completely reliant on racialized forms of power, but bourgeois legality itself, enshrining at its center the right to own property, fundamentally relies on racial structures of human nature to justify this right. Private property is a racial concept, and race, a propertarian one"; Vicky Osterweil, *In Defense of Looting: A Riotous History of Uncivil Action* (New York: Bold Type Books, 2020), 36.

8   As Frank B. Wilderson has put it, "I'm not against police brutality, I'm against the police"; see his 2015 interview with IMIXWHATILIKE. On the crucial distinction between restorative and transformative justice, see Ejeris Dixon and Leah Lakshmi Piepzna-Samarasinha, eds., *Beyond Survival: Strategies and Stories from the Transformative Justice Movement.*

At the Wendy's: Armed Struggle at the End of the World

1   The story of Natalie White is more sinister than often reported. Missing from the account that she was Rayshard's girlfriend is the fact that Rayshard was also married. The story after that is well known. Natalie was hunted down after videos circulated on social media of a white woman allegedly setting fire to the building, but the Atlanta Police Department didn't move to arrest her until after the funeral, which she wasn't present at. After the family went through its grieving process together, the state then moved in to take out the "extramarital" partner, further isolating her from Rayshard's Black family. The majority Black APD could, thus, attempt to align itself with Rayshard's family on the basis of Black identity, while attempting to isolate Natalie White from the family, in a bid to get the family to disidentify with the revolt that unfolded after Rayshard's killing.

2   From the French *zone à défendre*, or "zone to defend."

3   "On Black Leadership and Other White Myths," Ill Will, June 4, 2020.

4   James Carr, *Bad: The Autobiography of James Carr* (New York: Three Rooms Press, 2016 [1975]).

5   For two takes with seemingly entirely different understandings of civil war and conclusions about its desirability, see Idris Robinson, "Letter to Michael Reinoehl," this volume, pages 218–23; *Between Electoral Politics and Civil War: Anarchists Confront the 2020 Election*, CrimethInc.

Order Prevails in Louisville

1   On the *potlatch of destruction*, see Guy Debord, "The Decline and Fall of the Spectacle-Commodity Economy," in *The Situationist International Anthology*, ed. Ken Knabb (Berkeley, CA: Bureau of Public Secrets, 2006).

2   See Phil Neel, *Hinterland: America's New Landscape of Class and Conflict* (London: Reaktion Books, 2018), 99.

The End of the Summer

1   See Idris Robinson, "How It Might Should Be Done," this volume, pages 61–76.

2   See New York Post-Left, "Welcome to the Party," this volume, pages 78–85.

The Return of John Brown: White Race Traitors in the 2020 Uprising

1   C.L.R. James, *The Black Jacobins: Toussaint L'Ouverture and the San Domingo Revolution* (London: Penguin Books, 2001 [1938]).

2   W.E.B. Du Bois, *Black Reconstruction* (New York: Free Press, 1998 [1935]).

3   Frantz Fanon, *A Dying Colonialism* (New York: Grove Press, 1965 [1959]).
4   Cedric Robinson, *Black Marxism* (London: Zed Books, 1983).
5   Sylvia Wynter, "1492: A New World View," in Vera Lawrence Hyatt and Rex Nettleford, eds., *Race, Discourse, and the Origin of the Americas: A New World View* (Washington, DC: Smithsonian Institute Press, 1995).
6   Russell Maroon Shoats, "The Dragon and the Hydra: A Historical Study of Organizational Methods," 4STRUGGLEMAG, July 23, 2010. Russell Maroon Shoats, a member of the Black Liberation Army, was arrested in 1972 in connection with the shooting death of Philadelphia police sergeant Frank Von Colln. Sentenced to life, Shoats received compassionate release on October 26, 2021, less than two months before dying of colorectal cancer on December 17, 2021.
7   Noel Ignatin (later Ignatiev), 1972, "Black Worker, White Worker," Sojourner Truth, 1969–1986 Archives.
8   E.D. Mondainé, "Portland's Protests Were Supposed to Be about Black Lives. Now, They're White Spectacle," *Washington Post*, July 23, 2020.

Weapons and Ethics

1   Walter Benjamin, "Critique of Violence" (1921), in *Walter Benjamin: Selected Writings, 1: 1913–1926*, eds. Marcus Bullock and Michael W. Jennings (Cambridge, MA: Belknap Press, 1996).

Letter to Michael Reinoehl

1   Walter Benjamin, "Critique of Violence," in *Walter Benjamin: Selected Writings, 1: 1913–1926*, eds. Marcus Bullock and Michael W. Jennings (Cambridge, MA: Belknap Press, 1996), 250.
2   Robert Kenner, dir., "John Brown's Holy War," *American Experience* (Arlington, VA: Public Broadcasting System, 2000).
3   Ron Hahne and Ben Morea, "Chapter Report on the S.D.S. Regional Council," in *Black Mask and Up Against the Wall Motherfucker* (Oakland: PM Press, 2011), 141.

Memes without End

1   Paul Torino and Adrian Wohlleben, "Memes with Force: Lessons from the Yellow Vests," Mute Magazine, February 26, 2019; "Memes with Force: Transforming the Political Imaginary on the Subject," *Interchange Radio* (podcast).
2   "In contemporary insurrections…[the] hierarchical structure of command and its concomitant drive toward unity is being replaced by a form of immanent collective intelligence. Gestures and communication spread across an increasingly fragmented *socius* without consolidating any coherent organizational body or identity. Actions and tactics, shared on Telegram or social media and *detourned* to fit the needs of specific locales, spread in a memetic fashion"; Anonymous, "At the Wendy's: Armed Struggle at the End of the World," this volume, pages 145–61.
3   Gilles Deleuze and Félix Guattari, *Anti-Oedipus* (Minneapolis: University of Minnesota Press, 204), 315.
4   "Truckers shuttin it down outside Chicago!! #BlackSmokeMatters, #TruckerStrike," @MPHproject, Twitter, April 12, 2019.
5   "Neighborhood Water Gun Fight Leaves Atlanta Police Officers Soaked," 11 Alive News, June 3, 2019; available on YouTube.
6   For a timeline of events, see "Chronology on Chile's Inequality Crisis," Ciudadanía Inteligente.

7   "Yes, and: Results from the North American Contagious Antagonisms Inquiry (2007–2012)," Society for the Advancement of Criminal Science, April 2012; reprinted in *War in the Streets: Tactical Lessons from the Global Civil War* (Chicago: Ill Will Editions, 2016).

8   Occupy Wall Street was initially constructed on a memetic platform. The meme was as follows: "seize a plaza, set up autonomous circuits of social reproduction, make decisions through consensus, defend the occupation where necessary." In principle, anyone who showed up could take part; there was no "prior" belonging that authorized participation, nor were there central "demands" through which the movement indexed itself to any particular social subject in an a priori way. However, within a matter of weeks the movement had rigorously institutionalized *itself*: democratic proceduralism, activist virtue signaling, and endless "working groups" threw it back on itself, directing its energies inward rather than outward. When we showed up at the occupation, we were singularities, but to "participate" meant being drafted into constituent compositions modeled entirely on centralized decision-making and representational obsessions. Fairly soon, the only moments that felt powerful were when the state took the initiative to evict the occupations, thereby interrupting the democratic echo chamber. From Occupy, we learned two things: (i) the central contradiction today is no longer between vertical and horizontal organizing methods, nor is it between organizing inside or outside of *formal* institutional channels—all meaningful mass action today is horizontal, and only those movements that begin outside institutions will ever reach the point of constituting a threat; (ii) in fact, the central contradiction is between movements that retain the framework of classical politics—i.e., whose *means* rely on discourse and dialogue, and whose *ends* lie in the advancement of symbolic and hegemonic influence within civil society—and those movements that challenge the apparatus of "political speech," and representation by sidestepping any reference to a constituent subject and developing other modes of collaboration and communication. That said, although this basic difference remains decisive, we will most likely continue to see strange amalgams in the coming years.

9   The prefix *ante-* is intended to mark the fact that the event of revolt is not sui generis but mobilizes vital forms that were "already to some extent present"; see K.N. and Paul Torino, *Life, War, and Politics: After the George Floyd Rebellion* (Chicago: Ill Will, 2020), part 3; an analogous idea lies at the base of the concept of "the surround" in Stefano Harney and Fred Moten, *The Undercommons: Fugitive Planning & Black Study* (Wivenhoe, UK: Minor Compositions, 2013).

10   "What is a demand?... [It] is a contract, the guaranteed expiration date of one's struggle, the conditions for its conclusion"; Johann Kaspar, "We Demand Nothing," *Fire to the Prisons* no. 7 (Autumn 2009).

11   "It is gestures that use us as their instruments, as their bearers and incarnations"; Milan Kundera, *Immortality* (London: Faber & Faber, 2020 [1988]), 7.

12   By "politics," we understand those conflicts *within* everyday life that intensify to the point where sides must be taken, where neutrality is no longer possible. As such, there are no specifically political gestures or practices (speaking, debating, voting, etc.). The same applies in reverse: all gestures, all practices are potentially political, or ante-political, *including speech*—provided, of course, that one speaks from *within* a polarization, not from above it. When a conflict becomes intense enough, previously innocuous gestures and relations suddenly become hyper-potentiated and draw other forms and materials into the vortex. Later, once the

conflict subsides, the polarized practices or slogans are either reabsorbed into the banality of everyday life or else abandoned.

13 "*Mass* and *class* do not have the same contours or the same dynamic, even though the same group can be assigned both signs.... Mass movements accelerate and feed into one another (or dim for a long while, enter long stupors) but jump from one class to another, undergo mutation, emanate or emit new quanta that then modify class relations, bring their overcoding and reterritorialization into question, and run new lines of flight in new directions. Beneath the self-repro-duction of classes, there is always a variable map of masses"; Gilles Deleuze and Felix Guattari, *A Thousand Plateaus: Capitalism and Schizophrenia* (Minneapolis: University of Minnesota Press, 1987), 221.

14 To be a bit simplistic, the operative assumption here is that the spread of anarchy or ungovernability offers the most opportune path to opening up a new horizon of mass communist desertion and invention. However, since we cannot know what shape this horizon will take, nor do we wish to succumb to the prophetic trap of "waiting for the miracle," wagers on revolutionary potentiality must at the same time be rooted not in probabilistic projections but in our existing sensible contact with reality, our sense of what dignity and joy look like here and now, in the world that is, not the world that *ought* to be.

15 On the subject of right-wing co-optation of memetic movements, see Torino and Wohlleben, "Memes with Force."

16 Just as the transcendent status of merchandise under the sensory religion of the Spectacle depends in the "last instance" on the capacity of police to project their power far beyond their physical means, looting announces the profane restora-tion of both goods and cops to the domain of the sensible: henceforth, police *are* only where they appear, just as goods can be "had," provided one can transport them or consume them on the spot. By reducing power and consumption to the domain of free use, looting allows the absence of authority to be felt in a way otherwise impossible.

17 See "Welcome to the Party," in the present volume, pages 78–85; "After Peaceful Day in Reno, George Floyd Demonstration Devolved into Chaos, Vandalism," *Reno Gazette Journal*, May 31, 2020; "Police: Justice Center 'Attacked,' Set on Fire in Portland Protest, Riot Declared," KOMONews, May 30, 2020.

18 Although a full picture of the factors that played into this decision does not yet publicly exist, some specifics are recounted in an early interview with the Liaisons collective; see "'Everything Seems So Fragile and Powerful at the Same Time.' A Conversation About the Seattle Autonomous Zone," New Inquiry, June 16, 2020.

19 Some months later, Molotov cocktails were thrown through the smashed windows of the city courthouse in Kenosha, Wisconsin, but failed to ignite; a minor parole office was also put to flame; see Fran, JF, and Lane, "In the Eye of the Storm: A Report from Kenosha," this volume, pages 111–21.

20 "Dozens of Police Stations Attacked as Bogota Erupts in Violence," Bloomberg News, September 9, 2020; "Gunmen Blast into Nigerian Prison and Free 1800 Inmates," CBS News, April 6, 2021.

21 Anonymous, "From Freeway Shutdowns to Cop-Free Zones," Ill Will, July 22, 2016.

22 Phil Neel arrives at a similar conclusion: "Despite appearing as the opposite, the birth of the autonomous zone was itself a product of the movement's initial suffocation. While it provided a certain spectacular spur to events elsewhere and offered a brief, transformational experience for a small handful of people,

it also sealed in stone all the tactical regressions that had already taken shape as the social movement moved in to strangle the real movement beneath. In effect, then, this national rebellion ignited by the signal fire of a burning police precinct saw a symmetrical end to its first act when demonstrators refused to burn another precinct ceded to them by a similar police retreat"; see Phil Neel, "The Spiral," *Brooklyn Rail*, September 2020.

23 Tiqqun, "A Beautiful Hell" (2004), Ill Will, March 2021.

24 Tobi Haslett, "Magic Actions: Looking Back on the George Floyd Rebellion," *n+1*, May 2021.

25 Laurent Jeanpierre, *In Girum—Les leçons politiques des rond-points* (Paris: Éditions La Découverte, 2019), 19. As a particularly thoughtful, if ultimately inadequate, example of such a negative formulation, one might think of the recent description of the revolutionary movements of our times in Endnotes in terms of "nonmovements," following Asef Bayat; "Onward Barbarians," Endnotes.

26 "According to the majority of the Yellow Vests, politics does not derive its consistency in discourse, nor is it first of all a matter of opinions, demands, or programs"; Jeanpierre, *In Girum*, 27–29.

27 Maurice Blanchot, "Affirming the Rupture" (1968), in *Political Writings, 1953–1993* (New York: Fordham University Press, 2010), 88–89; incidentally, one finds here one of the first rigorous formulations of a concept of destituent power.

28 Hannah Black, "Go Outside," *Art Forum*, December 2020.

29 See Shemon and Arturo, "Theses on the George Floyd Rebellion," this volume, pages 25–29.

30 See Neal Shirley and Saralee Stafford, *Dixie Be Damned: 300 Years of Insurrection in the American South* (Oakland: AK Press, 2015). While none of these examples are free of contradictions, they testify to a persistent tendency among impoverished insurgents of various ethnicities toward "leveling," "mass desertions," and (according to the Council Report to the Governor following Bacon's Rebellion) "Vaine hopes of takeing the Countrey wholley out of his Majesty's handes and into their owne"; see Howard Zinn, *A People's History of the United States* (New York: HarperCollins, 2005 [1980]), 41–42.

31 Kiersten Solt, "Seven Theses on Destitution (After *Endnotes*)," Ill Will, February 2021.

32 Maurice Blanchot, *The Unavowable Community* (Chicago: Barrytown/Station Hill, 2000), 16.

33 Keno Evol, "Daunte Wright: A Billion Clusters of Rebellion and Starlight," Mn Artists, April 2021.

34 David Galula, *Counterinsurgency Warfare: Theory and Practice* (Westport, CT: Praeger, 1964), 95.

35 Jeanpierre, *In Girum*, 19.

36 As Phil Neel notes, it matters little whether or not the leftists who enact this substitutional repression are conscious of their true political role or whether or not they work explicitly with the police. The fact that "they earnestly see themselves as advancing the movement, even as they stifle it," makes the operation all the more effective; see Phil Neel, "The Spiral," *Brooklyn Rail*, September 2020.

37 For this claim, see "The 1619 Project," *New York Times Magazine*, August 2019.

38 Bartolomé de Las Casas was a Spanish colonist who later used his position as a religious figure to attempt to halt (or, where this proved impossible, to remediate) the tide of genocidal violence unleashed on Native Americans during the first phases of the colonization of Central America. In his audiences with the king

he adopted a strategic approach, challenging not the legitimacy of the Conquest *per se* but its methods, insisting on the moral and material-financial urgency of introducing order and oversight into the colonial missions, which he hoped would check the wanton violence of the settlers. In this, he may be regarded as an early progenitor of projects like police oversight committees and other policy reforms intended to curb state violence without deposing it. At the same time, Las Casas was *also* among the first Europeans to advocate the "just cause" of an armed war for self-determination on the part of the "Indians," and for this he has long been regarded as an early progenitor of decolonial and abolitionist politics. Whether one prefers to emphasize his role as a colonizer, a humanist reformist, or a partisan of decolonization (or an amalgam of all three), what is certain is that, in his budding awareness that "civilization is not a singular but plural" and in his sensitivity to the "discontemporaneity of historical developments and the relativity of the European position" (as Enzensberger once put it), Las Casas was not only the first truly *modern* subject but the figure who best exemplifies the apparatus through which modern political consciousness *covers over* this knowledge through its moral subsumption of alterity and the ruse of analogy by which modernity attempts to govern its own outside; citation taken from Hans Magnus Enzensberger, "Las Casas, or a Look Backwards into the Future," in *Zig Zag: The Politics of Culture and Vice Versa* (New York: New Press, 1998), 90–93.

39 "Thus did Las Casas and the planters come to terms. At daggers drawn over the labor of the Indian, they saw eye to eye on the labor of the Negro.... Justice to the Indians was purchased at the price of injustice to the Africans. The belligerent Protector of the Indians became a benevolent promoter of Negro slavery and the slave trade"; Eric Williams, *From Columbus to Castro: The History of the Caribbean, 1492–1969* (New York: Harper and Row, 1970), 43. Although Las Casas later regretted his suggestion, Williams notes that his regret still retained an anti-Black grammar, emphasizing an "empirical error" about African physiognomy rather than a lapse in universal moral judgment about the dignity of all life.

40 Frank B. Wilderson, III, "The Prison Slave as Hegemony's (Silent) Scandal," *Social Justice* 30, no. 2 (2003): 18–27.

41 Lawrence Clayton, "Bartolomé de las Casas and the African Slave Trade," *History Compass* 7, no. 6 (November 2009): 1526–41.

42 Ronald Judy, (*Dis)forming the American Canon: African-Arabic Slave Narratives and the Vernacular* (Minneapolis: University of Minnesota Press, 1993), 81.

43 "Thinking, as a part of man's essence, is held to be that which enables the distinguishing of good from evil, but it does so according to a universal order that translates the *prima praecepta* logically into secondary precepts that function *as the basis for all codes of social behavior*" (emphasis added); Judy, (*Dis)forming the American Canon*, 83.

44 This analogy lays the groundwork for the "intra-Settler ensemble of questions foundational to [the West's] ethical dilemmas (i.e. Marxism, feminism, psychoanalysis)"; Frank B. Wilderson, *Red, White, and Black: Cinema and the Structure of U.S. Antagonisms* (Durham, NC: Duke University Press, 2010), 215–19.

45 Ibid., 219.

46 The effort to place a rehabilitated vitalist politics in the service of an antifascist and anticapitalist youth movement has precursors not only in the "metropolitan Indians" (*indiani metropolitani*) of the Italian Autonomia movement (and perhaps already with the circle around Cesarano a decade prior) but also in American revolutionary groups of the 1960s and 1970s, such as MOVE and Up

Against the Wall Motherfucker. On left-wing versus right-wing vitalisms, see Alberto Toscano, "Vital Strategies: Maurizio Lazzarato and the Metaphysics of Contemporary Capitalism," *Theory, Culture & Society* 24, no. 6 (November 2007): 71–91.

47   Sonali Gupta and H. Bolin, "Virality: Against a Standard Unit of Life," *e-flux* 115 (February 2021).

48   See *Criminal Justice Matters* 77: "Exploring Penal Reforms," in particular Julia Sudbury, "Reform or Abolition? Using Popular Mobilisations to Dismantle the 'Prison-Industrial Complex.'"

49   "Lessons from Grant Park: Research Brief on Black Indigenous Solidarity Rally, Chicago Illinois," Black Lives Matter Chicago, August 2020; "Black Lives Matter on Chicago Looting: Black Lives 'More Important Than Downtown Corporations,'" NBC News, August 11, 2020.

50   In one of the finest texts produced last summer, "The Siege of the Third Precinct of Minneapolis: An Account and an Analysis," CrimethInc., June 2020, both dynamisms are theorized solely from the point of view of the agenda of the political riot. While the theory of composition offered in this text came the closest to describing the organizational animus "on the ground," it was too quick to subsume all aspects of the situation into a single type of crowd. According to the authors, the central feature that allows "looters" to be counted as a "role" within the composition of the political riot's crowd (medics, ballistic squads, laser pointers, sound systems, communications, etc.) is the fact of contributing to a general "ungovernability" of the situation as a whole. While this is understandable given the restricted frame of the article, which sought to map out the constellation of forces that led to the burning of the Third Precinct, from the point of view of a broader theory of the insurgent "crowd" in the twenty-first century it seems important to recognize the difference in kind between the two dynamisms at the level of their targets, motion, orientation toward the enemy, etc. The political riot and the storefront riot remain separate types of crowds. Even when they coexist on two sides of the same parking lot, as at the Target opposite the Third Precinct, to pass from one to the other involves a mutation and a becoming, a "tightening" and "loosening," as Elias Canetti said.

51   Of course, many local variations occur; sometimes the one riot dominates to the exclusion of the other. For instance, Portland's long summer was marked by an extremely sustained political riot, with few if any occasions of looting, whereas the storefront riots in Chicago took place without any attacks on state property or stationary clashes between crowds and police.

52   On the distinction between "good" and "bad" rioters, see Nevada, *Imaginary Enemies: Myth and Abolition in the Minneapolis Rebellion* (Chicago: Ill Will, 2020). Where the state doctrine speaks of "good" and "bad" rioters, we speak of political riots and storefront riots.

53   Jennifer A. Kingson, "Exclusive: $1 Billion-Plus Riot Damage Is Most Expensive in Insurance History," Axios, September 16, 2020.

54   Shemon and Arturo have contributed an admirable analysis of the use of car looting after Walter Wallace's killing in Philadelphia; see Shemon and Arturo, "Cars, Riots, and Black Liberation," Mute Magazine, November 2020. However, I would add that the genealogy of vehicular warfare is by no means limited to struggles around Black liberation. From the slow-rolls of "Black Smoke Matters" through the three thousand strong motorcycle and moped swarms during the 2019 uprising in Puerto Rico to the volunteer taxi mobs that spirited demonstrators out of

harm's way in Hong Kong, the tactical deployment of personally owned vehicles has become an increasing feature of the global grammar of action. While each of these cases represented tactical innovations in the mobilization of privately owned vehicles as a force of intervention, where their *weaponization* is concerned, it seems to me that a certain sequence begins in 2016, when, during the height of the clashes at Standing Rock, personal vehicles were transformed into barricades to block the main road to the DAPL construction site, before later being set on fire when police moved to attack the protesters who defended them. A year later, the right wing offered its reply to Standing Rock, when James Fields deliberately drove his car into a crowd of antifascists in Charlottesville in 2017, murdering Heather Heyer. Since then, vehicles have become a permanent tactical and affective element in street-level conflicts, from sideshows and COVID caravans to the first failed appearance of flotillas among Trump supporters. Nothing is more American than dragging everything in one's garage to the demo with you.

55 The concept of destitution was glossed in a letter published on Ill Will last year: "On the one hand, [destitution] refers to the emptying-out of the fictions of government (its claim to universality, impartiality, legality, consensus); on the other hand, it refers [to] a restoration of the positivity and fullness of experience. The two processes are linked like the alternating sides of a Möbius strip: wherever those usually consigned to existing as spectators upon the world (the excluded, the powerless) instead suddenly become party to their situation, active participants in an ethical polarization, the ruling class is invariably drawn into the polarization and cannot avoid exhibiting its partisan character. The police become one more gang among gangs;" August and Kora, "Quarantine Letter #1: Destitution, Interrupted," Ill Will, March 28, 2020.

56 For a representative sample, see *Short Circuit: A Counterlogistics Reader* (Olympia, WA: No New Ideas Press, 2015).

57 See Anonymous, "Order Prevails in Louisville," this volume, pages 162–75.

58 As Shemon and Arturo have recently observed, there is a "clear limit between the riot and the [logistics] strike," such that it may simply be unrealistic to expect BLM as a mode of action to authorize or invite a leap to the level of industrial actions at factories, warehouses, and ports; see Shemon and Arturo, "After the Tear Gas Clears: A Discussion on the Revolutionary Horizon Post-Rebellion," It's Going Down (podcast), April 29, 2021.

59 "The Great Screen Robbery: Chicago Looters Make Off with TVs & Other Expensive Goods from Moving Train in Broad Daylight," RT, June 4, 2020.

60 This fact is occasionally observed by ruling powers as well. As Chilean President Sebastián Pinera declared, "We are at war against a powerful enemy.... We are very conscious that they [protesters] have a degree of organization and logistic that is characteristic of a criminal organization" (public address), October 20, 2019; cited in "Chronology on Chile's Inequality Crisis," Ciudadanía Inteligente.

61 The occupation of the Wendy's in Atlanta is the outlier in this sequence, taking place in a poor and largely Black neighborhood, far from both the halls of power *and* the storefronts.

62 Anonymous, "Report Back on a Weekend of Actions against Police Weaponry," Ill Will, November 4, 2015.

63 On this point, see the discussion of destitution and place in Torino and Wohlleben, "Memes with Force."

64 As a middle school teacher explained to NPR at the time, "[We let through] cars, but not trucks hauling goods for major corporations like Wal-Mart and Coca-Cola"; "A Mexican Teachers' Strike Turns Deadly," NPR, July 9, 2016.

65 On this point, see K.N. and Paul Torino, "Life, War, Politics," Ill Will, November 2020. Among the best examples of the difficulty at stake in waging a "conflict over conflict" is the effort by residents of the ZAD in Notre-Dame-des-Landes, France, to shift the frame of their struggle after the state handed them a victory and canceled the airport they were blocking; see Mauvaise Troupe, "Victory and Its Consequences" (2019), *New Inquiry*, May 2020.

66 On the Chilean revolt and the idea of "rhythmic markers" by which it was able to expand, see Rodrigo Karmy Bolton, "The Anarchy of Beginnings: Notes on the Rhythmicity of Revolt," Ill Will, May 2020. It's worth noting that Karmy's concept remains ambivalently situated between the Trotskyist problem of a "convergence of struggles," which he evidently wants to avoid in his thinking about the event, and another viral image of politics for which he does not yet have a name. Far from a theoretical failing, this ambivalence is simply the structuring dilemma of our epoch.

Index

"Passim" (literally "scattered") indicates intermittent discussion of a topic over a cluster of pages.

About the Authors

Adrian Wohlleben is a writer and researcher living in the Midwest. His writings have appeared in *Commune*, Mute Magazine, and Ill Will.

Arturo is a writer and researcher living in Philadelphia. His articles have appeared in Mute Magazine, It's Going Down, and Ill Will. He is coauthor (with Shemon) of *The Revolutionary Meaning of the George Floyd Uprising* (Daraja Press, 2021).

Fran, **JF**, and **Lane** are revolutionaries living in the Midwest.

Idris Robinson is a PhD candidate in philosophy at the University of New Mexico. He is the author of several articles on revolt and crisis in European and American contexts over the past decade.

Inhabit is a collectively and anonymously written strategy emerging from a network of autonomous projects across North America.

Jarrod Shanahan is an assistant professor of criminal justice at Governors State University, the author of *Captives: How Rikers Island Took New York City Hostage* (Verso, 2022), and coauthor (with Zhandarka Kurti) of *States of Incarceration: Rebellion, Reform, and the Future of America's Punishment System* (Reaktion Books, 2022).

Nevada is a writer and communist living in Minneapolis.

New York Post-Left is the pen name of some pro-revolutionaries in Brooklyn.

Shemon is a writer and researcher living in New York. His articles have appeared in Hard Crackers, It's Going Down, Ill Will, and Mute Magazine. He is coauthor (with Arturo) of *The Revolutionary Meaning of the George Floyd Uprising* (Daraja Press, 2021).

Vortex Group is an anonymous collective of writers who desire an end to this world and the beginning of a new one.

Zhandarka Kurti is an assistant professor of criminal justice at Loyola University Chicago. She is the author of numerous articles on politics, race, and carceral policy and coauthor (with Jarrod Shanahan) of *States of Incarceration: Rebellion, Reform, and the Future of America's Punishment System* (Reaktion Books, 2022).

ABOUT PM PRESS

PM Press is an independent, radical publisher of books and media to educate, entertain, and inspire. Founded in 2007 by a small group of people with decades of publishing, media, and organizing experience, PM Press amplifies the voices of radical authors, artists, and activists. Our aim is to deliver bold political ideas and vital stories to all walks of life and arm the dreamers to demand the impossible. We have sold millions of copies of our books, most often one at a time, face to face. We're old enough to know what we're doing and young enough to know what's at stake. Join us to create a better world.

PM Press
PO Box 23912
Oakland, CA 94623
www.pmpress.org

PM Press in Europe
europe@pmpress.org
www.pmpress.org.uk

FRIENDS OF PM PRESS

These are indisputably momentous times—the financial system is melting down globally and the Empire is stumbling. Now more than ever there is a vital need for radical ideas.

In the many years since its founding—and on a mere shoestring—PM Press has risen to the formidable challenge of publishing and distributing knowledge and entertainment for the struggles ahead. With hundreds of releases to date, we have published an impressive and stimulating array of literature, art, music, politics, and culture. Using every available medium, we've succeeded in connecting those hungry for ideas and information to those putting them into practice.

Friends of PM allows you to directly help impact, amplify, and revitalize the discourse and actions of radical writers, filmmakers, and artists. It provides us with a stable foundation from which we can build upon our early successes and provides a much-needed subsidy for the materials that can't necessarily pay their own way. You can help make that happen—and receive every new title automatically delivered to your door once a month—by joining as a Friend of PM Press. And, we'll throw in a free T-shirt when you sign up.

Here are your options:

- **$30 a month** Get all books and pamphlets plus 50% discount on all webstore purchases

- **$40 a month** Get all PM Press releases (including CDs and DVDs) plus 50% discount on all webstore purchases

- **$100 a month** Superstar—Everything plus PM merchandise, free downloads, and 50% discount on all webstore purchases

For those who can't afford $30 or more a month, we have **Sustainer Rates** at $15, $10, and $5. Sustainers get a free PM Press T-shirt and a 50% discount on all purchases from our website.

Your Visa or Mastercard will be billed once a month, until you tell us to stop. Or until our efforts succeed in bringing the revolution around. Or the financial meltdown of Capital makes plastic redundant. Whichever comes first.

We Go Where They Go: The Story of Anti-Racist Action

Shannon Clay, Lady, Kristin Schwartz, and Michael Staudenmaier with a Foreword by Gord Hill

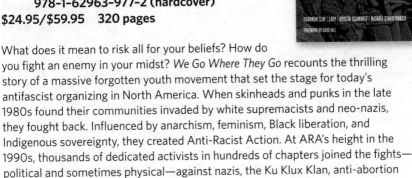

ISBN: 978-1-62963-972-7 (paperback)
      978-1-62963-977-2 (hardcover)
$24.95/$59.95   320 pages

What does it mean to risk all for your beliefs? How do you fight an enemy in your midst? *We Go Where They Go* recounts the thrilling story of a massive forgotten youth movement that set the stage for today's antifascist organizing in North America. When skinheads and punks in the late 1980s found their communities invaded by white supremacists and neo-nazis, they fought back. Influenced by anarchism, feminism, Black liberation, and Indigenous sovereignty, they created Anti-Racist Action. At ARA's height in the 1990s, thousands of dedicated activists in hundreds of chapters joined the fights—political and sometimes physical—against nazis, the Ku Klux Klan, anti-abortion fundamentalists, and racist police. Before media pundits, cynical politicians, and your uncle discovered "antifa," Anti-Racist Action was bringing it to the streets.

Based on extensive interviews with dozens of ARA participants, *We Go Where They Go* tells ARA's story from within, giving voice to those who risked their safety in their own defense and in solidarity with others. In reproducing the posters, zines, propaganda and photos of the movement itself, this essential work of radical history illustrates how cultural scenes can become powerful forces for change. Here at last is the story of an organic yet highly organized movement, exploring both its triumphs and failures, and offering valuable lessons for today's generation of activists and rabble-rousers. *We Go Where They Go* is a page-turning history of grassroots anti-racism. More than just inspiration, it's a roadmap.

"I was a big supporter and it was an honor to work with the Anti-Racist Action movement. Their unapologetic and uncompromising opposition to racism and fascism in the streets, in the government, and in the mosh pit continues to be inspiring to this day."
—Tom Morello

"Antifa became a household word with Trump attempting and failing to designate it a domestic terrorist group, but Antifa's roots date back to the late 1980s when little attention was being paid to violent fascist groups that were flourishing under Reaganism, and Anti-Racist Action (ARA) was singular and effective in its brilliant offensive. This book tells the story of ARA in breathtaking prose accompanied by stunning photographs and images."
—Roxanne Dunbar-Ortiz, author of *Loaded: A Disarming History of the Second Amendment*

The Mohawk Warrior Society: A Handbook on Sovereignty and Survival

Louis Karoniaktajeh Hall
Edited by Kahentinetha Rotiskarewake,
Philippe Blouin, Matt Peterson, and Malek
Rasamny

ISBN: 978-1-62963-941-3
$27.95   320 pages

The first collection of its kind, this anthology by members of the Mohawk Warrior Society uncovers a hidden history and paints a bold portrait of the spectacular experience of Kanien'kehá:ka survival and self-defense. Providing extensive documentation, context, and analysis, the book features foundational writings by prolific visual artist and polemicist Louis Karoniaktajeh Hall (1918–1993)—such as his landmark 1979 pamphlet *The Warrior's Handbook*, as well as selections of his pioneering artwork. This book contains new oral history by key figures of the Rotisken'rhakéhte's revival in the 1970s and tells the story of the Warriors' famous flag, their armed occupation of Ganienkeh in 1974, and the role of their constitution, the Great Peace, in guiding their commitment to freedom and independence. We hear directly the story of how the Kanien'kehá:ka Longhouse became one the most militant resistance groups in North America, gaining international attention with the Oka Crisis of 1990. This autohistory of the Rotisken'rhakéhte is complemented by a Mohawk history timeline from colonization to the present, a glossary of Mohawk political philosophy, and a new map of Iroquoia in Mohawk language. At last, the Mohawk Warriors can tell their own story with their own voices, and to serve as an example and inspiration for future generations struggling against the environmental, cultural, and social devastation cast upon the modern world.

"While many have heard of AIM & the Red Power movement of the '60s and '70s, most probably do not know the story of the Mohawk warriors and their influence on Indigenous struggles for land and self-determination, then and now. These include the 1974 Ganienkeh land reclamation (which still exists today as sovereign Mohawk territory), the 1990 Oka Crisis (an armed standoff that revived the fighting spirit & warrior culture of Indigenous peoples across North America), and the Warrior/ Warrior Unity flag, a powerful symbol of Indigenous resistance today commonly seen at blockades & rallies. The Mohawk Warrior Society tells this history in the words of the Mohawks themselves. Comprised of interviews with some of the key participants, as well as The Warrior's Handbook and Rebuilding the Iroquois Confederacy (both written by Louis Karoniaktajeh Hall, who also designed the Warrior/Unity flag), this book documents the important contributions Mohawk warriors have made to modern Indigenous resistance in North America."
—Gord Hill, Kwakwaka'wakw, author of *500 Years of Indigenous Resistance* and *The Antifa Comic Book*

Setting Sights: Histories and Reflections on Community Armed Self-Defense

scott crow with a Foreword by Ward Churchill

ISBN: 978-1-62963-444-9
$24.95 336 pages

Decades ago, Malcolm X eloquently stated that communities have the legitimate right to defend themselves "by any means necessary" with any tool or tactic, including guns. This wide-ranging anthology uncovers the hidden histories and ideas of community armed self-defense, exploring how it has been used by marginalized and oppressed communities as well as anarchists and radicals within significant social movements of the twentieth and twenty-first centuries.

Far from a call to arms, or a "how-to" manual for warfare, this volume offers histories, reflections, and questions about the role of firearms in small collective defense efforts and its place in larger efforts toward the creation of autonomy and liberation.

Featuring diverse perspectives from movements across the globe, *Setting Sights* includes vivid histories and personal reflections from both researchers and those who participated in community armed self-defense. Contributors include Dennis Banks, Kathleen Cleaver, Mabel Williams, Subcomandante Marcos, Kristian Williams, George Ciccariello-Maher, Ashanti Alston, and many more.

"This book is a must read. It looks like self-defense and resistance today, but it is more. It is about courage, lucidity, and tools to create new worlds under the storm, in the midst of disaster."
—Gustavo Esteva, founder of the Universidad de la Tierra and author of *The Future of Development: A Radical Manifesto*

"In Setting Sights, *scott crow pulls together an important collection of historic and contemporary essays and interviews on politically informed armed self-defense. Thoughtful, considered, compelling, and even provocative, this edited collection brings together many perspectives, raises important questions, and gives considerable attention to the ways race and gender inform these crucial issues."*
—Emilye Crosby, author of *A Little Taste of Freedom: The Black Freedom Struggle in Claiborne County, Mississippi*

Black Flags and Windmills: Hope, Anarchy, and the Common Ground Collective

scott crow with Forewords
by Kathleen Cleaver and John P. Clark

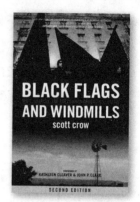

ISBN: 978-1-60486-453-3
$20.00   288 pages

When both levees and governments failed in New Orleans after Hurricane Katrina, the anarchist-inspired Common Ground Collective was created to fill the void. With the motto of "Solidarity Not Charity," they worked to create power from below—building autonomous projects, programs, and spaces of self-sufficiency like health clinics and neighborhood assemblies, while also supporting communities defending themselves from white militias and police brutality, illegal home demolitions, and evictions.

Black Flags and Windmills—equal parts memoir, history, and organizing philosophy—vividly intertwines Common Ground cofounder scott crow's experiences and ideas with Katrina's reality, illustrating how people can build local grassroots power for collective liberation. It is a story of resisting indifference, rebuilding hope amid collapse, and struggling against the grain to create better worlds.

The expanded second edition includes up-to-date interviews and discussions between crow and some of today's most articulate and influential activists and organizers on topics ranging from grassroots disaster relief efforts (both economic and environmental); dealing with infiltration, interrogation, and surveillance from the State; and a new photo section that vividly portrays scott's experiences as an anarchist, activist, and movement organizer in today's world.

"scott crow's trenchant memoir of grassroots organizing is an important contribution to a history of movements that far too often goes untold."
—Amy Goodman, host and executive producer of *Democracy Now!*

"This revised and expanded edition weaves scott crow's frontline experiences with a resilient, honest discussion of grassroots political movement-building."
—Will Potter, author of *Green Is the New Red: An Insider's Account of a Social Movement Under Siege*

"It is a brilliant, detailed, and humble book written with total frankness and at the same time a revolutionary poet's passion. It makes the reader feel that we too, with our emergency heart as our guide, can do anything; we only need to begin."
—Marina Sitrin, author of *Horizontalism: Voices of Popular Power in Argentina*